Lauren St John was born in Zimbabwe in 1966 and has lived in London since 1987. The first woman to be appointed golf correspondent of a national newspaper, she has worked for the *Sunday Times* for the past six years. She has also written for *Golf World*, *Today's Golfer* and *Golf Illustrated Weekly*. She is the author of *Shooting at Clouds: Inside the PGA European Tour* and *Seve*, a biography of the Spanish genius Seve Ballesteros. Her last book, *Out of Bounds*, was shortlisted for the 1995 Williams Hill Sports Book of the Year.

*Also by Lauren St John*

SHOOTING AT CLOUDS
SEVE: THE BIOGRAPHY
OUT OF BOUNDS

# GREG NORMAN

## —THE BIOGRAPHY—

## LAUREN ST JOHN

## CORGI BOOKS

**GREG NORMAN: THE BIOGRAPHY**
**A CORGI BOOK: 0 552 99787 0**

Originally published in Great Britain by Partridge Press,
a division of Transworld Publishers Ltd

PRINTING HISTORY
Partridge Press edition published 1998
Corgi edition published 1999

Set in Times by Falcon Oast Graphic Art

Corgi Books are published by Transworld Publishers Ltd,
61-63 Uxbridge Road, London W5 5SA
in Australia by Transworld Publishers, c/o Random House
Australia Pty Ltd, 20 Alfred Street, Milsons Point, NSW 2061
and in New Zealand by Transworld Publishers, c/o Random House
New Zealand, 18 Poland Road, Glenfield, Auckland.

Reproduced, printed and bound in Great Britain by
Cox & Wyman Ltd, Reading Berks.

*For J,*
*who makes everything possible*

# ACKNOWLEDGEMENTS

The success and authenticity of almost any biography of a living person depends largely on the co-operation of the people who have shaped and influenced him. For that reason, I am indebted to Greg and Laura Norman, who not only gave generously of their time, but were much kinder and nicer than they actually needed to be while doing so. Thanks also to Frank Williams, who is that rarity in professional sport – a manager who returns phone calls – and who went above and beyond the call of duty in attempting to ensure that this book depicted Greg fairly and as a whole human being, with all the charms and flaws that that implies.

I am enormously grateful to Merv and Toini Norman, to James and Lois Marshall (thanks for the lift to the station and the chocolate biscuits), to Hughes Norton, Tom Ramsey (I'm trying to dream up another book that will ensure I get to visit you and Carmel), Bill Longmuir, Charlie Earp, Robinson Holloway. Tom Callahan and Bart Collins. Thanks also to everyone at Transworld, especially my editor Adam Sisman, Shona Martyn, Hazel Orme, Sheila Corr, Shauna Newman, Nerrilee Weir and Katrina Whone. My heartfelt appreciation goes to Debbie Beckerman, without whom this book would never have happened; Rhod McEwan, the best bookseller in the world, and to my agents, Lyn Tranter in Australia, and Sara Menguc and Georgia Glover at David Higham, for keeping faith in me.

Anyone who has ever been through the nightmare that is writing a book knows that it is not only the author that feels the strain. Thanks to my Nashville family, Jack Daniels, Steve and Kim Byam, Jan, Steffi, Debra, Annabel and Michael and Jan Blaustone; my London support group, Joan, Liz, Jane and Chris; and my friends in the AGW, especially Peter Higgs and Derek Lawrenson. Lastly and most importantly, thanks to Ken Johnson, my mom, dad, sister, Lisa, and my cats Felix and Mommy-Cat, who weather the storms, cope with the crises and, hopefully, share in the good bits.

# CONTENTS

'I hate failure. The idea of failure is, I think, my driving force.'

GREG NORMAN, NOVEMBER 1989

# PROLOGUE

'Power is what it is all about and no one likes relinquishing that.'

MARK MCCORMACK, *GOLF WORLD*, 1988

GREG NORMAN HAD TAKEN New York. Eyes narrowed, black hat pulled down low, he stared down at the tramps, Trumps and shoeshine boys of Gotham from a king-sized neon billboard on Times Square. 'I had completely forgotten all about it,' Norman told *Golf World*. 'Then the limo driver told me to look up, and there it was. It was a lot bigger than I expected. It looked like a football field up there.'

In 1995 Norman was everywhere. His ice-blue eyes and Lone Ranger stance were plastered on buses rolling down Broadway and subway stations in Brooklyn. He was a sepia-toned success story on the cover of *Men's Journal* and the PGA Player of the Year. He put on his adventure hat for Chevrolet in America and Holden in Australia. He urged people to write with Le Boeuf pens, use Cobra clubs, consider Maxfli balls, play eighteen holes at the Medalist, buy Norman turf, sail Norman yachts, fly Qantas, wear a Rolex and *Attack Life* in Greg Norman clothes.

1

Two years earlier, in a villa on the other side of America, the corner-stones of this success story – International Management Group and the man they once marketed – had collided. Then, nobody was smiling. Norman, his chiselled face intent, was talking to his agent Hughes Norton. His elegantly beautiful wife Laura sat beside him. They were discussing the successful outcome of the biggest gamble of a career founded on risk. In 1990, Norman had invested $2 million of his own money in Cobra Golf Inc., acquiring a 12 per cent stake in the company. Even before the primary shares were offered in September 1993, it was clear that Norman's stake could be worth as much as $20 million. By 1 January 1996, it was worth nearly $44 million.

In the meantime, Norman had left IMG and the small matter of commission had arisen. Earlier, they had reached stalemate, but now Norton believed he had a temporary solution in mind, a destination for the $1 million in question, a safe house, as it were.

'Greg,' he said slowly, 'you're wrong not to pay IMG. But if you can't bring yourself to pay it to them, why don't you pay it to me?'

# CHAPTER ONE

## THE MILKY BAR KID

'The guys who want to be great players learn, from the age of fifteen, that if you're not willing to totally fall on your face with the whole world watching, and deal with it, and stay up, then you don't become a champion.'

DR BOB ROTELLA, SPORTS PSYCHOLOGIST, 1996

WHEN TOINI NORMAN PLAYED her last round of golf, the bougainvillaea were in bloom, crowding the tees with their scarlet and purple blossoms as she walked wistfully from the eighteenth hole, her pregnant belly heavy and awkward. She had managed to keep playing for over seven months, putting out weekly amid the ghost gums and sand greens of Mount Isa, but when the summer came, with scorching metallic skies, she was forced to admit defeat. On 9 February 1955, she was admitted to hospital with high blood pressure. Gregory John Norman was born the next day, arriving in the world with fine milky hair and a piercing scream. He weighed 8lb 11oz.

'He was a terrible baby.' Toini laughs. 'He cried all the time. He kept us awake for about twelve months. Finally we moved into a new house and I said to the neighbours, "I hope you aren't light sleepers because I'm going to just leave him to cry." Greg cried for two whole nights and then he never cried again.'

Both Toini and her husband Mervyn were of Nordic ancestry. Toini's carpenter father Seth and her mother Tyyne Hovi were Finns who had migrated to Australia in the thirties, while Merv's heritage was Norwegian, Danish, German and English. They met and fell in love on the tennis court, and when Greg was born Merv was working as an electrician at Mount Isa Mines in Northwest Queensland, a noisy jumble of slag heaps and shuddering pipelines. The largest city in the world, in terms of surface area, Mount Isa sprawls over rich deposits of zinc, silver, lead and copper. 'As the only place of consequence for 700km in any direction,' reports the *Rough Guide to Australia*, 'the smokestacks, concrete paving and sterile hills at Mount Isa assume oasis-like qualities on arrival, despite being undeniably ugly.'

Perhaps fortunately, the Normans moved away when Greg and his older sister Janis were still tiny, taking up residence in Townsville, an arid and muggy but altogether more convivial spot near the translucent waters of the Great Barrier Reef. Merv set up his own engineering practice, and Toini played golf again and tried to cope with Greg and Janis. 'Both my children were little horrors,' she says.

Her son was barely six when he discovered the joys of Magnetic Island, a vividly beautiful granite triangle just off the coast. The Normans had a small holiday house among the palms there and Greg and Janis spent every spare hour of their childhood skin-diving and spearfishing among the coral reefs, roasting their catches over an open fire. 'That's all I did,' Norman says, 'if I wasn't playing football or cricket or rugby or Australian Rules. I definitely wasn't studying, that's for sure.'

School was the bane of his life. He remembers a certain fondness for engineering, geography and physics, but his mind was always elsewhere. He despised French. 'He didn't like school,' Toini says. 'He'd rather have been outside. He didn't apply himself. His father tried to get him to, but he'd rather play sport, to the despair of his teachers. I ran into his headmaster years later and he said, "I often wondered what was going to happen to Greg." They always thought he could have tried harder.'

'He was always occupied and physically active,' recalled Merv. 'The bloke was never sitting down reading books. The simple thing is that his co-ordination was so good that any sport he touched he could have played it well. Picked up a billiard cue and he could play billiards well. Always had that good hand–eye co-ordination.'

As a young man, Merv had been a talented rugby footballer, who received several offers to go south to Brisbane and play, but his priorities lay elsewhere. Stern and uncompromising, with wide, powerful shoulders, he laboured towards a degree in electrical engineering and then threw himself into work at Mount Isa Mines. Norman describes him as 'dictatorial', the kind of man who would bang his fist on the table and say, 'That's it, boys. No more talk. Let's do it now.' A man to whom actions spoke far louder than words. 'To win anything,' Merv would inform his small son, 'the first thing you need to do is control yourself – then the environment around you. Do that, and you're on your way to improvement.'

At that age, the only thing Greg was interested in improving was his sporting skill. He proved an adept rugby-league footballer at Townsville Grammar and was chosen to represent Northern Queensland against South-east Queensland in a match in which he scored the only try. A series of ugly injuries persuaded him that rugby wasn't for him, and by that time he had developed a passion for bareback riding, galloping along the beaches in a wild flurry of spray. He and his friend Peter Rawkins kept horses in a paddock behind the Normans' house, a location that would have been convenient had it not involved a three-mile hike to the gate. To facilitate matters, Greg cut a hole in the fence and, after being caught red-handed by the furious park ranger, was banished for ever from keeping horses there.

Like a lot of young boys, Greg saw his father as dull and authoritarian. It came as a huge surprise to him to discover, years later, that Merv had been a bit of a prankster in his time, rigging up sticks of gelignite so that they exploded when the lighting he had fitted in the new Mount Isa Golf Club was switched on in a solemn ceremony. Merv's engineering skills also enabled him to build a little Sabot yacht for his water-mad children, who were members of the Townsville Sailing Club. Greg was already steeped in the machismo of Australian society and he immediately appointed himself captain of *Peter Pan*, shouting down his older sister. After they had sailed to victory in the B grade club championship, Janis punished him by joining the crew of a boat whose owner allowed her to be skipper.

'It was always the same.' Janis laughed. 'I'd beat him and he'd beat me up.'

Asked on the television programme *This Is Your Life* if there had been much competition between them, she said, 'Absolutely. I used to have bruises up my arms. He was a ratbag!'

'My sister and I were close, but like any brother and sister you've always got a love/hate relationship,' Norman says. 'We did a lot of things brothers and sisters wouldn't usually do together, like sailing. But, you know, we drifted apart. Distance is a killer for me because I live in the States. I've lost all my friends in Australia that I grew up with, which is tough. That's the other side of the coin people don't know or see or understand. You'd like to go back and see your friends you grew up with and see what happened and what they're doing. But I don't do that.'

Norman was influenced most by his mother, who remembers him as a 'thoughtful and considerate child. At one stage I was sick with flu. He was about seven at the time and he said to me, "Mum, you stay in bed and I'll make you some tea." '

'Greg and Toini have always been close,' says Charlie Earp, who would become Norman's mentor. 'They're the same sort of characters. Greg's lucky in that he's got his father's determination and ability to keep gnawing away, and he's got Toini's sporting gift.'

Merv was substantially stricter, not least because he was hoping that his son could still be persuaded to apply himself to his studies. At thirteen, struggling to puzzle out a maths problem, Norman recalls that he asked his father for help. 'Go in there and figure it out,' Merv said, pointing to his son's bedroom. Minutes later, the boy was back. 'Dad, I *can't* figure it out,' he said. Merv just pointed. 'Get back there and try again,' he snapped.

'They had their altercations,' Toini admits. 'Merv had his ideas of what he expected and he was a bit on the strict side.'

It was always something of a relief when the school holidays came and Greg could return to the rainbow reefs of Magnetic Island, or go out fishing and island-hopping for weeks on end with his schoolfriends Peter and David Hay, whose father, Dr Bob Hay, owned an ocean-going cruiser. It was on one of those trips, skin-diving and cautiously watching sharks feed, that Greg lost his front teeth for the first time. Rushing towards the killing pit – the hold where fish were dumped as they were heaved aboard – he slipped and fell against the edge. Amid the gore, it was discovered that one of his teeth was cracked diagonally from the bottom to the gumline, and the other had broken in half. Dr Hay charted a rapid course to Townsville, where the teeth were temporarily capped. Those caps were promptly knocked out in an Australian Rules game, and it was six years before Greg could afford to have them fixed properly.

On another, more successful, school holiday, Greg spent several weeks at an immense cattle station rounding up strays and indulging a brief flirtation with the idea of becoming a station hand, or what the Australians call a jackeroo. 'It was hard bush work and I loved the chase,' Norman recalled years later, 'but any thoughts I had of a jackeroo's life ended when I found myself assigned to a team castrating bulls.'

By 1969, Merv had resigned himself to the fact that it would be years, if ever, before his son was sufficiently educated to take over his thriving engineering practice and he reluctantly gave it up to accept another job with Mount Isa Mines Ltd in Brisbane. 'Greg was never that way inclined,' Toini says, adding, 'An engineer knows if a person's got the qualities needed. Greg didn't have the mathematics to be an engineer. I think Merv was a bit disappointed when he realized that Greg wasn't going to follow him into engineering. He would have kept the practice if he had done.'

In the breeze from the open window, the little aeroplanes twirled, straining at the twine that tethered them to the ceiling and the walls. There were P51 Mustangs, Spitfires, balsawood gliders and jets, all made with the same loving precision, some occupied by granite-faced pilots intent on circumnavigating the bedroom, others fitted with tiny motors that helped them bump along the paddock behind the house and reach for the sky on the sultry Australian evenings.

Greg Norman lay stretched out on his bed, picturing his future as a fighter pilot. He had tried collecting stamps and building balsa boxcars, but it was flight, and particularly fighter jets, that fascinated him. He had already joined the air cadets at his new school, Aspley High in Brisbane. 'That's my earliest recollection of what I wanted to be, a fighter pilot,' he says. At fifteen, Greg had long, finely muscled brown limbs, faraway blue eyes, a gap-toothed grin and a shock of straw-blond hair. He didn't dream, he focused. He didn't fret about getting from A to B. To Greg, B was attainable simply by wanting it badly enough.

'I was a very single-minded individual. Once I put my mind to it, I'd get the job done. I've never been a quitter in my life, even when I was a kid. I've always told the truth because that's what my father instilled in me – tell the truth whether people like it or not. You know who your friends are when you tell the truth.' But already he was discovering that not everybody enjoyed the truth quite as much as he did. 'At school I'd get the cane across my fingers because I was too honest.' Norman laughs. 'Because I'd tell them what I thought. But in the long run, it's been very beneficial for me.'

The Normans had moved into a two-storey house in Aspley, Brisbane, just a few months earlier, and that afternoon Greg was lonely and bored. His friends had been left behind in Townsville, and his mother had joined Virginia Golf Club and was on her way out to play. Hearing her gathering her clubs, he jumped up. 'Do you mind if I caddie for you?' he asked.

It was not his first introduction to golf. Janis still teases him about the time she beat him at crazy golf when they were kids, and there had been a nine-hole course on Magnetic Island where, Toini says, 'he would hack around and hit the ball a mile. But he wasn't really interested unless the water was too rough to go spearfishing.'

Prior to that day at Virginia, Norman's memory of golf is largely restricted to a shot he hit into a pandanus palm tree. In Brisbane, he carted Toini's clubs around the course, enjoying watching her play. Afterwards, when his mother went into the clubhouse for a drink with her partners, Greg borrowed her clubs and attempted a few holes on his own. Years later, he would say that he could reach par fives in two on the first day he ever played, but he also had his share of duffs and slices out of bounds. By the time his mother emerged, he was hooked.

'I'm a type-A personality,' Norman says, 'and it was one of those things that I knew I could beat. I just loved the challenge of it.'

'He only caddied for me once,' says Toini. 'He stole the clubs for himself after that. He had such dedication. He wanted to do everything well.'

At Aspley High School, Greg had started playing Australian Rules, a game based on Gaelic football, and eventually represented Queensland as a half-forward. But when he discovered golf, he realized that he preferred individual sports to team games. 'Everything I did outside surfing was a team sport,' Norman says. 'I could put in many great games playing Australian Rules and rugby and cricket and lose the matches, and you feel down. Or vice versa – put in a lot of poor performances, and when we won and everybody's elated, you know you didn't perform. Whereas in golf, you have all the highs and lows every time, every shot, every putt. It's so spontaneous. It's here and now and it's only you who experiences it, nobody else does. That's what I loved when I was a kid.'

At first, Greg borrowed Toini's clubs, but it soon become clear that golf was a passion that wasn't going to go away, and after he had left his mother waiting on the darkened clubhouse steps a few times his parents bought him his own set for $150. It was 8 August 1970. When he joined Virginia, his first handicap was 27.

'Once he made that decision, he went all out for it,' says Toini, who picked him up from school at 3 p.m. every day and drove him straight to the club, where he would hit balls until twilight obliterated them. 'He was there from daylight to dusk. Weekends, you wouldn't see him. He loved to practise. I don't think anyone in the world has practised more than Greg.'

His first action was to enrol himself for lessons with John Klatt, the pro at Virginia, who charged juniors twenty cents apiece for a group session. His second was to start devouring every piece of golf literature he could get his hands on, starting with Jack Nicklaus's classic *Golf My Way*. 'The [Nicklaus books] taught me the art of hitting down the line and using my body naturally. You want to keep the clubface going down the line and then let the automatic rotation after impact just happen.'

At school, he sat reading golf magazines behind his desk. Gail

9

Horne, a teacher at Aspley High, remembers confiscating them. His academic record plummeted.

'He would have failed my subject, Maths II,' Clive Evans told *Time* magazine, 'but that was the hardest of the lot. It wasn't a matter of ability, just not interested. His main asset was always his confidence.' He remembered Greg sitting sprawled out in his airy classroom, the louvred windows thrown open. 'He'd sit right next to the doorway with those long legs of his stretched across the aisle. Not the greatest student. Had ability, but you could see him sitting there dreaming. A natural sportsman, Australian Rules, cricket, everything. Always very respectful, polite. One of his favourite sayings if you suggested he might do better if he did some work was, "She'll be right, sir." And you know, he was darn right . . .'

The 1972 Aspley High Yearbook shows Greg Norman with a slightly bored smile on his face, his straw-blond hair framing a narrow face. He looks older than his years. The picture caption informs the reader that, 'Greg is such a good golfer that he made the state team at Easter. Lately he played with Billy Dunk. As well as golf, Greg has other interests. He is in Grade 12A and after matriculating would like to get a job with a golf firm or take up professional golfing. He is Kenny's House Captain this year. Greg also enjoys playing Australian Rules and has been centre half-forward for the past two years on the A-grade team.'

John Klatt remembers his athletic blond student as having 'a lot of raw talent, very strong. Hit the ball hard but not straight. He was very positive in his outlook. Believed in himself and that he could beat anyone.'

On 25 April 1971, nine months after taking up the game, Greg won his first trophy, teaming up with Merv in a fourball stableford event at Virginia for 50 points. 'That's the first cutting I have in the scrapbook,' Toini said proudly. Norman's 21 handicap was immediately slashed to 17. By 1 July, he was on 11, and Virginia nominated him for a Queensland junior squad for which the handicap limit was 6. By the time he left school in 1972, he was off scratch.

When he wasn't playing golf or Australian Rules, Greg spent his time surfing with his friend Greg Lyons. They were both prefects and they abused their privileges by playing truant in the afternoons, and riding the waves down at Noosa Heads. It was Lyons who found them holiday jobs at the Australian Match Manufacturing Company. They earned $50 a week for slicing up 30-foot logs with chain-saws and depositing the chunks in vats of boiling water, working stripped to the waist in jeans and army boots. Greg kept himself going through the back-breaking days with dreams of the gleaming set of clubs he planned to purchase.

'There was always something about Greg,' Merv said. 'I thought the kid had something special. He always enjoyed himself with his mates but he liked to lead.'

As a six-year-old, Greg had had all the fears that lurk in the minds of small children. In his nightmares, snakes lay coiled and deadly beneath the bed, and when darkness fell, his bedroom became a place of nameless terrors. But, unlike most children, he steeled himself to do something about it. One night he plucked up the courage to run from the door to the bed without turning on the light. Nothing grabbed him, no snakes reared their heads. The next night he walked a little slower and didn't cower beneath the covers. From then on, the darkness held no fear for him.

As he grew older he tested himself continually, and each time he walked away unscathed he grew braver. A lifesaving course at Magnetic Island had equipped him to deal with minor emergencies and ultimately it was that training which helped him save the life of a friend. Sitting around a swimming-pool with his Queensland Golf Union team-mates one afternoon, Greg, variously nicknamed the Milky Bar Kid, the Strawberry Bull and Buster, was watching Steve Perrin demonstrate his ability to swim six lengths underwater. After three lengths, Perrin slid slowly to a stop and sank to the bottom of the pool.

'He's in trouble,' Greg cried, and dived fully clothed into the water. While Glen Cogill ran to call an ambulance, Greg gave Perrin mouth-to-mouth resuscitation. When the ambulance arrived, Perrin was breathing again.

'I remember the guy in the pool,' Norman told the golf writer Chris Hodenfield. 'Everybody was either mesmerized or joking about the situation. Nobody wanted to take the responsibility of going in. From that day I never heard from him again. Completely disappeared from the game of golf, from surfing, from life.'

It was the second time he had saved a life. Janis's favourite memory of her brother is the time she was skin-diving and found herself tangled in deadly box jellyfish. Greg, 'my knight in shining armour', leaped in, pulled her free, dragged her aboard their boat and rowed as fast as he could to get help.

Norman's third brush with death had no happy ending. He and a young friend were at football training at Aspley High, running laps around a track in the Queensland heat when the other boy fell over suddenly. He had had a heart-attack. Norman gave him mouth-to-mouth resuscitation before the ambulance arrived but he died.

'He was my buddy, we were running together, and thirty-five minutes later I'm seeing his mother arrive at the hospital and I'm saying, "He didn't make it." I didn't go out and change my whole lifestyle, but it had an impact. It strengthened my mind . . . You never forget the face, the smell. Those are the things that build your stamina, your character, and all that stuff.'

Cogill remembers Greg Norman, who had his first victory in the 1973 Queensland Junior Championship at Royal Queensland (shooting 73, 74 to win by five strokes), as a confident, gregarious teenager. 'And he was very aggressive with the girls,' he said. 'Aw, yeah. Very aggressive guy. He used to get into a few scraps with the blokes over the girls. And he would not back off from anybody. Tough as nails.'

Toini's recollection is that her son was outgoing to an extent but also quite conservative. 'Greg was never one to party. I never had to worry about him coming home late at night, or drinking.'

Mostly, he just loved to be outdoors, soaking up the sunshine with his black Labrador Pancho, and breathing in the fresh-cut grass on the range at Virginia or the clean, salty smell of the ocean. He enjoyed being alone. Years on, long after he had achieved wealth and fame beyond his wildest dreams, almost nothing gave him greater pleasure than a hunting holiday with people he cared about in Queensland. 'I love to be out walking,' he said. 'May not even shoot a thing. Just to be out there in the solitude and the peace and quiet, where you can hear the birds and see the flowers and smell the rain coming from forty-five miles away.'

In the months after he left Aspley High, Greg took to pitching a tent on the beach at Noosa with his friends, lying in front of the campfire, waiting to catch a good wave. Bored and soon broke, he none the less enjoyed the untrammelled freedom of his existence. One morning, he left the camp and tripped down to the sea alone. The day before, a cyclone had blasted through the area and the surf was high, rising up in a towering wall of indigo and foam and then crashing lustily onto the rocks. He left his surfboard behind and took his flippers and hydrofoil hand controls.

'There was some great surf coming in,' recalls Norman, 'because any time you had a cyclone you had a great groundswell. At Noosa, the only way you could get out to the break was to go out onto the headland and jump in. I was a big body-surfer in those days and I wanted to go out where all the surfboarders were. When you're a kid, you never think of those things as being dangerous.'

Poised on the headland, Norman waited for a smooth, high wave and leaped. His last thought, before he was caught up in a churning tunnel of white water and smashed against the sea-bed, was that he'd chosen the wrong wave. The flippers and hand controls were ripped from his body, and the sea whirled him round like a washing machine. He was terrified. Clawing his way to the surface, he found that he had been swept half a mile out to sea. When he finally managed to half swim, half drift to the beach, he collapsed exhausted on the sand, unable to move for a quarter of an hour. It was the last time he ever surfed.

Lying drained on the beach at Noosa, with the sky curving silent and blue above him, Greg Norman realized that his life was going nowhere. When all was said and done, there was one thing he wanted more than anything else and that was to play great golf. 'Like I said, I'm a single-minded individual,' Norman says, with quiet determination. 'That challenge came to me, and there was nothing that was going to stop me getting to where I thought I could be.'

It was on a six-hour bus journey to Grafton for one of his last amateur events that Greg, full of optimism for the future, told his friends of his ambitions. 'Before I'm thirty, I'll be a millionaire, I'll be the best golfer in the world and I'll be married to an American,' he announced, suddenly, to Kevin Flanagan and Kevin Murphy.

There was a second's silence as they digested this. At that time

Greg was a one-handicapper and had never left the country. Then the jeers began. 'Who the hell do you think you are?' they demanded. 'What the fuck are you talking about?' And with the careless savagery of young men, they tore his goals to shreds.

Greg, lanky and tousle-haired, glared at them defiantly. 'When I've got my first million in the bank, I'll call you and let you know,' he promised.

A decade later, he did exactly that.

# CHAPTER TWO

# BLUE SKIES AND 65s

'I think we may have a helluva player back home. He may not win five Opens because the competition is greater, but this kid is going to be world class.'

PETER THOMSON TO THE BRITISH PRESS, 1976

THE ROAD TO ROYAL QUEENSLAND leads through a lonely wasteland of warehouses, scrub and run-down factories. A concrete arch dominates the horizon, rising out of the ground like a bridge to an uncertain future, and it is not until the visitor turns up the drive that the club's oasis effect is felt. Lush trees shade the low-lying grey clubhouse, palm fronds cast spiky shadows. Above the putting green, glass clinks on the balcony and golfers wilt in the relentless heat.

Nowadays, the shelves of Charlie Earp's pro shop are stacked high with Shark merchandise. Above the Akubra hats and boiled sweets, there are framed photographs of the teacher with Jack Nicklaus, Corrine Dibnah, Wayne Grady and Norman himself, and the changing-room door bears a crudely printed quote from Sam Snead: 'If a lot of people gripped a knife and fork like they do a golf club, they'd starve to death.'

In 1974, Earp's favourite adage was DIN and DIP: 'Do it now and do it properly.' A product of the red parched earth, as wiry and

15

sun-scorched as Crocodile Dundee, he would stand behind the counter dispensing homespun wisdom in a flat, earthy twang. He has never forgotten the day that Norman walked into his shop, broad-shouldered and loose-limbed, with a gap-toothed grin and determined blue eyes.

'I'm going to be the best player in the world,' he announced calmly.

Norman once said that as a teenager he 'turned to the surf as an escape route for the problems I was trying to sort out in my mind'. Exactly what those problems were he doesn't remember, but there is little doubt that his father's bitter opposition to his love affair with golf was the root cause of them.

Norman emerged from high school without any direction in life, feckless and fancy-free. Initially, he just 'lay around for twelve months, mostly doing nothing'. Nothing, that is, except surfing, hours and hours of skimming the waves in a bid to chase away the shadow that descended over the Norman household the day he turned down a career in the Royal Australian Air Force.

For the best part of twenty years, Norman has been describing how, in the grip of a 'burning desire to be a fighter pilot', he was sitting in the RAAF's Brisbane recruiting office with Merv, pen poised to sign the enlistment papers, when he froze. To this day, he has no idea what stopped him. 'I never consulted anybody, I never spoke to anybody, I just decided to say, "No." You've got to trust your instincts. And I'd have regretted it. If I'd joined the Air Force, I would have known deep down inside that I was doing something I didn't really want to do.'

But, according to his mother, Greg – whose academic record hardly suggests a fast-track entry into the top-gun ranks – was never on the brink of committing himself to a career as a fighter pilot. 'He and his father went to talk to the Air Force people and they suggested he finished his final year at school, his grade twelve, before apply-ing,' she remembers. 'But by then he was more interested in playing golf.'

Merv drove his son home, tight-lipped. He had hoped against hope that Greg would scrape through school with enough academic qualifications to be able to go to college and perhaps follow him into engineering and, when that failed, had clung to the idea that the boy would fulfil the ambition he himself had once had of being a fighter pilot. Now that hope too had been extinguished. Instead, he had to watch his carefree son, overlong hair in salty rats' tails, rise at his leisure every morning and saunter down to the beach with his surfboard tucked under his arm.

It was during this period that Norman became fixated on the idea of a career in professional golf. 'I was never particularly good up to that point. There wasn't much to go on except I had confidence in myself.' After nearly twelve months of sun and sand, he announced to his parents that he was thinking of becoming a professional golfer – 'the greatest player in the world'. Merv and, to a lesser extent, Toini took the news badly. 'I hadn't given them a lot of reason to believe I could make it as a professional golfer,' Norman says, remembering the scenes that followed this announcement. 'I was this big lump who hadn't done anything for a year.'

Laura, Norman's wife, who understands better than anyone the long-term effect Merv's disapproval had on his son, can see both sides of the story. 'His dad comes from the old school,' she says, of Merv's Depression-era severity. 'His dad really wanted Greg, his only son, to be successful, which is normal. Greg didn't play golf until he was fifteen years old, so when all of a sudden one day Greg wanted to play golf, his father was like, "Wait a minute, you can't just all of a sudden be a professional golfer . . ." I guess he didn't realize the talent that Greg had. No parent would . . . He was afraid that he would fail. It would have been different if he had been playing since he was nine or ten years old, but he was going to start playing golf and he was going to be the greatest golfer in the world. Well, his father was just afraid for him.'

Earp sighs. 'Old Merv didn't know anything about golf. Toini used to play. He's a workaholic, Merv, and he was a bit keen to get Greg into the Air Force, so he'd have some profession behind him. He'd be a bit like my father. My father had never heard of golf, so the second day I worked as a golf professional was the second day I'd been on a golf course in my life. I was never an amateur. And Greg was sort of in that situation. His father couldn't see the value of going into golf. In fairness to Merv, it wasn't that he didn't want his son to do that, he just thought: What future is there?'

'I'd be the same way if it was my son,' Norman says now. 'Believe me, now I have kids, I can understand how my father felt. Of course, I didn't at the time.'

In 1973, Norman took a job as a packer in the Brisbane warehouse of Precision Golf Forgings, an equipment manufacturing company run by amateur golfer called Sommie Mackay, the brother of the test cricketer Ken 'Slasher' Mackay. The atmosphere at home was strained, to say the least. With his pockets empty and his father's disappointment hovering like a palpable and accusatory presence in the house, Norman had been forced grudgingly out to work. Winning the Royal Queensland Club title had done nothing to allay his parents' worries. Merv, with his neatly pressed shirts and fanatical work ethic, saw Norman's golf dreams as a dilettante extension of his interest in surfing. Partly for that reason and partly because he was afraid of being left out of amateur teams if his ambitions were known, Norman felt he had no choice but to conduct his enquiries about turning professional in secret, and he used his breaks at PGF to make clandestine phone calls to golf's governing bodies. He planned to present his new career to his father as a *fait accompli*.

In the meantime, practice was Norman's priority. Soon after dawn broke he would make his way to the factory, and there in the cool grey light he would parcel equipment furiously, hurrying to subdue unwieldy golf carts, clubs and bags so that when his shift ended, he could be gone. It was a contest of wills. To Norman's mind, a four-hour shift was a four-hour shift but, as the hands of the clock ticked towards eleven, more and more tasks would suddenly be produced for him. Boiling with frustration, he would work even faster. At the last conceivable second, Mackay would acquiesce reluctantly and Norman would be out on the streets of Brisbane, racing for freedom, a breathless blur of healthy brown limbs and pale flying hair, dodging disapproving suits and women trapped in high heels.

He had more than a mile to run, and often the eleven-twenty train was pulling out of Roma Street station as he leaped aboard, collapsing winded among the hot, curious commuters. If he missed that train there were no others for an hour, and Virginia station was twenty minutes away. He was determined to practise for five hours a day.

Norman remembers approaching golf aggressively, even as a

youngster. He had only one aim and that was to beat the living day-lights out of the ball. 'Hit it three hundred metres without any problem,' he says. That year, he entered the Australian Open at Royal Queensland. To Norman, who had made rapid strides in an incredibly short period of time, it was an opportunity to gauge how much he had to improve as an amateur before he could consider the professional ranks. For the first three rounds, it seemed he was already there. He scored 71, 76, 71 and was drawn with Terry Gale, then one of Australia's leading amateurs. Norman was determined to beat him.

At the tenth hole in the final round, Norman's approach found a greenside bunker. He splashed out, not noticing that his friend Roger Dwyer, who was caddying for him, had left his golf cart unattended and was talking to someone in the gallery. His ball ran over the green, down the hill and struck the cart for a two-stroke penalty.

Norman was wild. He racked up an eight and, as he walked to the next tee, rounded angrily on Dwyer and demanded to know why he had been so stupid. Dwyer was mortified. 'One day, you're going to be a great player,' he said placatingly. 'Rome wasn't built in a day, and you will have many more bad breaks. I'm sorry.'

Norman burst into tears. He put a towel over his face to hide his misery and made a double-bogey at the eleventh. Gale finished leading amateur and Norman was runner-up after a 77. To the annoyance of the Australian Golf Union, he didn't appear at the presentation ceremony. 'I just wanted to get away,' Norman said.

Finally, his perseverance paid off and Billy McWilliam, the pro at Beverley Park in Sydney, took him on as an assistant. This was a coup for several reasons. Not only did McWilliam have a reputation for discovering and nurturing talent – Bruce Devlin and Bruce Crampton, the first Australian to win $1 million on the US Tour, had both benefited from his guidance – but the New South Wales Professional Golfers' Association had gone a step further than the PGA's Queensland division and assured McWilliam that Norman would be given releases to play in tournaments. To Norman, to whom three years as a trainee sounded like a life sentence, there was no better justification for heading south.

*

In March, a few weeks after his twentieth birthday, Norman put his belongings in the back of the Cortina he had bought for $2,300, kissed his mother, shook hands with his father and set off on the long drive to Sydney. Six hours later he was back again. He had left behind the $2,000 he had saved. His mother maintained it was telepathy, since he had not heard the message she had put out on local radio: 'Would Greg Norman, heading south to Sydney, please return home. He has forgotten his money.'

In Sydney, Norman shared an apartment in Kogarah with Doug Murray, another trainee. Initially, he set the alarm for 4 a.m. every day without fail and was hitting balls into the sunrise within the hour. At seven thirty, he would unlock the pro shop, and then he would repair clubs and sell balls to members until 5 p.m. But then McWilliam decided his assistants should help run his floodlit driving range. Since it rarely closed before 11 p.m., at which time Norman and Murray, working alternate evenings, had to gather up about four thousand balls, it was usually midnight before they were in bed.

Most nights they drifted off to sleep complaining about the drudgery of their lot. Their lives had become a monotonous regime of dealing with customers, with hardly a moment to spare for practising or playing. Norman felt he was going nowhere fast. He was. Three months after his arrival in Sydney, the New South Wales PGA reneged on their promise to grant him releases to play in tournaments while he was still a trainee. He would not be allowed to enter a professional event for three years.

It was a crushing blow. McWilliam, whose admiration for Norman's gift and hard work had been masked by his stern manner, was furious. 'Greg Norman is one of the most talented assistants I have ever had but he is going back home because he cannot play in pro tournaments in Sydney,' he told reporters. 'He has been waiting for invitations to play that have never arrived, so now he is going back to Queensland.'

The first Earp knew of it was when Norman phoned him and asked if he could see him. 'Is it important?' the older man asked.

'Very,' Norman said.

In Brisbane, Norman sat in Earp's lounge and begged him to let him finish his apprenticeship in Queensland. 'He had a girlfriend then and he was a fairly homely sort of boy,' Earp remembers. 'I said: "You're welcome to come back." And he got in his car, saw his mother and father, drove to Sydney to pack up all his gear and came back again. And that's when we really became close.'

In Sydney, Norman loaded up the Cortina and, determined not to waste another second of his life, set off on the long drive home at 10 p.m. Suburbs gave way to tropical beaches and barren red landscapes. Norman kept himself awake by wondering whether Earp would really be able to help him, and how his parents and the members of Royal Queensland would feel about him working in the pro shop.

The kangaroo came out of nowhere. Norman saw a blur, yanked the wheel hard left, hit a road sign and went into a spin. When the car finally stopped, jamming up against the embankment on the opposite side of the road, Norman sat in his seat trembling, the night unfurling around him.

The next afternoon, after a long, exhausted sleep, he went to inspect the car. It was a write-off. Somehow he had managed to drive it home but he wouldn't be driving it again. Uninsured, it cost $1,200 to repair and afterwards Norman sold it.

Life at Royal Queensland was fair but hard. Norman was paid $38 a week, for which he spent half the day in the shop and the rest hitting balls or working with Earp. 'The way you can hit a golf ball, we're not going to worry about the long game,' his teacher told him. 'We're just going to worry about your short game.'

Norman threw himself into his new practice regime with a discipline and ferocity that was astonishing even to the ambitious young assistants he worked alongside, Wayne Grady and Mike Ferguson. 'He was quite impressive,' recalls Grady, an enormously likeable, salt-of-the-earth Australian. 'He was a much bigger kid than the rest of us and could hit it a very long way at that time. It was always fun watching him hit the driver off the ground, because the old equipment and the old balls used to take off very low and then rise, peak and fall down. Greg was always a couple of years ahead of myself and the other guys, and he was the best.'

'His idea of practice was to practise,' said Glen Cogill. 'He didn't

just go muck around and have a drink. His hands would nearly bleed.'
He remembered Norman as being very organized. 'He knew where
he was going and he wanted it real bad. That's the kind of guy he was.
You could nearly call him cocky. At the junior pennants he'd say, "I'm
going to beat this guy 5 and 4." He was cocky for an Australian.
We're a pretty negative people.'

In the first six months at Royal Queensland, Norman sat and
passed all the trainee exams he would normally have been expected
to complete in three years. In September he won the Queensland
trainee championship in a play-off at McCleod Country Club, a
course built for women by women. 'He had that flair,' Earp says.

Encouraged, Norman beat balls behind the bamboo curtain of the
practice range at his own club with religious intensity. Soon he provoked the ire of the greens committee. There is something about
exceptional youngsters that arouses the pettiness inherent in all golf
clubs, and at Royal Queensland it was led by the chairman of the
greens. He wanted Norman banned from the range for taking so
many divots it looked as if it had been mauled by pigs. 'We had a bit
of a barney,' recalls Earp, who refused to stand by and see his most
disciplined assistant punished for his dedication.

Incidents like these cemented their relationship. While the other
assistants were letting their hair down in the pubs or on the beach,
Norman wrestled with his game. He gave himself projects. There was
gnarled old Moreton Bay Fig near the practice ground and he liked to
see how close he could stand to it and still clear it with a five-iron.
'He learned to play the shot that made him under that tree,' says Earp.

Watching his pupil one morning, Earp said, 'Gregory, you need to
learn to hit the ball lower.'

'I'll be all right,' Norman said, launching a ball into the blue. 'I'm
designing my game for America.'

'Yes,' retorted Earp, 'but if you play that shot in Britain, it'll end
up in Paris.'

But Norman always required proof for everything. It was not
enough for him to be told that a technique was wrong or a clubhead
was right. He had to know why. On that particular occasion, Earp
called over a Scottish member who assured Norman that, when playing at Turnberry or Troon, 'You'll be needing to keep it quail high,'

but there were numerous others. He needed confirmation from Kel Nagle that Earp was right when he said the shaft in his driver was too stiff to work the ball effectively, and he nearly had a stroke when Earp suggested he should change his grip.

'Nobody plays with a grip like that,' growled Norman.

'Well, Jack Nicklaus does, Norman von Nida does, Kel Nagle does, Gary Player does, Arnold Palmer does,' Earp snapped back.

Secretly, he thought Norman had it all, power, talent, focus. 'Determined, really determined,' Earp told *Time*. 'He'd look at you with those palomino eyes that he's got and you knew, you could see him pumping up.'

Earp had a fuse as short as Norman's, which inexorably led to clashes. One lunchtime, when Norman had worked hard all morning and felt he was owed a few hours' practice, Earp ordered him into the back of the store to clean some sets of clubs. Norman exploded. Any assistant who didn't measure up was shown the door and occasionally helped there by the scruff of his neck, and Norman might have received the same treatment had he not grabbed Earp by the front of his shirt and lifted him off his feet. Reason prevailed before any damage was done. When his mother came into the shop ten minutes later, Norman stood sweetly behind the counter and sold her a golf ball.

He grins at the memory. 'Charlie always pushed me, which was great. There were times when I wanted to fight him, but you knew that the guy loved you and knew where you wanted to go, so he was just being your blinkers for you.'

When Norman wasn't hitting balls or waiting on customers, he went fishing with Earp and a couple of friends in a little wooden dinghy with an outboard motor. Earp remembers those trips as being among the few social settings in which Norman was truly comfortable. 'A lot of people who are shy are outgoing until they get to a certain barrier, then they go back the other way. He was never a person to be pushing in. He'd wait till he was invited, which is a sign of shyness.'

Earp encouraged him to come out of his shell on the course, teaching him the value of sport as entertainment by coaching him to adopt 'the aura of a clown . . . The clown in the circus is making people happy. Gary Player is like that, and so are Seve and Greg.'

One area where Norman showed no sign of reticence was in his on-course gambling, which he had started while still a boy at Virginia. Playing for money that he could not afford to lose, often with Cyril King, a local businessman, taught him to handle pressure and win, and the bets grew larger by the day. The most he ever earned in one round was $1,200 and, in April 1976, when the Queensland PGA announced that he was now eligible to compete in state-controlled tournaments, he used the money for his travel expenses. He won his first pro-am title in Dalby in June. Even now Earp can remember the hostility that greeted Norman's success in those early events. 'They didn't like him because he was good. In Australia, we have that: knock the tall poppy down.'

In August, the PGA of Australia invited him to join the circuit. Norman celebrated by regaining his state trainee title at Keperra by fifteen shots. His first real event was held in Bateman's Bay and had a prize fund of $15,000. He finished third. The following week, he returned to Keperra for the Queensland Open, shot 70, 73, 74, 70 and shared third place again.

'Throughout the tournament he missed only ten greens,' reported the *Courier Mail*. 'He laid into his tee shot off the eighteenth for a gain of 360 metres and hit a nine-iron in. For a twenty-one-year-old not yet out of his time it was downright arrogance.'

It was a lightning beginning. Brimming with confidence, Norman finished in the top ten for the third successive week in the New South Wales Open. He was ready.

When the starter called his name, Norman strode onto the tee box and smashed his drive down the first hole at the Grange. Glen Cogill was caddying for him. Norman was up against the cream of Australian golf in the $35,000 West Lakes Classic, his first major event, and he felt he needed all the help he could get just to make the cut.

It was not a day conducive to settling the nerves of rookies. Not only was Norman paired with Bruce Crampton, who attracted a large gallery, but there was a strong gusting wind and a forty-minute delay. Norman eyed the tree-lined fairways with alarm. A Perth player named John Clifford had set a course record of 67, an outstanding score in the conditions, particularly when the field featured players like David Graham, Graham Marsh, Jack Newton, Bruce Devlin and Bob Shearer. Norman calmed himself by focusing on Clifford's score. I'll have to beat that, he thought.

Until he teed off that day, Norman's progress had gone largely unnoticed by the media and even by most players. The only reason Bill Longmuir, a young Scotsman in the group ahead, had heard of him was because his friend Doug McClelland had been paired with Norman the week before. 'Doug said, "Have you heard of this Greg Norman?"' Longmuir recalls. 'He said, "God, he's just unbelievable. This is the best player I've ever seen."'

Longmuir, struggling in the high winds that swept through Adelaide's Grange club that first day, shot 77. 'I got in and this kid had shot sixty-four. I thought: That's just not possible on this course, not on a day like that. My memories are that it was a score that just wasn't on. A sixty-nine would have been brilliant, but a sixty-four was phenomenal.'

In the second round, Longmuir struggled to concentrate and kept glancing back at the group behind, awed by the length of Norman's drives. Norman, who was determined not to have to protect his lead, played aggressively, and twice incurred Crampton's wrath. First, he was shouted at for memorizing rather than marking his ball's original position when he dropped away from a path at the short eighth. Fortunately Norman was supported by an official who had also noted the exact spot. But Crampton found fault with him again when they reached the green.

'You're not allowed to do that,' Crampton snapped, as Norman carefully brushed a few grains of sand off the green.

'Yes, I am,' Norman said. And a small row developed.

Once again the official stood by him, assuring Crampton that the rules of the Australasian Tour differed from those in the US and that Norman was quite correct.

'I watched him come up the last,' Longmuir says, 'and he hit it in the water off the tee. I thought: He's gone today. He's probably shot seventy-six or seventy-seven. He put his scorecard in and he'd had a sixty-seven, with a ball in the hazard at the last. It was mind-blowing stuff, really. That was my introduction to him. Everyone was going: "This is definitely the next Jack Nicklaus." He was always going to be great was how it was viewed. I mean, it was a bit like Tiger Woods now. Everywhere he goes, people are talking about him and watching him. Well, it was the same with Greg.'

After two rounds, Norman was leading by five strokes. After three, he led by ten on 16 under par, an unbelievable achievement in a field of that strength. He had made twenty-two birdies in fifty-four holes and his nearest challengers were Crampton and Chris Tickner. Marsh and Devlin were a distant twelve shots behind. It was national news. Even the conservative Peter Thomson, winner of five Open Championships and the greatest golfer Australia had produced, was moved to say that Norman was the best-looking young player he had seen.

'He was an instant star,' Thomson remembers. 'I thought he was phenomenal. We're now in awe of Tiger Woods coming out of the forest, but Norman was the same at the time. He was a long hitter and he seemed to have everything in his favour, good looks, good physique, nice personality. I thought that he would be the dominant figure after Nicklaus. In fact, I was the one who said he would beat Ballesteros, but everybody in Europe scoffed at that because right away it was Ballesteros who started doing things. Of course, Greg didn't.'

Rodger Davis, another successful Australian, was struck by the dramatic improvement in Norman's game. 'Within a matter of eighteen months, he had gone from being one of the wildest long hitters to one of the straightest long hitters.'

On the final day, Norman woke up with Gary Player's words running through his mind: 'The toughest, loneliest place in the world is out in front of a golf tournament.' Cogill did his best to reassure him, and together they decided that Norman should stick to the aggressive strategy that had rewarded him so far.

And so it was that when the gun went off, Norman played with complete abandon, sending every tee shot past the 300-yard marker with scant regard for the consequences, aiming every iron shot at the pin. It was an expensive play. He notched up six bogeys and a double-bogey and, had he not also managed five birdies, would have handed the tournament to David Graham.

'It might have destroyed him for ever if he had blown a ten-shot lead,' Graham said melodramatically.

'I felt the pressure today,' admitted Norman, who had a new car and $8,000 in the bank after just four events. 'My stomach was tied in knots.' He described victory as 'an unreal feeling. It's been a great experience and now I know what to do – I think.'

Peter Thomson was lavish in his praise. 'His rounds of sixty-four, sixty-seven, sixty-six, seventy-four speak for themselves, but the manner of him getting them revealed that here we have a young golfer in the Nicklaus mould – dare I say better? What incredible heights must now be before him . . . What an income this man will earn by the time he reaches thirty.'

Back in Brisbane, his mother was beside herself with joy. No win before or since in his career has brought her greater pleasure, and it was compounded when she sank a putt to win the mixed foursomes championship at Virginia just as Norman won the West Lakes Classic. Her partner was Sommie Mackay, Norman's old boss.

'When I put on the radio and heard that Greg had won, it was so incredible,' Toini says. 'I couldn't believe it. I was stunned.'

So was Norman. 'It was a great catalyst for my career, winning as quickly as I did,' he says now. 'I was Tiger Woods. I went through the same thing that Tiger's going through, I got off to a fast start . . . At West Lakes, when I blew away the field – ten shots in front in a field with the strength of the Bruce Cramptons, the David Grahams and Bruce Devlins, those guys who were the icons of Australian golf – I went straight up to the roof and then I was off. I just knew. When I won that seven-thousand-dollar cheque I thought I was the richest man in the world.'

Norman was twenty-one, weighed 13st 3lb, and had the unstoppable momentum of greatness. He not only played like a young Nicklaus, he looked like him. A photograph of Norman meeting his hero at the Australian Open a couple of days after West Lakes shows an uncanny resemblance – the same broad faces and tanned, uneven features, the same eagle eyes and chapped lips, the same rough-cut, wind-streaked blond hair and the same stubborn stance. But none of it helped when Norman was drawn with the Golden Bear in the first round of the tournament. So nervous that he thought he 'might die', he shot an 80 to Nicklaus's 72 and died only of embarrassment.

Angry and disappointed and scarcely able to speak, he retreated at the first opportunity to his hotel room. Lying in bed, he relived the anguish of the round over and over again, beginning with his first tee shot, which he had cold-topped, dribbling it 30 yards into a tree. What must Nicklaus have thought of him?

Nicklaus actually thought a great deal of him. 'He shot an eighty today but you'd never know it by his manner,' he said of Norman, who was already being nicknamed the Golden Cub. 'The score was not a reflection of his game. He's potentially a very good golfer.' He described Norman as having 'the physique of a durable athlete'.

When Norman recorded a 72 the following day, Nicklaus spent twenty minutes talking to him in the locker room, telling the young Australian that he felt he was good enough to play the PGA Tour in America. 'Why don't you think about doing that?' he suggested. Norman was overwhelmed. He would have loved to have told Nicklaus that the first golf book he had ever read was his, but instead he just nodded shyly. The trauma of the previous day had been entirely worth it.

Norman finished second behind Bob Shearer on the Australian Order of Merit that year, presenting a unique problem for the PGA. For the first time ever they had to select a trainee professional to represent Australia in the World Cup, held at Mission Hills, California, in mid-December. When Norman and Shearer finished a respectable seventh, the former was given permission to play the professional circuit full time. If he ever decided he wanted to teach or work in a pro shop, he would have to complete the last eighteen months of his three-year apprenticeship.

Even at that stage, it was unlikely that Norman would ever find himself so down on his luck that he would be obliged to go back to selling tee pegs, but he was already discovering that life on the road had its own set of problems. Six months after the West Lakes Classic, the company whose equipment he used had still not honoured its agreement to pay him a win bonus of $750. In the most short-sighted decision any business ever made, the company heads resorted to blackmail, telling him that unless he entered into a contract with them he would forfeit the bonus. The contract? A return fare to

Europe and $1,500. Norman told them he would 'rather die' than sign for that amount.

It was Peter Thomson who came to his rescue. He was already guiding Norman through the formalities of full membership of the PGA, and when he heard about his predicament, he phoned Norman at a motel in Melbourne where he was staying and asked him to meet him on the tenth tee at Victoria Golf Club.

At the appointed time, Norman waited on the tee. When Thomson appeared, he was walking briskly through the shady avenue of trees from the ninth, talking to the British player Guy Wolstenholme and another sturdy man. Up close, the young Australian took the stranger's measure, noting his sharp eyes and aura of no-nonsense strength. He was smoking a pipe. They shook hands.

'Meet James Marshall,' Thomson said.

# CHAPTER THREE

---

# NORMAN CONQUEST

'He will become the world's greatest golfer. He has weaknesses in his game but these will not prevent him from reaching the top.'

NORMAN VON NIDA ON GREG NORMAN'S POTENTIAL, 1980

IT WAS BARELY DAWN when Norman rose, pulled a thick shirt over his wide shoulders, whistled to the dogs and set off across the fields with his shotgun, dew spurting from his heels. Behind him, Beaurepaire House was etched against the skyline. Its castle-like structure, moat and manservant lent it an austere but faintly exotic air. Peacocks paraded round the garden, dark trees huddled on the grounds. It resembled a building from fiction: Wuthering Heights or Northanger Abbey.

'It was like one of those English jumble sales,' recalls the Australian golf writer Tom Ramsey, who once stayed in Norman's bedroom there, 'full of antique furniture and antlers. Parts of the house looked like it belonged to the Addams Family. You just expected the hand to come out of a box and grab you as you walked past.'

In a matter of months, Norman's life had changed out of all recognition. It had been doing so ever since he first laid eyes on James

Marshall at Victoria Golf Club. A former stevedore in Canada and lieutenant in the British Army in Malaysia, Marshall was now a director of two Rolls-Royce engineering companies and an Australian company, and it was through his friendship with Peter Thomson and Guy Wolstenholme that he had become interested in golf management. Thomson had remarked that his business experience provided the perfect background.

Marshall was something of an entrepreneur and he thought it was an excellent idea. He spent several months studying the form of the British players and, after trying and failing to sign up Nick Faldo in scenes that Colin Snape, the former executive director of the WPGA, describes as a sort of real-life *Carry On Golfing*, decided that the rest were lacking in ambition. According to Jack Newton, one of Australia's best players at the time, Marshall then attempted to persuade him to become a client. Newton declined but claims he recommended Norman. 'If you're ever going to get hold of someone with raw talent, it's him,' he said. Meanwhile, Thomson was busy arranging for Norman to meet Marshall in Melbourne.

At Victoria, Norman, his blond Beatle haircut falling over his eyes, was wandering along animatedly discussing rugby and football with the Englishman when Thomson handed him a driver. 'Show James how good you are,' he urged, as they stepped onto the eleventh tee. Norman was in his street shoes, but he casually unleashed a huge drive that bounded far past the 300-yard marker. Marshall had never seen anything like it. His assessment of the young Australian then and in the ensuing months was that he was 'a very rough diamond. Bit of a Jack the lad. Totally unpolished. The sort of fellow you'd expect to find around Bondi Beach. He was a very outgoing, gregarious, rough-at-the-edges type of guy.'

But he was astute enough to realize that there was a lot more to Norman when it came to the course. 'There was something about him that was very different from the English and European players that I had met. I had a gut feeling that he was a winner. He was very ballsy, very tough and he had enormous self-confidence. He was a very exciting guy to watch hitting golf balls. And he was very young. It took a lot to get Peter Thomson enthusiastic about anybody. Peter Thomson is never the kind of guy who throws bouquets around all over the place. But Peter thought he had a good chance at being very good, and I liked Greg's attitude and I liked Greg very much when I met him. I thought it would be quite a lot of fun. I thought I could do quite a lot for him.'

That evening, Marshall invited Norman to dinner at the Hilton. 'He was very charming,' Norman remembers. 'He said all the right things at the right time.'

Marshall claims to have had no thought of managing Norman at all, but he did bear in mind that Ed Barner, whose management of Johnny Miller and Seve Ballesteros would eventually end in tears, was circling like the proverbial shark. Over dinner, he questioned Norman closely about his goals. Norman was impressed by Marshall's worldliness, his autocratic air. Here was a man he felt he could really talk to about business. He told Marshall that he felt as if he was being blackmailed by his sponsors. Would Marshall consider helping him? Marshall shook his head. Without a contractual agreement between them, he had no right to intervene.

Norman studied him thoughtfully across the table. Mere hours had elapsed since he had gripped Marshall's hand at Victoria, and yet the glimpse he had caught of Marshall's world – a sophisticated whirl of butlers and landed gentry, first-class flights and fine dining – had left him in no doubt that he wanted to be part of it. He decided to trust to fate. Shyly, he told Marshall that Thomson had spoken highly of him and asked the Englishman if he would be interested in managing him.

'Not particularly,' Marshall said bluntly.

Norman was crushed. It was the last answer he had expected, and disappointment rose like bile in his throat. Marshall smiled. He liked a man with ambition. He probed Norman further about what sort of arrangement he had in mind and, at the end of the evening, agreed to think it over.

Curiously, it was not Norman's beachboy gaucheness that made Marshall hesitate. It was the awful possibility that Norman, being so young, would have meddling, overbearing stage parents. He had been through that already with Faldo. He made it brutally clear to Norman that he wanted his decision to be made independently, without any prior consultation with his family or advisers. 'What I didn't want was to get involved with parents and uncles and aunts and brothers and all of that sort of stuff, because one of the problems when you manage a young player is you get a lot of parents who are on an ego trip and suddenly they're on the bandwagon: "It's my son and I want to know what he's doing." '

But Marshall knew intuitively that he was on to a good thing. He drafted a contract in his hotel room that night and the principles were agreed with Norman the following morning. Then he told the Australian to get himself a lawyer.

The first Norman's parents knew of it was when he blithely informed them he was about to sign his life away. Their reaction was one of total shock and disbelief. As far as they were concerned, Marshall was a stranger not only to them but to their son. One round of golf did not constitute a relationship; one meal at the Hilton was no basis for unconditional trust. Charlie Earp rang Marshall and demanded in no uncertain terms to know his intentions. Norman's parents entreated their son to think again. But his mind was made up. The fact that Marshall was a friend of both Thomson and Wolstenholme was endorsement enough for him. On 17 February 1977, forty-eight hours after meeting the Englishman, he signed on the dotted line, 'against the wishes of Charlie Earp, against the wishes of my mom and dad and against the wishes of all my friends in Brisbane. And they all tried to talk me out of doing it.'

The die was cast. Under the terms of the contract, Marshall was entitled to 25 per cent of Norman's non-tournament earnings, a reasonable deal by sports-management standards. Within a fortnight, the $750 bonus cheque due to Norman was in his bank.

'My whole approach to management was very different from, perhaps, some, in the sense that I didn't have to make a living so I wasn't relying on Mr Norman being successful,' Marshall says. 'So I never, for example, took a penny of his prize money. Ever. My whole basis was (a) obviously to negotiate good commercial deals for him, and (b) to try to get him set up mentally – just like a father with a son – steering the guy in the right direction . . . My whole objective was to keep his feet on the ground and turn him into a winner who was able to cope with the pressures of winning and losing, and the press and life in general. Because he had led a very sheltered life.'

Norman's prospects had now taken on a rose-tinted hue. The Australian Golf Writers Association had voted him the outstanding young player of 1976 and presented him with a return ticket to London, and Marshall had arranged for him to play in three events in Japan. Travelling with Guy Wolstenholme, he shot a closing 66 in the thirty-six-hole Kuzuha International in Nagoya to win by two strokes. He was paid in cash. 'I remember sitting on a bed in this hotel room with like a zillion yen all over the room,' he said. 'I thought I'd never need to work another day.'

Nervous that he would be robbed, Norman packed it all into a briefcase and carried it on the plane with him, later depositing it in a foreign bank account at American Express in London. On one of those leaden March days when the wind blows cold enough to freeze the breath in your lungs, Norman arrived in England to start his new life. Marshall picked him up at the airport in a big black Bentley and ferried him home to Hampshire through a patchwork of green and white. When they turned up the long driveway that led to the magnificent Beaurepaire House, Norman felt a rush of euphoria. Lois, Marshall's warm, smiling wife, and the Alsatians Bruno and Celia were there to greet him. He pinched himself. If he hadn't arrived yet, he was well on the way.

Norman was frozen to the marrow. His skin was stretched taut across his bones like a cold compress and his rain-jacket restricted his backswing. His hands had lost all feeling. He stared miserably across the bleak moonscape of Royal St George's, gripped and regripped the club, and contemplated another bogey. There was no doubt that he was going to miss the cut in the PGA Championship, his first British tournament. He tried to convince himself it was because the course didn't suit him.

'I dislike the type of golf test Royal St George's presents because I believe luck plays too great a part,' he said, nearly six years later. 'I dislike St Andrews and Muirfield for the same reason . . . I prefer to play "target" golf on a course where I know that there is no hidden pimple in the middle of the fairway to send my ball into strangling rough.'

In 1975, Severiano Ballesteros had formed exactly the same impression. 'It was horrible,' recalled the Spaniard who, despite winning three Opens on the links of St Andrews and Royal Lytham, has never found a place in his heart for St George's. 'So cold, so much wind, so different from any other course I had ever known. Especially I didn't like the fact that there were no trees for my eyes to get reference . . . I tell you, by the time I had played one round I didn't like *anything* about Sandwich.'

After all Marshall's support Norman felt embarrassed to have missed two consecutive cuts. He subjected himself to a harsh post-mortem of each costly shot and set off to Blairgowrie for the Martini International determined to justify his manager's faith. There, on the heather-lined fairways, Norman found his feet. He stretched to the watery sun, flexed his golfing muscles and played with as much joy and abandon as he ever had in Australia. After three rounds, he was two strokes behind the leader Howard Clark. He felt comfortable and confident. At the tenth on the final day, he seized his chance. He made five birdies in six holes for a course record 66 and victory by three shots over Simon Hobday. His 277 total earned him £3,000. 'I've been trying to forget him ever since,' said the Zimbabwean.

Ken Schofield, the executive director of the European Tour, has a vivid recollection of seeing the Australian's name next to his final round score: 1066 (10 under par, 66) – the date of the Norman Conquest.

The media embraced him with open arms. Bored rigid with the ageing European stalwarts who had not yet surrendered to the new guard, they saluted him as a surfer-boy incarnation of Jack Nicklaus. 'Dazzler Greg Storms In,' cried the *Sunday Express*. The *Sunday Telegraph* described him as 'the most exciting newcomer to hit the world professional scene for some considerable time. Norman catches both the eye and the imagination. With his blond hair and Nicklaus hairstyle goes a lovely looping swing and a slide into the ball that generates enormous power with no apparent effort.'

Marshall was ecstatic. He rewarded Norman with a shotgun and, while Norman tried it out on an assortment of unfortunate rabbits and grouse, spent days on the phone to potential sponsors. He had known the Australian for less than a month and already it was hard to imagine life without him. Norman radiated energy and a kind of irrepressible exuberance. They played golf together, went shooting together.

'He lived with me literally as a son might have done,' Marshall says. 'He was a fun, normal guy, sort of like a great big teddy-bear. He was very kind and considerate.'

From the outset, Norman, Marshall and Earp had been in agreement that Europe was the ideal proving ground for him. Norman's plan was to go to the States when he was twenty-five and had some experience behind him. 'He had a lot of growing up to do, golf-wise and otherwise,' Marshall remembers.

A few days after Norman's victory in the Martini International, Marshall ordered him to pack a bag. They were off to Los Angeles to talk business with Wilson, the sporting-goods company. It was Norman's first introduction to the thrust and parry of deal-making and it left an indelible impression on him. When he returned to London, he had a three-year contract worth $100,000, plus bonuses.

'I fully expect Greg to be a millionaire by the time he's thirty,' Marshall told reporters.

Norman reacted to his newfound wealth with unabashed glee. He embraced it, celebrated it and reached eagerly and unashamedly for the trappings that accompanied it. Later, he recalled that the contract with Wilson 'paved the way to an extravagance I had never been able to enjoy previously' by making him feel secure and prosperous. He decided he simply had to have a new wardrobe. Naturally, Marshall knew just the place and had all the right connections, and before Norman could say 'American Express', he was being shepherded around Harrods with the store manager at one elbow and his own manager at the other. There followed a shopping spree which – although insignificant beside some of Norman's later indulgences – was the biggest he had ever been on at the time. Suits, sports jackets, shirts, ties, trousers, underwear and a fine watch piled up at the checkout, and the eventual tally was a staggering £4,000.

It didn't stop there. He loved the speed and superior lines of Marshall's Ferrari, and a second-hand Ferrari of his own was the next item on his agenda. Stewart Ginn, another Australian managed by Marshall, remembers Norman's infectious delight when he picked out the sleek red car and paid the salesman. 'He wanted to drive it straight out the showroom.' Ginn laughs. 'He couldn't bear to wait two days for it to be delivered. He said: "Give me the keys, I want to drive it *right* now!" '

Norman enjoyed nothing more than to put his foot flat and feel the wind in his hair. Fined £150 for doing 112 m.p.h., he took to playing a dangerous game of hide and seek with police on the country lanes. Within months, he had decided that the red Ferrari was too conspicuous and bought a silver one, which he treasured. Although he pushed it to 162 m.p.h., he was only once stopped for speeding, and the policeman asked for his autograph and let him go.

Bill Longmuir recalls Norman's passion for his cars with amusement. Whenever they went into London's West End, Norman insisted on driving, and he had Longmuir and the Italian player Baldovino Dassu in the car one night when he went straight through a red light. 'It was just turning red,' recalls Longmuir, 'but there was a police car behind us and this police car was straight on our tail and pulled him over. I thought: Oh, my God, he's going to have the book thrown at him here!

'But Greg jumped out and he said, "Before you say anything, if I had tried to stop at that light, I would have caused an accident." And the policeman was sort of taken aback. He thought, Holy shit, who is this guy? And let him off! It was great.'

By the time Norman finished, he had spent more than $100,000 on the Ferraris. Commenting on this spree in 1981, he told Australia's *National Times*, 'That was stupid. I had the money and I thought, Now I'll go out and live like a king. But I'm over that now. I've sold both Ferraris and I want more of a sedan-type car. I also went mad buying good clothes. I have shirts I've never got out of their wrappers.'

His erstwhile manager remembers that period well. 'He had two things that were always bubbling to the surface, that needed controlling,' Marshall says. 'One was that he had a *phenomenal* ego. I don't think I've ever met anybody with quite such a big ego, even at that age. Secondly, he was ultra materialistic. Very impressed by money, very impressed by people who had money, and very materialistically oriented. Those, to me, were slight danger signs. I tried to get him to get life into perspective.'

But Norman's perspective had already been irrevocably altered. Even now he can recall feeling 'like I was King of the Hill. All of these things you get enamoured with. You don't see the forest for the trees. I had all these things around me and showered on me. I felt like I was some Lord of the Manor.'

While Marshall opened the door to a lifestyle Norman had only dreamed of, taking him to publicity launches and dinners with Muhammad Ali (his twin brother John produced the renowned Ali documentary, *The Greatest*), Norman set about conquering Europe with his raw talent and uncomplicated charm. There was no side to him; what you saw was what you got. 'He was very green between the ears,' Jack Newton says. 'I mean, he hadn't been playing that long and he sort of burst onto the scene, had a lot of success early, and was pretty confident and brash.'

But as Derek Pillage, who managed Sandy Lyle and Lee Trevino early in their careers, observed, 'There was something about him that was different from anybody else, almost like a young Sean Connery.'

To the British press, Norman bore more than a superficial resemblance to the Golden Bear, and they were constantly comparing them. 'He looks like Nicklaus, he swings like Nicklaus and he hits the ball as far as Nicklaus,' they reported on the eve of the Open Championship. Norman, whom Nicklaus was trying to persuade to move to America sooner rather than later, tried to play it down.

'Sure it's good to get the flattering publicity and attention,' he conceded. 'But I don't want to be a bighead. That's my greatest fear.'

Missing the cut at Turnberry went some way to ensuring that didn't happen immediately, but his game and his physique were so extraordinary that he couldn't help but attract comment. 'Greg had a lot going for him,' said Marshall, who was fielding off endorsements from day one. 'He was unusual-looking, he was tall, he was blond, he was an extrovert and he generated a lot of excitement wherever he went.'

But already Norman's gifts were the target of resentment. There was a perception among certain players that he was snobbish and standoffish. 'He had a huge amount of style and I think the British players looked upon him in a jealous manner,' Longmuir says. 'In some ways, the European Tour was a little bit cliquey in those days. It was very British. And he blew them apart.'

Analysing Norman's swing, Lou Miller, the head pro at Pinehurst, North Carolina, and one of the leading teachers at the time, was astounded to hear that the Australian had only taken up golf in his late teens. 'He has talent beyond those few years of experience and once he has harnessed his tremendous power he will be an outstanding player,' he said. His only concern was that Norman's legs might occasionally be too active, causing him to 'hit a big push shot to the right'. For the most part, Norman's 'amazing hand and eye coordination' helped him to correct any problems, but Miller worried that under pressure that facility might desert him.

Ken Brown, who first played with Norman in the Uniroyal International at Moor Park, where he finished equal ninth, says that, while his technique wasn't nearly as good as it is now, Norman was a 'very impressive hitter of the golf ball. He did hit it absolutely enormous distances and the equipment we used then wasn't very good. But each round, he'd miss two or three putts, and his short game then was just like a miniature full swing. Now he has one of the best short games in golf.'

He warmed to the Australian immediately. 'Whenever I played with him, I always thought that he took the game in a nice spirit. Although he tried his hardest, gave it a hundred and ten per cent, even in the early days I thought he was a very sporting person. He took it all in his stride, all the ups and downs. He took it as a game, rather than an obsession. It wasn't life and death. As a personality, he was larger than life. He came over with James Marshall and he had the air of already being a superstar and a millionaire, even though he hadn't proved that he was a star.'

Under Marshall's guidance, Norman blossomed. Marshall was firm with him, patient with him, coaxed him, gently educated him. When Norman came home after missing a cut and wanted to sit around venting his frustration and disgustedly telling his manager he could have beaten half the field, Marshall would shut him up by telling him, 'Well, you didn't. There's no point in saying you might have done.'

Marshall was quite protective of his young protégé, and right from the start there was a sort of distancing of Norman from the other players – even Australians he knew. He discouraged Norman from hanging around the golf club after his rounds. To Marshall, the course could be likened to an office or even a boxing ring, and long lunches and drinking sessions with players one was trying to beat were not conducive to a tough competitive attitude.

Another area he worked on with Norman was media relations, explaining to him that he couldn't just be nice to the press when it suited him. 'You had to be able to be civilized to the press whether you had a good round or a bad round. I tried to get him to see that also in other people, that the local caddie was just as important as the local president in his own way. I tried to sort of instil in him a sense of values, I suppose.'

To anyone who had ever known Norman as a sun-kissed surfer, with hardly a worry in the world as he took his first steps in golf, the change in him was dramatic.

'Marshall gave Greg a lot of sophistication,' Tom Ramsey says. 'I think Marshall almost taught Greg to hold a knife and fork. That was my feeling at the time.'

Norman freely admits it. 'He actually took me under his wing and taught me the finer side of life. You know, because I didn't have any refinement about me, about how to dress and how to eat at dinners and all that stuff, and he actually taught me all that. It was wonderful. From then until now, the things he taught me all those years ago I use every day. So there was a lot of good that he did and a lot of bad.'

There was one other person who had almost as much influence over Norman at that age as Marshall: Stewart Ginn, Marshall's other client. Ginn first got to know Norman when he was paired with him for the first two rounds of the West Lakes Classic. 'I thought, My God, this guy's unbelievable,' says Ginn, now playing on the Japanese Tour. 'As a fellow competitor, you knew he was something special. It was scary to watch him play in those days. He had no fear. He *still* has no fear. I'd never seen a player go at a golf ball the way he did at that time.'

The week after West Lakes, Ginn and Norman met up for a beer and a meal and they had been firm friends ever since. During Norman's first few years on the Tour, they shopped, played golf and hung out at Beaurepaire House together. 'He was a lot of fun,' Ginn says affectionately. 'A real character.' Ginn would borrow one of Norman's Ferraris, Norman would drive the other and they would tear off to tournaments like some high-speed version of Jack Kerouac and Neal Cassady (alias Sal Paradise and Dean Moriarty) in *On the Road*, footloose and in love with life.

'Ginny taught Norman how to be Hollywood,' says Mike Clayton, an Australian player, course designer and columnist. 'Ginny had the big hair and the Ferrari. Ginny wore the most outrageous clothes in the seventies. Ginny is the only guy who you can look at in photos from the seventies and he doesn't look ridiculous. He could carry it off . . . Greg cultivated his image pretty early on and he could pull it off, too. He had the presence to pull it off.'

Ginn, who nicknamed Norman 'Hollywood', described him as a quick learner when it came to style and fast living. 'When he was twenty, twenty-one, he was a wild boy.' He laughs. 'He was mad. He was a bit crazy. He was like a wild horse – you couldn't tame him. In a lot of respects Marshall was quite good for him. He helped him out, taught him what to say and how to say it. Before Marshall came along, his nickname was "Bomber". One reason was how hard he used to hit the ball. He didn't care what was in the way, trees, skyscrapers. But it was also because he was a maniac in a car and he was a good joker. He loved to play pranks – he still does. He was mad.'

'He had his wild moments,' Jimmy Barden, a friend from Norman's youth, told Chris Hodenfield in *Today's Golfer*. 'Once we were towing Merv's boat back of my car and we got stuck in a traffic jam. So Greg says turn here, now turn here, and soon we were pulling this boat over the back nine at Virginia. I had no idea where we were going. He just kept pushing me along.'

One of Norman's favourite party tricks was ripping on the hand-brake while travelling at an unsafe pace. 'I remember coming up the drive to the golf club at the Australian Open with him,' Ginn says. 'We were in a souped-up yellow Ford or something, from one of the cowboys, and he locks the brakes, and the engine is screaming and smoke's pouring out, and he doesn't care. He was an idiot.'

Norman always claims that, as a young man, he was an introvert. 'I absolutely had to force myself to speak to people, no question about it,' he told *Fore!*. 'I was so shy it was almost painful. I was into myself and I was terrified to bring myself out. The only time I felt sure of myself, the only time I felt confident, was when I was on the golf course.' He has a clear recollection of sitting by himself after the presentation ceremony at West Lakes, dressed in white trousers and a green shirt, knowing that he was supposed to mingle with sponsors but not knowing how. 'I said to myself, "Son, you've got to change," ' Norman remembers. ' "If you want to be the best player you can be, and go on and win golf tournaments, you're going to have to learn to mingle and make conversation . . ." That was harder for me than working on my golf game because it went against my grain. It probably took me five years.'

His mother says that he was only 'shy-ish. He always says that when he won the West Lakes Classic he sat in the corner by himself having a beer, but I think that's a bit of an exaggeration. His friend was caddying for him so he was probably there.'

On the Tour, Norman was popular with those players good enough not to be jealous of him, namely Sam Torrance, a rough, talented Scot; Michael King, universally known as Queenie; an Irishman with a talent for fun called John O'Leary; and, of course, Bill Longmuir. There was a tiny pub behind the racecourse in York that was a favourite haunt of the five of them, and they spent time there whenever they were in town. 'Greg used to do lot of nice things for people,' Ginn says, remembering Norman's kindness towards the owners, 'and one of them was always staying there. It was only a tiny place and he could have stayed anywhere he liked, but he always made a point of going back there, even when he became who he became.'

Years later, Norman told *Sports Illustrated* that Merv's muted response to his early achievements preyed on his mind. 'Even when I started climbing the ladder, he didn't think I'd be anything,' Norman said. 'I had a point to prove to him, to everybody.'

Today, Norman believes that his first three victories were crucial to his success. 'The West Lakes Classic, the Martini and the tournament I won in Japan – my first three tournaments I won on each respective Tour – were the most important for me.'

In the second half of 1977, he was eighth in the Scandinavian Enterprise Open, third in the Irish Open and racked up five top-five finishes in Australia. He also went across to America to play in the Memorial Tournament in Dublin, Ohio, at the invitation of Jack Nicklaus. When he missed the cut, he was totally distraught. Larry O'Brien, vice-president of Nicklaus's Golden Bear International, recalled that 'every morning he'd get up early and go hit three hundred or more balls on the practice tee. He was so determined that this would not happen again.'

The only hitch in a very well-laid set of plans was the $180,000 Australian Open pro-am, to which Norman was not invited. It was a petty snub and James Marshall was justifiably angry on his behalf. 'Here is a guy who has made a terrific impression for Australian golf in Britain and Japan this year,' he told the press, after heated confrontations with various officials. 'Yet he is kicked in the backside like this.' When the officials claimed there had been an oversight and allowed Norman to play, he got his own back by winning.

Looking back, Peter Thomson believes that Norman's first few years on the European Tour were some of the happiest of his career. 'I don't think there was any pressure on him at all. He was enjoying himself immensely. The "majors", as we call them, didn't come into his thinking. He was out there having a ball, playing golf, which he wanted to do more than anything, plenty of social life, big flash cars and a lot of money flooding in. He was on top of the world.'

# CHAPTER FOUR

# LOVE AND WAR

'The envy brigade is very strong in golf.'

COLIN SNAPE, 1997

IN THE 13 DECEMBER 1978 edition of the *Sun*, there is a picture of Norman with a big smile on his face and his arm around Sue Barker, the British tennis player who had been the world number three the previous year. They make an attractive couple. The headline reads, 'It's Sue With Her New Beau In Tow', and Norman is reported as saying, 'She's going to teach me tennis and I'll teach her golf.'

For a sportsman who was routinely described as movie-star handsome and charming to boot, Norman seems to have had few, if any, serious relationships before he married. Bill Longmuir has a dim recollection of an Australian girl, left behind during his first season, but essentially Norman was quite reserved. On the golf course, he had a natural presence and a ready smile that made him seem more gregarious than he was, but away from it he preferred to race his car down the narrow country lanes, walk the dogs, or sit with his gun on the bonnet of Marshall's jeep in the dark grounds at Beaurepaire House, picking off rabbits in the headlights.

'When he came back from a tournament, he wasn't interested in getting into the car and driving into the city to the nightclubs,' Marshall says. 'He wasn't like that.'

To some extent that changed when he met Barker at a golf tournament in Brisbane in November 1978. Introduced by Marshall, they liked each other on sight. When they left Australia, they left together, and Barker followed him to the World Cup in Hawaii, Mexico City and New York before they returned to England for Christmas.

Barker, who had recently split with her coach and suffered a slump on the tennis court, had also broken off her engagement to a tennis player just six weeks before she met Norman. In February she told the *Daily Mirror*, 'It worries me that I'll be away from Greg, but we both realize that our careers are the most important thing at the moment.' In the *Daily Mail*, she described her relationship with Norman as 'an easy thing. Not intense. We're very similar.'

'The guy who said absence makes the heart grow fonder was dead right,' grinned Norman. 'I'd hate to see my telephone bill.'

In 1978 Norman had won four times in Australia and once in Fiji, beginning by making seven birdies and an eagle in a course record 64 to beat Ian Stanley by three strokes in the Caltex Festival of Sydney Open in January. In seventy-two holes, he made just three bogeys. Elsewhere, he felt he had met ill fortune at every turn.

'I'm not using that as an excuse,' he said in September at Pacific Harbour, the Fijian resort he had signed a two-year deal to represent. 'It's just a totally new experience for me. I seem to have been dogged by bad luck since my two Australian victories in January. Take the Swiss Open last week. I was a shot behind playing the eighth hole and I knew I could reach the par five in two for an eagle chance. My shot hit a small stake fifteen yards in front of me, flew back, hit my caddie and rebounded into deep rough. Any chance of winning went out the door right there. And that's the sort of luck I've been having.'

Three days later, he won the South Seas Classic on the third hole of a play-off.

Marshall remembers Norman's brief romance with Barker as a rarity in his life. 'I wouldn't say he was a lady-killer by any stretch of the imagination. As I say, the Greg I knew and managed and who lived with us was very, very different from the Greg he became, but leopards don't change their spots. They can only change them super-ficially. I mean, there are numerous things that Greg will say about things that just plainly aren't true. For example, if you were to say to Greg, "Did you know Sue Barker very well?" he'd brush it off and say, "Very superficially." But of course it's not true. He was very keen on Sue. It was Sue who finished the relationship.'

In point of fact, Norman was denying that his relationship with Barker had ever been anything but the most casual of acquaintance-ships by May the following year. 'We were just friends,' he said firmly. 'It's hardly worth mentioning.'

The line of traffic stretched far into the foggy distance on the moun-tain road that led to the New Territories. Norman and Marshall sat resignedly in the back of the limousine, staring out at the fine mist rain that blurred the Hong Kong skyline. They had allowed an hour to get to Fanling Golf Club but it was taking two. Norman glanced at his watch and swore. 'We're going to be lucky to make it,' he said.

In three years on Tour, Norman had learned several useful lessons, one of them being that the first rule of travel was to be patient in situ-ations he could do nothing about. However, he had also become much more outspoken. Take the subject of appearance money, which was an issue very early on in his career. 'Players can't bitch about what the sponsor wants to do with his money,' Norman said, after hearing that Bob Shearer planned to boycott the 1979 Australian PGA because David Graham was getting $10,000 to play. 'If the Yanks get it certainly the Aussies should get it if they've proved themselves. I know Melbourne is Bobby's home town but he's won nothing really big yet. David has won the Australian Open, he has proved himself in America and won the World Match Play Championship.'

It was the first of numerous rows in Australia over appearance fees. By 1981, he was paid everywhere he played, with the exception of the World Match Play, the Martini and the US. His fees in his own country had rocketed to $15,000, although Marshall claimed he didn't receive a cent to play in the Australian Open. Significantly, Norman was one of the only players to support his arch-rival Ballesteros during the Spaniard's dispute with the European Tour

46

Players Division that year, describing him as 'the Arnold Palmer of Europe' to officials. It made no difference. Ballesteros resigned from the Tour in protest over the appearance-money ban and was controversially left out of the Ryder Cup.

In Hong Kong, where Norman was appearing early in 1979 as part of his Cathay-Pacific deal, Marshall climbed out of the car and enterprisingly organized a police escort. They arrived at the club with five minutes to spare. Norman was three strokes off the lead and paired with Little Lu, the nephew of the diminutive, pork-pie-hatted Mr Lu who had been narrowly beaten by Lee Trevino in the 1971 Open. The gallery was large and vociferous and, when the referee awarded him a free drop from GUR at the ninth, they took on a mob mentality. Upset by their perceptible anger Norman topped his next tee shot, but held on to win with a 16-foot birdie putt at the last. The $20,000 cheque was the biggest of his career so far.

Five years later, when he won the Hong Kong Open again, Norman whiled away a rain-out by hitting balls out of his hotel window into the harbour far below.

When the first-class passengers were called, Norman and Marshall made their way out to the plane. Norman smiled perfunctorily in the direction of the flight attendants as he headed towards his seat. His heart stopped, skipped a beat, started again jerkily. A strange feeling of euphoria swept over him. He fastened his seatbelt. Then he looked over at the beautiful brunette who had caught his gaze.

'I remember telling James Marshall, "I bet you I'll marry that woman,"' Norman says. 'And I had never even met her, never even said one word to her.'

It was the summer of 1979. Norman and Marshall were flying from Detroit to New York after his first US Open at Inverness, where he had finished forty-eighth. His disappointment vanished at a stroke when Laura Andrassy came down the aisle. Marshall cast an amused glance at his face and shook his head.

'What can I get you?' Laura asked.

'A 7-Up, please,' Norman said.

Marshall jumped up.

'You sit down, honey. I'll get the drinks,' he said, and reached for

Laura's tray. Ignoring her protests, he steered her briskly into his seat. 'I'd like to introduce you to Gregory Norman,' he said, and departed to help several open-mouthed flight attendants mix drinks for the passengers.

Norman flushed with embarrassment. He hated being called by his full name. Recovering his composure, he began politely to ask her where she was from and about her job at American Airlines. 'He was shy and so was I but we managed to get a conversation going,' Laura recalled.

Laura had done several charter flights with athletes, notably the Oakland Raiders and the New York Knicks, most of whom had left a bad impression on her ('They're all kind of grubby guys'). Her first reaction when she heard Norman was a golfer was, ' "Oh, not another one of those athletes." But he was such a gentleman. He didn't drink and he wasn't a rowdy type of guy, and I was very impressed by that.'

Later in the flight, she went up to the cockpit. 'I said, "Guys, I think I'm in love. There's this golfer out there named Greg Norman." They said, "He's pulling your leg. There's no such golfer." They said he was giving me this story so I'd go out with him.'

Fate hasn't often been kind to Norman but it was kind to him then. The forty-minute flight was extended to eighty by air-traffic controllers and he asked Laura to have dinner with him when they reached New York. At first she was hesitant, but Norman persisted and when they landed at midnight she agreed to meet him in Manhattan. He was checking into his hotel when she paged him. There was a fuel strike and she couldn't get a taxi. Refusing to be diverted, Norman decided to call a cab and collect her. None were available for love or money. He was standing on the empty street, cursing his luck, when a limousine pulled up and two passengers stepped out.

'When he showed up in front of my hotel in this long black limousine, I thought, Who in the heck is this guy?' Laura says. By then, it was nearly 2 a.m. and every restaurant they tried was closing. Norman and Laura sat in the back of the limo with the lights of Manhattan flashing in, and laughed until they cried. 'I thought he was wonderful,' says Laura, who wondered afterwards whether she would ever hear from him again. 'We had such a nice time. We got along just like that, immediately. He was a real gentleman. Not pushy. Very appealing, in fact.'

The bill for the limousine was $200. 'You're crazy,' Marshall told Norman gruffly when he put him on a plane to Bermuda the next day. Norman didn't care. He had already tried to persuade Laura to come to Britain for the Open. 'I thought, This guy's crazy,' Laura said. 'I don't even know him.' She suggested that he should come to New York again instead. Norman, who had returned to Britain for a few days before leaving again for Japan, arranged to spend three days there on his way back. On their first evening together, they had a moonlit dinner at the Twin Trade Towers restaurant.

'I guess that's probably when we fell in love,' Laura says.

Norman did convince Laura she should come to Britain, but after the Open not before it. 'The tournament is too important to you and I would only be in the way,' she said, so Norman went to Royal Lytham well before the tournament started. Out in the twisting sea breezes, he mapped the soft ochre links and tall grasses and puzzled over the greens. When he finished eighth, he was disappointed. That was the year that Ballesteros, the raven-haired Spanish genius, combined some of the wildest driving and most magical recovery shots – notoriously a birdie from the car-park near the sixteenth on the final day – ever seen at an Open to become the youngest winner this century. Norman, who felt he was in with a chance, scored a 76 that day and complained that the last round 'did not treat me kindly'.

The day after the Open, he drove his red Ferrari to Heathrow Airport to fetch Laura. She was in London for only four days but they made the most of them, taking long walks through the woods at Beaurepaire House, sightseeing at St Paul's, Madame Tussaud's and the Tower of London, and enjoying cosy dinners with James and Lois Marshall. They felt very comfortable with one another. The only bad moment came when Norman's Ferrari was damaged by vandals when they were at dinner in the West End one night. The bill for restoring it came to £1,000.

Towards the end of the season, Norman strained his back and was out for six weeks, but he recovered in time for the Australian Open. With the exception of the majors, there was no title on earth he wanted more and, when he shot 73, 69, 73 to take the lead going into the last round, he was overjoyed.

On Sunday, a duel developed between Norman and Jack Newton. To Norman, Newton was 'a character of enormous magnetism who treats the game with an outwardly casual approach, chain-smoking his way from tee to green and, when the day's work is finished, is always ready to slap a dollar on the bar and enjoy himself'. That there was a little more to Newton was demonstrated by his performance at Metropolitan. Norman, who could have won with a birdie on the eighteenth, three-putted from the lower tier some 20 feet away to hand the tournament to his rival.

To this day, he can remember his mind going black and his body turning ice-cold as the putt that would have left him tied for the Australian Open slipped past the hole. 'Disappointment and disbelief were merged into a nightmarish experience I will never forget.'

Up in the stands, his mother burst into tears. Newton was engulfed by jubilant well-wishers. Sportingly, Norman put an arm around him and said, 'Great work, Newts,' before stumbling away to the locker room, where his father and caddie were waiting. Told an hour later that he had been fined $50 for failing to reappear for the prize-giving ceremony, he blew his top in the tournament director's office, claiming that nobody had come to tell him it was taking place.

'The next day the Australian papers all carried the same story: "Norman lacks the guts to become a champion," ' he recalled in his instruction book, *Shark Attack!*. ' "He missed his chance, and now he'll never win a big one." When I saw those headlines, I was livid. I vowed to [teach] those newspapers a lesson, and the next year I did.'

He took a break then and enjoyed the summer, fishing and shooting kangaroos to his heart's content. His antidote to all the activity was the occasional lie-in. 'I've been known to sleep for twelve hours when I'm not playing golf.' He grinned.

Due to a dispute between Marshall and the sponsors (Marshall claims it was due to Norman rather than him, and that, after a 'dust-up with Cathay-Pacific, Norman almost became *persona non grata*' in the region), Norman did not defend his Hong Kong Open title. Nor did he get to the Spanish Open. He and Stewart Ginn flew into Madrid from the Italian Open, unaware that they needed visas, and were put straight on a plane to London.

In the end, both incidents were minor blips in a brilliant season. Norman cut a swathe across the European circuit, finishing ten shots clear of the field in the French Open, winning the Scandinavian Open and the World Match Play and racking up more than a dozen top tens. 'Each tournament you win is like going up another step,' he said. 'Then all of a sudden you come to major championships . . . By the time I'm thirty or thirty-one, I'll know if I'm going to make it to number one.'

At the Irish Open in August, Jackie Lee, who had followed Paul 'the Singing Caddie' Stevens on to Norman's bag, turned up late for duty and was promptly sacked. Scotty Gilmour, a grizzled veteran of more than twenty years on the US circuit, offered his services. He had started caddying during the Second World War, had been evacuated to Turnberry during the Blitz, and later carried the bags of some of the best players in the game, including Tony Jacklin, Tom Weiskopf, Gary Player and Arnold Palmer.

Norman reminded him of Raymond Floyd. 'Same kind of mind as Floyd,' says Gilmour, who earned £175 per week plus 5 per cent for a place. 'Completely zoned. Just cut everything off in the world. Kind of a Jekyll and Hyde on the course and sometimes in his social life . . . Same type of personality as Floyd. They can be the nicest guys in the world one day and the next day they're the complete opposite.' He had lot of fun with Norman in the beginning. 'He was a bit crazy. Quite wild. He'd jump in a car and go a hundred miles an hour down a country lane. Reckless. I had some good laughs with him.'

When Norman finally won the Australian Open at The Lakes that year, Gilmour told reporters, 'I've caddied for the best, and let me tell you, he's going to be the one to beat around the world. Next year, he'll be a household name.'

'He's a great believer in me,' said Norman, for whom victory had brought the promise of the most priceless award of all, an invitation to the US Masters. 'He never thinks I'm going to shoot a bad round. He's done a lot for my game.'

He had been desperately disappointed when he lost the European Order of Merit by just £278 to Sandy Lyle, but it hadn't altered his lifestyle. In Australia, the *National Times* reported that Norman had bought and sold property in Honolulu, London and Queensland. His most recent purchase was a $175,000 Australian Gold Coast house, with a pool and a jetty leading down to the sea, which Laura was helping him to decorate. In the US, he stayed with Laura in her apartment in Washington DC. 'Laura's very upset with me because I don't know how much money I've got,' laughed Norman, who was heading off to Divot, his new home at Paradise Point. 'I've got bank accounts here and in England and America. When I get a cheque I put it in the bank in whatever country I'm in. I don't know what it adds up to.'

The envelope that would influence Norman's destiny arrived at his parents' home in Brisbane early in 1981. The card inside, with its distinctive symbol – a yellow flag inside an emerald green outline of the United States – was more than just an invitation to the Masters. It was a passport to agony, ecstasy and history.

Norman was delirious with excitement, promptly winning the Australian Masters by seven shots at Huntingdale, and setting off to Augusta with hope in his heart. Years before, Arnold Palmer had said that 'From the moment I set foot on Augusta National, my whole view of the game of golf changed. In fact, I think Augusta National actually set the tone for my entire career. It was such an immaculate place with everything done first class. And the grass was just beautiful. It was pretty awesome.'

In a slightly different sense, Augusta set the tone for Norman's career. As soon as he turned up Magnolia Drive, breathed in the heavenly scent of the pines and saw the pristine white clubhouse, the pink, white and scarlet splash of azaleas, rhododendron and dogwood, and the snowy bunkers etched against the flawless emerald fairways, he felt the same way Palmer did. 'I'll never forget how I was struck by Augusta that first year,' he told *Golf Digest*. 'This was what golf was meant to be, pure golf. This was the purest form of golf tournament. Everything about it was first rate. That stroke up Magnolia Drive, with the clubhouse ahead, the practice ranges on either side, it just gets you in the perfect frame of mind for a tournament.'

Standing on the first tee a few days later, Norman struggled to recall his earlier enthusiasm. He felt sick. Nerves gathered like termites in his stomach and gnawed away at his innards. His clubs felt like lead weights in his hands. He avoided the eyes of his partner, stared glumly down the fairway and executed a stiff practice swing. When the starter announced his name, he pushed his drive woodenly down the first and walked after it with his eyes fixed firmly on the hill in front of him.

A smile tugged at Nicklaus's mouth. He put an arm around his young partner's shoulders and said quietly, 'I don't know about you, but by the time we reach the top of this hill, my feet will just about be back on the ground. I'm so nervous.'

Norman had never felt so grateful to anyone in his life. Relief flooded through him, the nauseous feeling receded and all of a sudden Augusta looked beautiful again. He felt he could focus, could think about putting his name on the leaderboard. 'Take a deep breath and let's enjoy the golf,' Nicklaus said encouragingly.

Norman did just that. When the round ended, he was tied for the lead with Johnny Miller, Keith Fergus, Lon Hinkle and Curtis Strange on 69. 'Just being here is probably the greatest thrill of my life,' Norman told reporters.

It was the first time many of the Americans had seen Norman play, much less had the chance to speak to him, and Norman felt slightly overwhelmed by the size of the press corps. 'What should I say if they ask me what I do?' he panicked.

'Oh,' said Marshall airily, 'tell them that you love hunting great white sharks.'

In his press conference, Norman, lighting up the room with his sunburned, muscular physique and toothpaste smile, painted a picture of blissful childhood, surfing and skin-diving on the Great Barrier Reef, casually remarking that he would love to have shot the sharks that ate the fish he caught. The next morning, the headline on the *Augusta Chronicle* read: 'Great White Shark Leads Masters'.

In the second round, Nicklaus took control of the tournament, shooting a 65 that could easily have been a course record and left him with a four-shot lead. Norman recorded an impressive 70 and played Augusta, where experience is everything, as if his game was made for

53

the spacious fairways and enigmatic greens. The third round developed into a duel between Nicklaus and Tom Watson, but Norman held on to record a 72 and lie third going into the final round.

Afterwards, he described his six-iron to the sixteenth on Saturday as 'one of the best six-irons of my life. Jack had the honour and he hit a shot in there close. Jack *is* Jack at Augusta. The people went nuts. I stepped up and hit a six-iron inside of him. I'll always remember that shot. I felt like King of the Hill.'

Had it not been for a double-bogey at the tenth on Sunday, Norman might have been able to overhaul Watson. At the seventh, a perfect pitch shot earned him a birdie and moved him alongside Nicklaus on five under par. At the turn, Watson was just two in front. But at the par four tenth, Norman pulled his drive into the trees, and was three under par when he emerged from them. He finished fourth on 283, three behind Watson and one behind Nicklaus and Miller, an extraordinary achievement for a player with so little experience on American courses and none at Augusta.

The US media greeted his arrival as rapturously as their European counterparts had four years earlier. 'With his platinum-blond Prince Valiant hairdo, Norman looks more like a surfer than a golfer,' wrote Herbert Warren Wind in the *New Yorker*, 'but . . . [he] should do very well if he decides to campaign in this country.'

'Norman's an awfully strong young player,' Nicklaus agreed. 'I think he will get a Green Jacket one of these days. He's also got something golf needs – charisma.'

'He's like a big cat, almost ferocious in his intensity,' said the teacher Paul Runyan. 'I thought his swing looked very sound.'

These accolades were all very well, but Norman, who had been close enough to the Green Jacket almost to feel its cool silk lining sliding over his shoulders, was bitterly disappointed. It's hard to imagine that he wasn't heartsore as he drove away from Augusta, and yet it was the first of numerous occasions in his career when he appeared to put it into a locked room in his mind and move on almost instantaneously. That night, he asked Laura to marry him.

'I'm the kind of guy who just lives for now,' Norman said. 'I can forget about everything. When I lost the Masters, I went back to the house and [Laura] and my friends were all sad. I had to cheer *them* up. There was nothing to be done except learn from it. I have.'

The invention of Norman's Great White Shark label had a bizarre twist. Norman felt that, during the press conference where he talked about hating sharks and wanting to destroy them, a misunderstanding had arisen and the journalists gained the impression that he had actually shot a few. Since this was not the case, the inaccuracy bothered him. 'When I got back to Australia later that year, I decided to put my conscience at ease,' Norman recalled. He put a .303 rifle in the cabin of *Divot II*, his 28-foot ocean-going cruiser, spent several hours patrolling the coastline in Queensland and, when he spotted a dorsal fin, 'buried several bullets into the thick skin of an ugly hammerhead and hoped those American golf writers understood'.

As to whether the shark – massacred to lend veracity to an unpleasant embellishment – understood, he doesn't say.

His conscience clear, his dream partly realized, Norman launched into 1981 with gusto. 'No-one could ever accuse Greg Norman of being modest,' Louis T. Stanley observed in the *Pelham Golf Yearbook*. 'His self-confidence and belief in himself is tantamount to a pep talk. When he arrived in Britain this year he mentioned as an aside that he intended to win three tournaments. Just like that. And the remarkable thing is that he almost did so.'

Item one on Norman's agenda was to win another Martini at Wentworth. All week long, rain slanted across the fairways of the Burma Road course and Sunday was no different. By the time Norman reached the eighteenth, delays had stretched his final round to nearly six hours. He was cold and wet, but he felt good on the greens. His mother had posted him the putter he had vented his rage on after the Australian Open two years earlier. Once again, his drive died where it pitched, kicking up a muddy spray. 'You need an eagle to be sure of winning,' his caddie told him.

Norman hesitated. He selected a one-iron, gave it everything he had and it soared 228 yards down the fairway. It landed 18 yards from the pin and Norman stroked it in for an eagle three. When Bernhard

Langer's birdie putt turned away from the hole, the Australian won his third Martini with a total of 287, the only score under par.

To Norman, there was no reason he couldn't win three successive events, but Nick Faldo had other plans. The Englishman's willowy swing and methodical approach were suited to Ganton and, in the final round, when unruly galleries crowded the fairways, he swept to 10 under par to win the PGA Championship.

'Faldo always had an edge over Greg, mentally,' Scotty Gilmour remembers.

It was a bittersweet triumph. Faldo and his partners, Ken Brown and Norman, finished forty minutes after the previous group. Faldo and Norman were fined £50 each for slow play, and Brown, a frequent offender, £100. They were outraged. 'It wasn't our fault,' cried Faldo. 'We had a big gallery and had to wait at least thirty-six times for the fairway to be cleared. It's really upsetting. We put on a damn good show, but instead of a slap on the back we get a slap in the face.'

In those days, Brown was something of a rebel without a cause, a gifted player with a knack for finding trouble, and Norman, angry at his uncaring attitude, chose the interval when their penalty was being decided to take him to task over it. He informed him that 'unless he changed his habits he would destroy himself on the golf Tour' and that 'other players on the Tour would grow to hate playing with him'.

Brown's memory of the conversation is hazy, but he does know 'it would have been water off a duck's back. I was forever being chastised for something or other.'

The next week, Norman bounced back with an easy victory in the Dunlop Masters, taking his earnings to £27,000. 'Two out of three isn't bad.' He grinned.

'Norman is not only a successful player,' remarked the *Daily Mirror*, 'he has taken over from Severiano Ballesteros as the darling of the crowds. And, unlike the Spaniard, the big, fair-haired Australian always has time for a wave and a smile, whether he has just birdied a hole or dropped a shot.'

His free-wheeling, happy-go-lucky style of play had won him a huge following, particularly among women. 'Greg does appeal to the girls,' said his mother. 'We get heaps of fan mail from women all over the world asking for pictures and autographs. But Greg only has time for two women, me and his girlfriend.' Norman phoned Toini for half an hour every single day from wherever he was in the world.

'I'd be telling a lie if I didn't say I'm amazed at how well I've done so quickly,' said Norman, who was in the process of signing a deal to represent the Rolls of Monmouth club and drive a Rolls-Royce. 'I'm feeling pretty good.' He had won nineteen of the hundred events in which he had played as a pro. 'I don't think I've ever played a bad round of golf, even when I first picked up the clubs at fifteen,' he told *People* magazine in Australia. 'It's probably true that I'm a natural, but that doesn't mean it was all easy.'

He told *Woman's Day*, which featured him in a swashbuckling pose at the wheel of a speedboat, that he never dreamed of staying in anything but the best hotels. 'Can't see the point in it.' That, he said, was why there was so much 'bitching' about him. 'I know there are some people who are not very nice about me. That's understandable. I've come a long way in a short time. I've tried very hard and succeeded.'

Tony Johnstone, the Zimbabwean, remembers playing with Norman at the Italian Open. 'He started eagle, hole-in-one, and I'd never heard of him. The night before, John Bland and I were looking at the noticeboard and I said, "Who's this G. Norman?" He said, "You've never heard of Greg Norman? He's going to be a superstar." After two holes with him, I knew that. He shot a sixty-four and made it look easy.'

'The secret of his success is an outsize ego,' Louis T. Stanley observed cuttingly. 'His belief in himself is off-putting, but it does the trick . . .'


On 1 July 1981, Norman and Laura were married at St Mary's Catholic Church in Old Town Alexandria, Virginia. James Marshall was Norman's best man and his parents flew in for the ceremony. Because of the time constraints – they had brought the wedding forward from September to July to coincide with Merv and Toini's trip to the US Open – it was a small, intimate ceremony, with only a few of Laura's friends and her immediate family invited.

'I'm fantastically happy,' Norman said.

Marshall's reaction to their marriage had been mixed. 'He said he was excited but I don't think he was excited,' Laura says, with a laugh, speculating that he viewed her as an interloper in the close relationship he enjoyed with Norman.

Stewart Ginn, who could see the cracks appearing in the Marshall/Norman relationship, suspects she was right. 'The writing was on the wall. When Greg got married, there was someone else to help him and advise him.'

The couple held three receptions, one in Washington, one in England and one in Australia, and were planning to buy a house in the United States. 'One of the wonderful things about Laura is that she hates golf,' Norman said. 'When I come back to the hotel after a gruelling day of competition we can relax over a meal without talking golf.'

'Laura has given Greg a more level-headed approach to life,' his mother concurred.

But not even Laura's influence was fail-safe. The more desperate Norman became to win a major, the more pressure he put on himself, and now he grew agitated days before the Open began at St George's. 'He was pacing up and down waiting for the gun to go off,' Laura said. 'I tried to tell him in a subtle way that it wasn't a race.'

The previous year, he had been exactly the same way at Muirfield, saying he felt 'like a dog straining at a leash' days before the event started. Walking to the first tee in the first round, he felt drained. 'So far the Open has not been the happiest of experiences for me, but to win it still remains my biggest ambition in golf.'

At Sandwich, the Open kicked off amid the usual flurry of silly-season stories. In twenty years, the Americans had won the title thirteen times, but they complained that the event was prohibitively expensive. What with first-class air-tickets to procure, wives and children to bring, coaches to pay and five-star hotel accommodation to be found, only those who finished in the top fifteen broke even. On a more serious note, Lee Trevino said that the course was playing so long, the power players would do well: namely, Ballesteros, Norman, Nicklaus, Watson and Floyd.

For Norman, at least, it was not to be. He was two behind the leaders, Nick Job and Vicente Fernandez, after an opening 72, and in the second round crashed to a 75. There is a picture of him standing knee-deep in grass, Rupert Bear trousers splayed, teeth gritted, his huge hands struggling to hold on to his follow-through after extracting a clump as big as a haystack from the rough.

He had peaked too early again. And although he had come to the realization that he had to find 'the key that unlocks Britain's seaside links', regardless of whether or not he liked them, because those were the courses on which he would ultimately be examined, he flew into a rage and refused to speak to the press.

'Greg Norman fell by the wayside with the second-round seventy-five and put on a display of petulance that would have done John McEnroe proud,' an Australian newspaper reported. 'More seriously for the future of Norman's golf, boiling temperament off the course spilled on to it the next day. Making a charge back into contention, he misjudged a drive that wound up in a fairway bunker. Cursing as he strode after it, Norman slashed at the sand all too hurriedly and had a bogey. He could not curb the tide of self-destruction and picked up more bogeys on three of the next four holes. It was a crucial time in the world's premier Open tournament and Norman blew it.'

As a teenager, Norman had indulged his temper freely on the golf course until the day his father had walked away from him in disgust. Playing in a club match at Virginia, he had thrown a series of tantrums, finally sending a seven-iron cartwheeling down the fairway. Merv went straight home. When Greg returned, sheepish and repentant, Merv told him a home truth that turned him white beneath his tan. 'No self-respecting golfer would think of doing what you did today,' Merv raged.

'He used to get mad with himself if he didn't hit the perfect shot,' Toini says. 'I used to caddie for him a bit and I'd tell him that he had to learn not to expect perfection all the time. But he always did expect perfection.'

Norman, who had never thought of how his behaviour might look, much less considered the effect it might have on his game, was almost in tears. He made a mental resolution never to throw a club again. 'Certainly, I have a temper. Sometimes I think I graduated with straight As in this department,' he admitted, years later. But in golf, he learned to keep it in check.

Off the course, he was less successful. Little things sent him berserk. In a classic case of road rage, he chased down a car that swerved recklessly in front of him in Britain in the early eighties and punched the driver on the jaw.

'He had a very quick temper,' James Marshall recalls, 'which I spotted very early on and which I tried to get him to control. For example, he might be going through an airport and somebody would brush against him completely by accident, and Greg would almost turn around and hit the guy. He was funny like that. He had a very short fuse.'

A definite flashpoint was smoking, which Norman hated. Bill Longmuir and Michael 'Queenie' King avoided lighting up anywhere near him because they knew it irritated him, but it could not always be avoided. One evening, Norman and Longmuir went with Queenie and a couple of his wealthy Sunningdale friends to the Thatched Tavern, a low-ceilinged old pub, rich in character. The moment they sat down, the woman in the party lit up a cigarette. Discreetly, Norman opened the door to let in some fresh air. She stood up and closed it. Norman opened it again. She closed it.

'She kept making comments,' Longmuir recalled. 'She was moaning and bitching about Greg and Australians, and he finally snapped and he chewed her out in front of everyone. It all went very quiet after that. But that's Greg. He's only being honest. He wanted some fresh air in the room.'

Norman did not win again that season but a tie for fourth place in the US PGA Championship helped him feel he was inching nearer to his goals. Peter Thomson was sceptical. 'Jack Newton's got tennis elbow, Stewart Ginn is a walking hospital case, Kel Nagle suffers from old age and Greg Norman, our best hope, is a shadow of his former self,' he wrote in the Melbourne *Age* on the eve of the Australian Open.

Looking back, Thomson claims that he only said those things 'to sting him a bit, make him try a bit harder and get a bit more ferocious'. Norman was determined to prove his worth, but for the second time in three years an aggressive birdie attempt at the last when a par would have sufficed cost him his national title.

Afterwards, Norman put his clubs in the cupboard, loaded

provisions on his boat and planned the honeymoon for which he and his wife had not had time during the season. Norman charted their course along the Great Barrier Reef and they cast off in high spirits. It didn't go quite as planned. Laura was seasick, and nothing made her more nauseous than the gentle bobbing of the boat when Norman stopped to fish. He teased her gently about it but there was nothing to be done.

Christmas more than made up for it. They relaxed in the Queensland sunshine with Norman's family, and Laura impressed her in-laws with Christmas lunch. Over the next few weeks, barbecuing steaks, lying by the pool and drinking beer with friends, Norman unwound. The Australian Open receded to the back of his mind. And that was how 1981 ended, on a high note.

CHAPTER FIVE

# THE YEAR OF LIVING DANGEROUSLY

'Greg fires everyone who gets close to him.'

AMERICAN GOLF WRITER, AUGUST 1997

THE 'DOORBANGERS' NORMAN used to call them. They arrived, unsolicited and uninvited, sometimes well-meaning but almost always intrusive, walking boldly along the soft pale sand to the Normans' front door, scaring the pelicans into the bay. They wanted autographs, they wanted advice, they wanted to chat, to look around. Soon Paradise Point became Paradise Lost. Their refuge ruined, the Normans were forced to sell.

That was how 1982 begun. An atmosphere of menace hung over everything. Even a friendly fishing competition almost ended in disaster. Norman, out on the Great Barrier Reef with Cyril King and his three sons, Greg, Gary and Steve, decided to see who could catch the biggest fish. The idea was for Cyril and Steve to fish along the coastline, while Norman and the others headed out to sea. East of Glasshouse Mountain, they dropped anchor. Absorbed in their tasks, they failed to notice a subtle change in the conditions. Waves slapped warningly at the boat. The wind picked up. Norman was opening a beer when a blue wall of water came out of nowhere, curling above them like a biblical tidal wave and crashing down on the deck.

Pandemonium ensued. Gary was hurled into the engine casing, fishing gear flew and Norman and Greg grabbed frantically for anything that would save them from being swept overboard. Several terrifying minutes elapsed while the boat fought to right itself. When the waves died down sufficiently for them to move, they abandoned the competition without a qualm and headed shakily for the shore.

Unsurprisingly, Norman sold *Divot II* a fortnight later. What happened next was symptomatic of his increasingly cavalier attitude towards expensive toys. Having invested almost immediately in a sea-going cruiser, he sold it after just two weeks, deciding that it didn't make sense to be tied up unused and neglected for the majority of the year. He and Laura then went house-hunting near Surfers Paradise and purchased a large colonial-style property on five acres of land, with four bedrooms, a separate guest-house and a swimming-pool. One boundary fence was long enough for a five-iron shot, so Norman built a practice fairway and could hit balls all day long in the sunshine for the entertainment of the wallabies and roos.

Ten weeks after his last competitive stroke, Norman returned to the fray to find that the endless distractions had taken their toll on his game. Inwardly, his head spun with financial transactions. He finished a disappointing eighth in the Victorian Open behind Mike Clayton and did worse still in the Australian Masters, scoring two 73s and a 78 in the third round. He complained that he couldn't concentrate. After each poor performance, he tortured himself, putting distractedly on his hotel carpet for hour upon hour. Eventually, unable to sleep, he would sit on the bed with his head in his hands, analysing the tournament shot by shot, punishing himself until dawn.

When March came, it was almost a relief to escape to the Hong Kong Open, to be alone with Laura, to be able to sit peacefully in a hotel room, high above the frantic city, and feel the joy come flooding though him when she told him she was expecting their first child.

'James,' Norman almost shouted down the phone to Beaurepaire House, 'I've got some great news. Laura's pregnant and we're going to have a baby in October.'

There are differing accounts of what happened next. According to Norman silence echoed down the line. 'James?' Norman repeated uneasily.

'Well,' said Marshall at length, 'I can see this is going to throw a spanner in the works.'

Norman went white with rage. In a single motion, he ripped the telephone out of the wall and threw it across the room, smashing it to pieces. A gaping hole in the hotel plaster bore vivid testimony to the beginning of a vicious end. 'It devastated me and it devastated my wife,' Norman says. 'Because we couldn't understand why he would make a statement like that.'

The bailiffs came at 3 a.m., knocking on the door with a subpoena.

'They came then because they knew they would get him,' Laura says, remembering Norman standing bleary-eyed on the front step, staring at the court summons that was all that was left of his five-year relationship with James Marshall.

It is ironic that the end came at a time when everything, at least on the surface, was perfect. Marshall's prediction about the enormity of Norman's financial success had come true. Since taking him on, Marshall had negotiated endorsements with Spalding in Australia, Slazenger internationally, Qantas (who were horrified when a loophole in the smallprint allowed Norman to sign with their rivals Cathay-Pacific), BMW in the UK, Korralybyn Golf and Country Club, Schweppes and others. In 1981, Marshall told journalists that if Norman chose to quit playing then, he would be comfortable due to property in the Gold Coast and London and a share portfolio that brought in an annual return of 25 per cent. On the Tour, Norman sailed from event to event in a Rolls-Royce, with the aura of a man who had already made it.

'James gave Greg this style almost of how to play the Tour,' Longmuir says. '"You don't want to be like everybody else – here's a Rolls-Royce." It did have a positive effect, I'm sure, on the way he played and the way he was perceived by other players.'

Perhaps because of all this, Norman was gaining in stature and confidence with each passing day. The seasons had burnished his skin and filled out his frame and now he seemed to tower over lesser players like a Viking. He expressed opinions in a forthright, uncompromising way that left those unused to such frankness shaken. He was his own man, and the more he took charge of his career, the more inevitable it became that it would eventually end in conflict with Marshall. '[James] wanted to be too much involved in Greg's life, I think,' Longmuir observed.

It was a classic case of an irresistible force meeting an immovable object. Marshall felt that he had treated Norman like a son and made him a star, while Norman thought that, although Marshall 'took a personal pride in the moulding of Greg Norman', he was also 'possessive' and that, among other things, was a slippery slope. But it took the telephone call from Hong Kong to end it. 'There was a lot more to that situation,' Norman says, 'but that was the straw that broke the camel's back.'

Marshall has no recollection of the phone call. 'Why would I have said that? Let's look at it logically. If I had said that Laura being pregnant might present a problem – and I don't believe I did say it – I would only have meant it would be hard for Laura with Greg travelling all the time. It's a lovely story. I find it very amusing. But it isn't true.'

When Norman had arrived in Britain for the new season, he and Marshall went straight from the airport to a sponsors' dinner at the Grosvenor House Hotel. Afterwards, Norman suggested to Marshall that they go upstairs for a quiet drink. Then he informed his manager he was leaving him.

To Marshall, it was a bolt from the blue, the very last thing on earth he expected to hear. 'It came as a complete surprise.' Minutes later, when the cruel words and bitter recriminations finally died on pinched lips, beneath icy gazes, Marshall got up from the table, told Norman he would be hearing from his lawyers and walked out of his life for ever.

'Just let's say that we decided that he was going to go his own way, and that was that,' Marshall says shortly. 'We settled out of court.'

Asked how he felt, he replied, 'I don't know how *he* felt. I was sad that things turned out the way they had. I felt, without being dramatic . . .'

'Betrayed?'

'Possibly. I felt sad that somebody who had lived in my house and been treated almost like a brother behaved the way he did.'

'I'm not going to get into it,' Norman says. 'I'll just tell you one thing about people in life . . . The key ingredient in life with anybody is loyalty . . . Most of the time people fall out with you because of lack of loyalty . . . To me, if somebody wants to sever a relationship and says, "Look, Greg, I need to move on, I've been offered another job", or, "I'd like to go and do this," fine, go. We've had a great relationship, I'm happy for you to go and find another job or do something different or new. That's not showing lack of loyalty, that's just showing that you want to move on in life.

'Lack of loyalty is when someone uses you, manipulates you, does things behind your back that you find out later on. You can build up wonderful long-term relationships with loyalty. Soon as somebody crosses that loyalty line with me, I've got no time for them. Because I give so much. I'm a giver, not a taker. I'm a very generous individual with my time, my effort, my money, my emotions . . . My cards are on the table and when they're on the table everybody knows exactly where they stand.'

Marshall felt he had been 'one hundred and fifty per cent loyal to Greg'.

Laura compared Marshall to a 'jilted lover . . . Greg was very hurt by what happened. We really loved James and Lois a lot. They were like family to Greg and they became like family to me. He was Greg's best man at the wedding. So I look back on it and I feel sorry that it went the way it went, but I still have great memories of James and Lois and always will and I'm never going to let anything come in the way of that . . . I think he cared about Greg so much and he felt so devastated because Greg wanted to go on his own that he could never get over that . . . Greg just needed a change and that was the way it was. He has no bad feelings about James whatsoever.'

The change Norman wanted was the freedom to go to International

Management Group, the Mark McCormack organization that has looked after the careers of everyone from Arnold Palmer to Tiger Woods. According to Marshall, IMG began trying to poach Norman within a year or two of Marshall taking him on, and Norman was signed by Ian Todd and John Simpson, now Faldo's manager, at the Open in July, months after leaving.

'I was always conscious that IMG were sort of hovering around but that's something I didn't bother to think about,' Marshall says. 'It didn't worry me, and I have to say I had complete trust in Greg so that gave me a double reason not to worry. I'm not bitter about it. If I was to look back on what happened, I would only say that I was very disappointed that it happened the way it happened.'

They have never spoken since.

'James Marshall was the guy who really started the ball rolling for Greg Norman,' says Scotty Gilmour, Norman's caddie. 'He was a super guy. It was his idea: "The Shark". He took Greg Norman and was developing him into a superstar. He managed him great and McCormack got all the benefits.'

Bill Longmuir's recollection is that Norman was very guarded on the subject and he suspected a great deal of money was changing hands. 'I guessed it was hurting him . . . I just remember Greg being pissed off by the end of that situation.'

Marshall felt equally aggrieved. He maintains that Norman got away lightly. 'I know of many cases of people who he's alienated along the way, who were very kind to him in the early days. I think money can change a lot of people, and undoubtedly it has changed Greg . . . The Greg Norman that is portrayed on the screen or through the press as being the great sportsman, the great loser, the really nice guy, the down-to-earth, kind, straightforward, honest person, well, there's another side to Greg, and I think over the years people who know him have seen that side. The Greg I like to remember was the Greg that I managed for five years and had a great time with, and was great fun to be with. I prefer that Greg to the Greg who went to IMG and took on another sort of guise.'

On 2 June the split was announced in the British papers. 'We have parted on good terms,' Norman said, and tried to turn his attention to his golf game. But by now it was clear that he was experiencing his first real slump. The principle cause of it was his putting (statistics show that, at 286 yards, he was second in distance from the tee, seventh in driving accuracy, second in greens in regulation and out of the top twelve when it came to putting) but a sharp decline in confidence didn't help.

At the Martini, he hit rock bottom. In the final round at Lindrick, he hooked his tee shot into the trees at the seventeenth and racked up an impressive collection of penalties for a 14. The gallery thought it was hilarious. Norman, who eventually finished with an 82, nineteen strokes behind Bernard Gallacher, found it difficult to believe his game could get any worse. 'I felt desperate about my situation and, for the first time in my career, desperate about the problems in my game,' he recalled later.

'Golf's chief pommie-basher this week celebrates an anniversary he would rather forget,' sneered the *News of the World*. 'It's exactly a year since Aussie Greg's last win . . .' There followed a cheerful cataloguing of Norman's recent ills: his surgery for piles, the 'huge' abscess in his mouth, his break-up with Marshall and, last but not least, the 14 he notched up at the Martini. Norman, who had played just seven events since 1 November, an average of one event per month, acknowledged that his biggest problem was lack of competition.

Elsewhere, Laura was asked if it concerned her that so many women followed Norman on the course. 'I trust him,' she answered simply. 'And do you know something else? I'm so pleased other women find him attractive. It means all of us are right. But the difference is, he's all mine.'

It was Laura who finally came up with a solution to Norman's woes, suggesting he call Dr Rudi Webster, a 'mental skills coach' he had met the previous year. Webster believed that ridding the mind of disruptive influences was critical to success on the sportsfield and he had worked wonders with the West Indies cricket team.

One telephone conversation turned Norman's year round. Counselled by Dr Webster, Norman realized that his mind and how he controlled it were as important as any shot, and that he should never think of golf in terms of numbers but in terms of hitting the ball. Years later, when Webster interviewed him for his book *Winning Ways*, he asked Norman if he ever had problems concentrating. Norman confessed he did. 'When the pressure becomes too great or if I get tired mentally, my concentration goes ... My mind often wanders at crucial times. If I've parred an easy par five instead of getting a birdie, I say to myself, "Damn it, you should have birdied that hole." '

He told Webster that he tried to focus by thinking 'rhythm, get good rhythm' over the ball. 'Once I put that thought in my mind, everything else is blocked out. It's like putting a protective bandage around my head to keep out distractions.'

'When you do this you make a common mistake,' Webster said. 'You leave your concentration in the past and you forget the present. The same thing will happen if you project it too far into the future. Remember, the point of power is the present.'

After an hour on the phone with Webster, Norman felt his confidence seeping back. Laura thought there was more to it. 'You're not working hard enough at the game,' she told him frankly.

Thirteen days later, Norman shot a record-equalling 65 to take a three-stroke lead into the final round of the Dunlop Masters at St Pierre. 'It could have been a sixty-one,' said Norman, who had followed Laura's advice by hitting thousands of short-iron shots and putts at Wentworth during his week off. 'I missed four putts inside seven feet.' The following day, he won by eight strokes from Bernhard Langer with another 65.

All the while, the Marshall situation gnawed at Norman's mind. No sooner had he made up his mind to try to qualify for the US Open – the USGA had not seen fit to invite him – and inspect the house they were buying in Florida at the same time than he was forced to cancel due to an unpostponable business meeting/courtroom date.

Throughout the legal toing and froing of that season, Norman continued to perform, winning the State Express Classic the week before the Open. During the tournament, he spotted a plaque at the Belfry showing that Ballesteros had driven the green at the 292-yard tenth, and he took great delight in not only driving the green but holing from 60 feet for a two. Laura had not seen him win since they married, and there were tears in her eyes when he hugged her and said, 'That was for you.'

At Troon, Norman shot a 65 in practice with Jack Nicklaus, Tom Weiskopf and David Graham to win all side bets, but couldn't reproduce that scoring in the tournament. Rounds of 73, 75, 76, 72 left him a distant twenty-seventh. Across the Atlantic Norman fared better, finishing in the top twelve in the Canadian Open, despite being left in the lurch by his caddie. Norman was cross then but he was madder still when he reached the US PGA in Tulsa to find no Scotty Gilmour and no word from him.

Desperate to win his first major, Norman opened with a 66, and after two rounds was only three strokes behind Raymond Floyd. Playing with Floyd on the final day, he arrived at the eighteenth knowing he needed a birdie to have a chance of finishing second. Firing at the flagstick with a three-iron, Norman watched as the ball pitched just short and bounded over the green into deep grass. His recovery chip limped onto the putting surface, finishing 25 feet from the flag. His putt hit the hole but stayed out to give him a share of fifth place. Floyd took six and still won by three shots.

At the Irish Open the next week Gilmour was back in service, but Norman declared himself unsatisfied with his caddie's explanation for his absence and they parted company. Gilmour claims it was the excuse Norman needed to get rid of him and take on Pete Coleman, Ballesteros's caddie. Coleman says that Norman had been trying to lure him away from the Spaniard ever since he worked for him during a week off in the 1980 French Open at St Cloud and they won by ten strokes.

'I didn't turn up in Tulsa, the reason being that he promised to pay for my flight and never did,' Gilmour says sourly. He claims that Norman only ever gave him one air-ticket and that was a flight to Australia donated by Cathay-Pacific, his sponsors.

Back in London, the Normans were robbed of £15,000 of jewellery, cash and credit cards by a gang of call girls at the Hyde Park Hotel. Norman had half woken as they rifled through his belongings and, unable to focus in the darkness, mumbled in sleepy protest, 'Laura, what are you doing?'

'Go back to sleep,' a woman's voice told him calmly.

When he teased Laura about her midnight adventures the next morning, she stared at him in surprise. 'I never stirred,' she said, and Norman felt an icy surge of anger and dismay as it dawned on him that they had been robbed.

As detectives scurried about the room with fingerprint powder, Laura shuddered. 'It's horrible to think they were creeping about the room as we slept,' she said.

On the eve of the Hennessy Cognac Cup in September, Norman received a phone call from Laura. She was alone at their new home in Orlando and she felt as bad as she could possibly feel. 'Another call like that and I'll be on the next plane home,' fretted Norman, captain of the Rest of the World side.

Both he and Laura were keen for the baby to be born in Orlando, close to Laura's parents, and Norman had devised a complicated schedule of flights to ensure that he would be at his wife's side for the birth. He was quite prepared to quit mid-tournament if necessary. During September and October, he criss-crossed the Atlantic six times in four weeks. 'It's costing me two thousand pounds a week but it's worth every penny,' said Norman, told to expect the baby on 13 October.

In between, he lost the European Open when an earthworm popped out of the grass behind his ball in the split second before he was due to launch his tee shot at the seventh. Adjusting the club minutely in mid-swing, so as not to send the worm into the next world, Norman ended in a bank of heather and gorse. He never recovered.

On 5 October, he flew to England for a televised match with Jan Stephenson, Beth Daniel and Bernhard Langer at Woburn. He was practising prior to the start of it at 9.30 a.m. when he was summoned to the clubhouse for a phone call. Norman panicked. His first thought was that something had gone wrong. Laura told him that she was in hospital and in final labour. Norman was shaken to the core. He walked to the tee, his mind in turmoil. 'I'm just about to become a father,' he said.

There was no way he could leave before the end of filming, and no way he could concentrate. A radio link to the clubhouse gave him a progress report every half-hour from the Orlando hospital and, when he returned to his hotel, he was told he could speak to Laura at 6 p.m.

'Darling, we have a baby daughter,' was the first thing she said.

Norman and Langer were beaten 4–2 in the series by the women the next day, and Norman was at Heathrow Airport thirty minutes after holing out on the eighteenth green. He flew Concorde to New York, connected to Orlando almost immediately and was with his wife and daughter, Morgan-Leigh, just nine hours after leaving Woburn. Lawrence Levy, his chain-smoking, extrovert and much-loved British photographer friend, was Morgan-Leigh's godfather.

In the weeks that followed, while he waited for the medical clearance needed to take his daughter to Australia, Norman negotiated appearance money with the AGU. After some debate, he agreed to play the Australian Open without an appearance fee but insisted on being paid for two other events.

Arriving back home, he caused a storm of controversy by publicly condemning Graham Marsh for playing in the Dunlop Phoenix in Japan instead of supporting the Australian Open. A year later, Norman did exactly the same thing himself.

Marsh got his own back. In a barbed statement, he said that Australian golf fans knew that, barring date clashes and sponsor pressure, he would 'continue to play in Australia without making appearance-money demands, an attitude which Greg Norman does not hold despite his professed concern for the fans and Australian golf'.

All through that long, tense Australian summer, Bill Longmuir stayed with Norman and Laura in the calm timber house on the Gold Coast, where kookaburras and rainbow parakeets whirled through the trees and danced along the perimeter fence. Norman had him out mowing the practice area, a four-hour exercise, and they tinkered with clubs in the workshop and hit balls, bare torsoed under a canopy of blue sky. They were never still. Even Pete Coleman, who stayed with Norman briefly, was assigned to paint the snooker room.

'Greg's one of these guys who's a workaholic,' says Longmuir. 'He wakes up early and he's got to be active. He's not the sort of person that can sit down and relax very easily. You very rarely see him sitting down. And on that particular trip, if we weren't playing in a tournament and he wasn't showing me something in the car, the countryside or the golf courses or the coastline, if we weren't working in the garden or hitting balls, then we were in the snooker room, playing snooker.'

In friendly matches on his table at home Norman was as competitive as he was on the golf course. Longmuir, who had thought of himself as fairly handy with a cue, was crushed with relentless efficiency during any spare minute of his stay. He was used to it. Norman had used him as a practice opponent on the eve of the World Match Play. They had played for £50 but Norman fought as hard as he would when the real competition started. On the seventeenth, Longmuir hit his second shot stone dead and Norman holed a putt from across the green to level the match. At the last, they both reached the green in two. Longmuir sank a 30-footer for a three, and Norman, carefully scrutinizing the line, followed him in triumphantly from 20 feet.

'I could *not* beat him, even on my best day,' Longmuir says ruefully. 'He'd put a lot of emphasis on a match like that. He'd sort of walk away from it feeling good.'

That November, flying along the palm-fringed white beaches of Surfers Paradise with Norman, Longmuir thought that he had seldom been happier. There was an easy familiarity about the Norman household, with its beautiful but unfussy décor, that was conducive to homeliness. 'There was always a really comfortable atmosphere. There was a big kitchen and that's where you lived your life. A little bit old-fashioned, I suppose. You didn't feel as though you had to dress up for dinner. I felt as though I could have walked down in my underwear and just sat down on the settee and put my feet up. It was a very liveable home.'

It had come as an enormous shock to Longmuir when the Australian decided to get married the previous year. 'Here Greg was in the prime of his life, in terms of his condition and golf, and he had sort of latched himself up,' he recalls. 'I didn't think he would ever settle down that early on.' Now he began to see things rather differently. 'Looking back at it, for Greg, it was the stability he definitely needed at that time in his life. He would have been a wandering nomad without it. He probably would have kept on being successful because his talent was so tremendous, but his condition would have gone. He probably would have fizzled out. Laura gave him the sort of tunnel-vision to success. She gave him a reason to do well, and then he began to win the big tournaments. He became a complete player when he met Laura. He was pretty wild. She quietened him down.'

For the duration of his stay, Longmuir felt that Norman went out of his way to make him feel welcome and ensure he had a good time. 'He used to take me up to the loft and it was full of golf equipment. I'd get hold of a wedge and say, "That's fantastic," and he'd say, "Take it. If you like it, take it." He was incredibly generous. If you went out to dinner, he would always pick up the bill, *always*, or try to do it. Later on, when I stayed with him at Bay Hill in America, I'd go down and use the golf facilities there and he'd say, "Anything you want, put it on my tab." You just couldn't put your hand in your pocket. He'd give me the keys to the car. It was like, what was his was mine while I was staying there, which is another side of Greg Norman I don't think people really know.'

Curiously enough, it was Norman's generosity that sparked his next explosion. Away from Surfers Paradise, things had been going rather less well. Norman and Coleman were not hitting it off nearly as happily as they had in France. 'We had a stormy relationship . . . so it's not hard to remember,' the caddie says wryly. 'Basically, we never got on. We were both sort of domineering people, I suppose.'

The problem started when Coleman gave an interview to Tom Ramsey, who asked him how Norman compared to Ballesteros.

'Seve's a better player, but Greg's a better payer,' joked Coleman.

Norman was furious. He confronted Coleman as soon as he saw it. 'Nice piece in the paper,' he said sarcastically.

'I said, "Well, that's the way I see it," ' Coleman recalled. 'I didn't say, "It's not true," because it was true. But it wasn't what he wanted to hear.'

Norman's first real encounter with Ballesteros had been at the 1977 World Cup in Palm Springs, the year the Spanish team won. When the tournament was over, Norman and Shearer had decided to pay a visit to a local nightclub. There, in the half-light, propped up against the bar, was Ballesteros, smoking moodily and nursing a drink. Norman felt disappointed in him. To him, a champion athlete like the Spaniard should have had more self-discipline. 'Hell, that's not right, a twenty-year-old boy smoking and drinking like that,' he said to Shearer.

He had already formed the opinion that Ballesteros's swing put too much strain on his back and was too uncontrolled to make him one of the world's best players. Obviously, that opinion was revised pretty rapidly, but his assessment of the Spaniard's character remained unchanged for a long time. Norman insists that it was four years before they exchanged a single word. When Ballesteros addressed him at the 1980 World Match Play, wishing him good luck as he laced up his golf shoes in the locker room prior to meeting Nick Faldo in the quarter-finals, the Australian nearly fell off the bench. 'He remained aloof and distant as far as I was concerned,' Norman said. 'I thought it was strange behaviour.'

Pete Coleman says that Ballesteros's taciturnity was nothing unusual, and certainly wasn't directed at Norman in any malevolent way. 'Seve would blank most everybody. Seve, unless it was a Spaniard, wouldn't converse with anybody.'

'In those days, there was no question that the star of the European Tour was Seve,' Marshall says, 'and I think Greg was very jealous of him. He used to say, "Oh, Seve never says, 'Good shot,' when you play with him," and "I could have beaten him." And I'd say, "Hey, if you feel like that, go out and beat him." You've got to bear in mind that in those days Seve didn't speak much English and was a young guy and a foreigner. I think Seve handled himself extremely well. He was always very courteous, but I think in the early days he was a bit of a bugbear to Greg and they certainly weren't chums. Seve had very little in common with Greg.'

Norman claimed that it was in fact Ballesteros who was jealous and said that, during what he described as the four-year 'ice-age' between them, 'I had no doubt that he was practising a type of long-term gamesmanship on me . . . He obviously recognized me as a threat to the supremacy he had established in Europe.'

Coleman laughs. 'Seve *always* thought he was number one. He might not have liked the flashy way that Greg used to carry on, but I don't think he was worried about being second to Greg Norman.'

None the less, as Coleman observed to Ramsey, if there was one area in which Norman consistently upstaged the Spaniard, then it was his generosity towards the people around him. Ballesteros is notoriously mean, and nobody has suffered the consequences more than his caddies. When Ballesteros finished runner-up in the 1976 Open, his caddie received the princely sum of £250 for the tournament. When Coleman caddied for him in the late seventies, he was paid the minimum wage of £120, plus 5 per cent for a top-twenty place – 2 per cent less than the average.

'At the time, [Greg paid] nearly twice what anybody else was paying,' Coleman remembers. 'Plus, I had to look after his Rolls-Royce when he was in England. I used to turn up at the local pub in it. His percentage was also ten per cent, whereas a lot of the guys only paid five per cent.'

The drawback was the abuse Norman delivered on the course. 'People like that are basically never wrong,' said Coleman, citing a time when he spent two days before a tournament preparing yardages for Norman and then had the Australian turn on him when an iron shot pitched by the flag and bounded through the green.

'Wrong yardage,' snapped Norman.

'I said, "One thing that wasn't was a wrong yardage. It might have been the wrong club but it wasn't the wrong yardage." But he kept on and on, and that belittles you when you're trying so hard to get the right yardage.'

As much as Coleman admired Norman's game, his ability to 'kill the course with his driver', there was only so much he could take. He stayed a couple more weeks and then returned to England to work for Bernhard Langer.

Two days before the start of the Australian Open in Sydney, Longmuir went to Greg and Laura's hotel room for a drink before the three of them attended a function. He knocked on the door. It flew open and Laura, panic-stricken and emotional, cried, 'Thank God, you're here, Bill.' She grabbed his arm. 'Greg's on the floor.'

Longmuir rushed into the room to find Norman writhing on the carpet, as white as a sheet. 'I thought, God, he's dying,' remembers Longmuir. The hotel doctor had been called but it was clear that Norman needed to get to a hospital urgently.

In those days, Norman was much bigger than he is now. Muscles bunched on gladiator arms and across his broad chest, and there were the beginnings of a beer belly. He hung like a deadweight across Longmuir's shoulders as the Scotsman, bent double and staggering under his bulk, battled to lift him.

'I physically carried him downstairs,' Longmuir said. 'That's how I *know* how big he is. What a job I had. He couldn't move, he was in so much pain. I've never seen anyone in so much pain. I put him in the back of a taxi and when we got to the hospital and they said, "What's wrong?" he sort of blurted out, "Give me something for this f–ing pain," in typical Greg fashion, just demanding that they make it all right.'

The following morning, Norman underwent a cystoscopy to remove a kidney stone at the Masonic Hospital in Ashfield. When he came round, he was absolutely adamant that he wasn't withdrawing from the tournament. If he could walk, he wanted to play. Reporters phoning the hospital were told by Laura that Norman, who had been diagnosed with a urinary-tract infection several weeks earlier, had had a small stone removed. 'It was a damn big one,' shouted Norman from his bed.

At the sixteenth hole in the first round of the Australian Open, Norman withdrew from the tournament. His face was a sickly yellow, his body racked with pain. Doctors watching his progress on television said they could see his legs shaking. It was blowing a gale. Norman felt weak and nauseous as he struggled to 12 over par, but he forced himself on, taking frequent rests on the shooting stick Coleman carried. His parents were watching and he didn't want to disappoint them.

In the end, he had to admit defeat. It was not the way he would have chosen to end that tumultuous season but he had a lot to be proud of. He had won the Order of Merit in Europe in only eleven appearances, earning £66,405.71 and beating Sandy Lyle and Sam Torrance who had each played twenty-three events.

# CHAPTER SIX

---

# STORM WARNING

'I find the practice fairways around the British Tour very lonely places, because quite often I am the only one there.'

GREG NORMAN, 1983

THE FIRST INDICATION THAT something was horribly, perhaps irremediably, wrong was the wall of silence. Norman walked onto the putting green at Royal Birkdale on the eve of the Open, greeted a couple of players cheerily and was startled when they pretended they hadn't heard him and turned away. For a minute he thought they were kidding. He hadn't seen them since having cartilage surgery on his left knee in May, and he limped after them with a teasing comment on his lips. A wave of hostility stopped him dead. Several of the players walked off the green, leaving Norman embarrassed and alone. Then came the final indignity. A man he had counted as a friend shouted over his shoulder, 'You should be sent to Coventry for what you did.'

There had been no indication of what was to come. By 1983, after a seemingly endless stream of ailments – 'Growing pains,' he said, with a laugh – Norman had recovered all his old bounce and exuberance.

He swept to victory in the Australian Masters at Huntingdale with a final-round 66, won the Hong Kong Open by three and, had it not been for an 'absurdly rushed putt' in the play-off against Mike Nicolette in the Bay Hill Classic, would have triumphed in his first American event.

Peter Dobereiner, the late *Observer* correspondent, remembered being unsure how to approach him afterwards. 'My trepidation was groundless. Norman sought me out and said, "Come and look at something." The something was a blood-red Ferrari that had just been delivered, an event of much greater importance in Norman's mind than losing a play-off.'

Earlier in the year, Norman had overheard a conversation between two test cricketers that had convinced him (momentarily) that his relish for the spectacular option – huge, lashed drives that drew gasps from the crowd, and do or die five-irons – had sometimes proved expensive in major championships, particularly with regard to the 1981 Masters and the US PGA the previous season.

'What part of batting do you enjoy most?' one cricketer had asked the other.

'Hitting fours and sixes.'

'How much of the time do you do that?'

'About ten per cent.'

'So you don't really enjoy the other ninety per cent?'

'I never thought of it like that.'

Norman hadn't thought of it like that either. He realized he had to come to terms with a more businesslike way of putting a score together – or pay the price. But that was easier said than done. He wasn't yet ready to relinquish the sweet high that accompanied a high-risk shot delivered safely to the pin. He lived for the tingling rush of adrenaline and the flush of pride. 'I've always loved the intense pressure of the last moments of a tournament,' he said. 'You know, when anybody can win it. The money, the cars and the recognition are nice, but that's not why I'm in this game. It's for those rare moments when I'm on that knife edge. There's no feeling like it.'

Although he did not experience it at the Players Championship at Sawgrass, where he was sixty-third, or at Augusta, where he was thirtieth, his smile flashed easily that spring. Married life agreed with him. Possibly expecting the reverse, he found that Laura and his young daughter had a calming effect on him when they travelled together, and now he took them with him whenever he could.

'I remember him telling me, "You have to understand, if we get married, golf will still be my most important thing in the world," ' Laura says. 'I didn't really think about it then because I wasn't really thinking about marriage. We were just having a great time. But as soon as we got married he changed. His focus was towards me, and then when we had children, his focus was towards his family. So it was nothing I had to work on him to do. He didn't know anything else when he met me, he knew golf. That was his focus.'

It was a steaming July. In April, Norman had wrenched his knee playing with Morgan-Leigh, aggravating an old football injury. He had been out of competition for two months at an estimated cost of up to £70,000 in lost prize and appearance money when he returned to Europe for the Open. After one day in the sunshine practising, with Laura, Morgan-Leigh and his big yellow Rolls-Royce near by, at Sunningdale, he walked straight into a storm of controversy. But it wasn't, as might have been expected, the State Express Classic that caused the furore (Norman had refused to defend his title after sponsors refused to pay him £6,000 in appearance money). Rather, it was the publication of his book, *My Story*.

The problem with autobiographies is that it's difficult to tell whether the tone used in them is that of the subject or the author. In *My Story*, Norman, through his Australian ghost writer Don Lawrence, comes across as smug and full of himself. Anyone and everything that doesn't marry up to his high standards are laid to waste. Jack Newton is attacked for his playboy lifestyle, Jerry Pate is someone who throws himself into ponds to celebrate victories 'because those wins aren't very frequent', and Ken Brown is 'a tragic figure in the game'. Sacred cows, including Royal St George's and virtually the entire British circuit, are slaughtered without compunction.

'So many talented golfers on the British Tour have not got the drive, have not got the guts or that inner power that is needed to go on and win when victory is in sight,' rued Norman, who said that only

Sandy Lyle and Nick Faldo were exceptions to this rule. 'The desire is there, but the raw courage required to turn that desire into a reality is sadly missing. There are too many good-time players on the British Tour who would be better off spending their spare time on the practice fairway, honing their skills to the point where they can stand up under the pressures that winning a golf tournament demands. Nobody can do it for them. They have to do it themselves.'

It would be an understatement to say that his comments were met with outrage. For weeks, there was hardly a golf article in Britain that did not include the words 'gutless poms', and all the nationalism and pent-up vitriol at the disposal of both media and players was heaped on Norman's head. But nothing hurt him more than the reactions of those people closest to him. It is said that there's no worse enemy than a former friend and, in the cases of Sam Torrance and John O'Leary, Norman learned the truth of that. By all accounts, they were ready to hit him.

Brian Barnes, the former Ryder Cup player, took exception to Norman's remarks about being surprised to see Ballesteros smoking and drinking after the 1977 World Cup. 'Who is Greg trying to kid? Does he think he is a monk?' Barnes raged. 'All this is sheer bloody nonsense.' Norman, he said, had 'become a bit too big for his boots, especially since he has not won a major tournament'.

'To be honest with you, a lot of the pros wouldn't speak to him over that,' Longmuir says. 'But when you knew Greg Norman, you knew why he was saying it. He felt that the British pros were lazy in terms of not going to play the world circuit. I always thought that Sam Torrance and Howard Clark should have been full-time US Tour players. They didn't want to do that. Fair enough, but to become a great player, you have to take that step, and I think that was the point he was trying to make.'

Norman was genuinely bewildered. He had excepted Lyle and Faldo from his criticism and he couldn't understand why the rest couldn't take it in the spirit it was meant, as a gentle spur to encourage them on to greater heights. 'A couple of guys, who I thought were good friends of mine, have walked right past me without saying a word,' Norman said. 'What's the matter with them? I just wrote the truth as I saw it. If they don't like it, they should tell me to my face.'

He was completely unrepentant. He admitted that his golf hadn't been the same since the operation, and that his short game had suffered, but felt that he'd rather tee off at Royal Birkdale playing mediocre than peak too early. 'I'm here for one thing, to win the Open,' he said. He eventually finished equal nineteenth.

Ken Schofield describes the whole 'gutless poms' episode as a storm in a teacup, but the effects were much more far-reaching than that phrase implies. Oddly, it was only Ken Brown, whom Norman singled out as a classic example of the poor attitude and wasted talent he was referring to, who thought that the Shark's criticism was well founded.

'At the time, the British players, and to some extent the Europeans, hadn't been brave enough to go to America, and unless you commit yourself to doing that you're never going to be a world beater,' says Brown, now a respected television commentator. 'That was what he was saying and there was some justification for it. You'd have to say we did have a track record of not finishing the job off.'

Reminded of the time Norman lectured him on his attitude at Ganton, Brown laughs. 'I would say that there was probably some justification for that as well. I never really did believe in myself.'

If Brown's response had been the norm rather than the rare exception, things might have turned out rather better than they did. But of Norman's friends, only Bill Longmuir and Queenie stayed loyal. 'John O'Leary, particularly, took it upon himself to put Greg down, and you know you can't ever cross Greg that way,' Longmuir says. 'You're going to lose a friend for life. It got to a point where it had all sort of blown over for a bit and we were playing in York at the B & H International. I was staying with Greg that week and we were in a restaurant. Sam [Torrance] and John O'Leary were on the other side of the restaurant and they sent a bottle of wine over to Greg. This was the sort of olive branch to make up. But the damage had been done by then because John O'Leary had made a comment that was out of line. And it was typical Greg, because he told the waiter to tell them to shove it up their arse. It was very funny the way it happened. I sort of grinned and thought, God, what's going to happen next? I know Greg will still speak to Sam and John but it left a severe dent in their relationship.'

It is possible that Norman does speak to Torrance and O'Leary but it seems doubtful they are bosom buddies. So sensitive is the issue of Norman's criticism, even fourteen years on, that when Torrance was questioned about it for this book, he froze. 'There is absolutely no way on earth that I would ever talk about that,' he snapped. 'No comment,' he reiterated darkly and then, muttering expletives, he wheeled and walked away.

Looking back, Norman says of his remarks in *My Story*, 'It was only what I saw at the time. I probably regret saying it because it affected some of the relationships I had, but you know I said it. I've always spoken the truth and maybe some of those guys reacted to the truth.' He claims, 'I never wanted to do that book anyway. I was against it, I fought it, but the deal was done before I knew anything about it.'

Marshall, who organized the deal, dismisses that as 'a complete and utter lie. The book was done with his compliance. I said to Greg, "It's far too early for you to do it," but Greg didn't think it would be too soon. He thought it would be great . . . And he was involved in it from start to finish.'

That tournament at Fulford was the last time Longmuir and Norman ever stayed together in Britain. Frustrated and disillusioned, Norman announced at the B & H that he was quitting Europe 'for personal reasons . . . Next year you'll see me just for the Open,' he said. 'The rest of the time I'll be on the US Tour. I'm finished.'

He was forty-fifth on the Order of Merit at the time and nursing a shoulder injury. 'They say things come in threes so I hope things are going to change now,' Norman said. 'It's been a pretty miserable season so far.'

At the European Open, where he finished fifth, Norman gave Longmuir a holdall full of brand-new golf grips and other belongings, leaving the Scotsman with the distinct impression that he was going for good. An atmosphere of finality pervaded the whole week. It went without saying that there would always be a bond between them, but the absence of the fun and vitality Norman had brought to both golf and their relationship left Longmuir feeling empty.

'He'll always be a friend,' Longmuir said sincerely. 'I'll always feel

The Milky Bar Kid: Greg, aged ten, grins for the camera. *Merv Norman*

Greg, complete with pudding-bowl haircut, dreams of stardom in his school uniform. *Merv Norman*

Family Portrait: Greg poses with his parents, Merv and Toini, and his sister, Janis. *Merv Norman*

Norman, blossoming under James Marshall's
direction, swings his way to success at
Fulford in 1978. *Phil Sheldon*

Norman, nicknamed Hollywood by his friends, shows off the strength and power that led Nicklaus to describe him as 'a durable athlete'. *Phil Sheldon*

Young Love: just days before he proposed, Norman embraces Laura at Augusta. *Phil Sheldon*

Showman: with eventual winner, Tom Watson, looking on, Norman aims for success in the 1981 Masters at Augusta. *Phil Sheldon*

Young Lions: Norman and Seve Ballesteros, the stars of the European Tour, battle it out at Royal St George's in 1981. *Phil Sheldon*

Norman rushes ecstatically across the seventy-second green after a brilliant putt ties
him with Fuzzy Zoeller at the 1984 US Open at Winged Foot. *Phil Sheldon*

The strain shows as Norman and his famous teacher, Charlie Earp, battle for the play-off
that would eventually go Fuzzy Zoeller's way at Winged Foot in 1984. *Phil Sheldon*

Favoured Son: Norman drives past Turnberry's famous lighthouse on his way to victory in the 1986 Open. *Allsport*

Norman chips from the gallery after hitting a four-iron right to lose the 1986 Masters to Jack Nicklaus. *Phil Sheldon*

Jack in the Box: Tway bursts joyously from the bunker after holing out to beat Norman at the 1986 US PGA at Inverness. *Phil Sheldon*

Norman reels in agony as he misses a putt that might have won him the 1987 Masters. Larry Mize would go on to defeat Norman with a miracle chip on the second play-off hole. *Phil Sheldon*

The Shark and the Bear: Norman and his mentor, Jack Nicklaus, clown around during the semi-finals of the 1986 World Match Play. *Phil Sheldon*

Heaven Sent: Norman savours sweet success after winning the 1986 Open at Turnberry.
*Phil Sheldon*

comfortable with him because I know where he's coming from. You read a lot about Greg being arrogant and unfriendly, but when you understand who he is, you understand where he's coming from. He's just being himself. Success hasn't changed him. He's always enjoyed his money and he's enjoyed being generous to people.'

Benevolence is a persistent theme in Norman's life, except in one notable case: that of his erstwhile caddie, Scotty Gilmour. All Norman's other employees, from Pete Coleman on, are unanimous in their praise of him as an exceptionally good payer. Gilmour appears to have encountered him before he became one.

In Gilmour's version of the events that led to their split, he had agreed to return to work for Norman at the beginning of the 1983 season on condition that the Shark set right his principal grievance: his failure to reimburse Gilmour for at least some of his flights and hotels. But as the months ticked by and Gilmour's wages were once again negated by his expenses, resentment began to simmer in the dour Briton's breast. At the US PGA Championship at Riviera it surfaced with a vengeance.

The tournament had not gone well. Subconsciously, Norman was still favouring his injured knee and he finished well down the field in forty-second place. 'He gave me a cheque and just vanished,' Gilmour recalled. 'He was just at the point of going mad. He used to have a terrible temper. I looked at the cheque and it was for a hundred and seventy-five pounds.'

Standing beside the putting green, Gilmour's face fell. He had no way of paying either his hotel bill or his flight to Glasgow for the tournament the following week. Upon hearing his plight, a wealthy businessman came to his rescue, but Gilmour had had enough. When he arrived in Scotland for the next event, he marched up to Norman and confronted him. 'Greg,' he said pleadingly, 'you've got to square up with me for the flights for this year. I'm broke. I don't have a penny.'

Norman's face hardened. 'Tom Watson says he doesn't pay for his caddie's flights, and I don't think I should either,' he argued.

'So that was us finished,' Gilmour said flatly. 'That was the day we finished.'

The relationships between golfers and caddies – particularly the intense bonds that form at the highest level – are a lot like marriages. Divorce can be acrimonious. The relentless pace of the professional circuit and the stress of competition mean that caddies are common casualties, but there are always two sides to every story.

James Marshall's experience was that Norman 'behaved terribly with caddies. I don't think Greg has been very good about remembering those people who helped him on the way up. Say he was staying [at my house] and I said to him, "You know, the local guy at the golf club would just love you to come and say hi." Greg wouldn't do that. But if I said to him, "Lord Bathurst, who owns Gloucestershire, would be very interested in having you come to dinner," he would be there like a shot, and I think that is one of the things that people possibly resent.'

Gilmour takes the same view. 'I'm a little bitter about it. He treated me pretty bad and I was pretty loyal to him.'

To Gilmour, the final straw was when he wished Norman happy new year in Dubai in 1997 and asked after his family, and Norman failed to do the same in return. 'He didn't say, "How's your wife?" and my wife travelled with me everywhere. My wife and Laura got along great. She used to babysit Morgan. But that's what kind of guy he is . . . I was more than a caddie, I was a friend. It's Greg's fault that he doesn't have any friends. He's stamped on a lot of people. He's stamped on people all his life. I don't feel sorry for him. He's brought it all on himself. He's got a wonderful life, he's got all the money in the world, but I wonder if he's really a happy guy.'

From each fresh crisis, Norman emerged stronger and more determined. He overcame Ballesteros in the semi-final of the World Match Play, after the Spaniard suggested he should get through the ball more with his right hand when he was putting, and beat Faldo 3 and 2 in the final. Andy Prodger, Faldo's caddie at the time, remembers it as one of the few occasions when they met that Norman did not allow himself to become agitated by the Englishman's deadly slowness. There was no love lost between them. 'Complete opposites,' Prodger says. 'An introvert and an extrovert.'

Two weeks later Norman won the Cannes Open. He flew back to

Australia and into a row with the AGU. They were refusing to pay him an appearance fee to play in the Australian Open, although they did not draw the line at paying Nick Price, Jim Thorpe and one or two other relatively nondescript foreign players.

'I don't give a damn about the Australian Open any more,' Norman said sullenly at the New South Wales Open. He threatened to boycott his national open for the next four years and had already entered the Dunlop Phoenix, held concurrently in Japan. 'I don't hold it against Nick and Jim for getting appearance money. Good luck to them. I just can't work out what the AGU have got against me. I'm getting paid my normal fee, about eight thousand dollars, to play this week and I'm getting it next week at Tweed Heads.'

He went on to win the tournament. 'They can't stop him,' David Graham, the 1981 US Open champion, said after losing a sudden-death play-off to Norman at Concord. It was Norman's fourth victory in five events.

Soon afterwards, Norman announced that he was selling his house on the Gold Coast so that he could buy a bigger property in America. He was on the brink of signing a $500,000 three-year deal with Spalding, the largest contract ever procured by an Australian sportsman and the fourth largest by a golfer. Out of a season of chaos, Norman had manipulated a triumphant departure.

When Norman left Marshall he put himself into the hands of Hughes Norton, the suave, astute head of IMG's golf division. Norton had managed a string of top players, including Lanny Wadkins, and had a reputation as a brilliant wheeler-dealer, as cunning as he was charming. Norton had been in dialogue with the Australian for several years before he left Marshall and was thrilled to be master-minding his advance into the New World.

'I thought he was the most attractive, charismatic, talented player I'd ever seen, perhaps since Arnold Palmer. He had a lot of the same characteristics – not only gifted but with great desire to work hard and improve. He had everything, absolutely everything. To me, you couldn't have created a better persona: Australian, which certainly Americans love; blond, which is always appealing; long-hitting, powerful, gutsy. The whole nine yards. He was the total package, ten out of ten.'

Norman, who had been tempted to leave Europe in 1982, was convinced that his timing was perfect. 'The best thing I ever did was holding out that extra year and playing different courses. Just take Sunningdale, Wentworth, Royal Birkdale and St Andrews . . . Every week is a new adventure. I've always been a believer that anyone coming from overseas should play at least two Tours. Once you've got your blooding, then you go to the States. Because you've got to keep going forward all the time in the States. One average round in the States and you get lapped by about twenty guys.'

With Norton watching over him like a dark angel, Norman launched his assault on the PGA Tour. He had begun the year by winning the Australian Masters, with what David Graham described as 'the most awesome exhibition of driving a golf ball I've ever seen. Absolutely phenomenal.' But when the Florida swing and Augusta came and went with only a missed cut at the TPC and a twenty-fifth place at the Masters to show for it, his confidence waned dramatically. None of the old keys helped. His swing slipped out of synch, his short game grew ragged at the edges and his putts rimmed out.

Norman had been in the US all of five minutes, but already there was a small contingent who were pleased to see him struggle. Playing at Atlanta Country Club, Norman had just hit the par five eleventh in two when an American star, who had required three shots, walked over to him and said, 'Son, you're not good enough to play over here. You just pack your ass up and go home.' Norman felt his blood boil. Welcome to America, he thought.

In the last round of the Memorial, Norman shot a 73 to finish 10 over par. Desperate to stop the slide, he phoned Charlie Earp in Australia and entreated him to fly to the US as soon as possible. Earp told him to extend his backswing and hold on until he got there. A week later, Norman won the Kemper Open. He opened with a 68, was seven strokes ahead of the field after three rounds at windswept Congressional, and eventually won by five in a show-stopping display of controlled aggression and effortless style.

'We won seventy-two thousand dollars minus what I spent shopping all week,' Laura recalls with a laugh. When Earp flew in a day or so later, the cheque was still pinned to the fridge door, more than ten times what Norman had earned for his victory in the West Lakes Classic.

Across America, they were waking up to the arrival of a new super-star. After just three years of trying, Norman was an overnight success. His power game, movie-star orthodontics and ability to convey moneyed sophistication and wholesome Aussie friendliness simultaneously gave him the kind of popular appeal only Arnold Palmer had ever generated. Bill Longmuir remembers going out to an Italian restaurant in Orlando with him and being taken aback by the scale of attention and affection he received from the notoriously parochial locals dining there. Jim Murray, the renowned *LA Times* columnist wrote:

> He's as unselfconscious as a puppy with a ball of yarn. He's flashy. He's got this shock of platinum hair that makes him look like Jean Harlow from a distance. When he smiles, which is a lot, his teeth light up like a keyboard. He could give Liberace lessons in glitz. Best of all, he looks like what you think a world-class athlete should look like. The way you'd like to look if you made your living in sports. If you think this is common, you don't know golf. They've got guys in this game who can't see without glasses. They've got some who can't see too well with glasses. They've got guys who look like department store Santa Clauses and guys who look as if you could mail them home or clean cannons with them. Not our Greg. Greg Norman looks as if he was made by Michelangelo. He's got this wide, sloping shoulder of the practised surfer. He has no rear end to speak of, and so little waist-line you wonder how his pants stay up. He could pass for a light-heavyweight boxer in any bar in the world.

'The thing that impressed me the most is that he had a certain air, a positiveness, an aggressiveness on the golf course,' says Nick Price, the Zimbabwean player who lived near Norman in Florida and would become one of his closest friends. 'He just had superstar written all over him, even in those days. He had that debonair attitude.'

With Earp at his side, Norman had every reason to be debonair. 'I caddied for him in 1984 in the United States Open, which we should have won,' Earp says ruefully. '*Should* have.'

For a moment, Greg Norman's mind was a blank. He could not recall the packed galleries and narrow greens of Winged Foot, could not recall the nearness of his dream. With less than a month to go before the 1997 US PGA returned to Winged Foot, the scene of his duel with Fuzzy Zoeller in 1984, he could remember almost nothing about the tournament. ' 'Eighty-four?' he says slowly. 'You remind me.'

'Well, starting with the closing holes of the final round . . .'

'Of?'

'The US Open in 1984.'

'What was that? That was . . .'

'You made some incredible birdies to get into the play-off . . .' Silence.

'The one with Fuzzy Zoeller,' interjected Bart Collins, president of Norman's company Great White Shark Enterprises.

The slow light of recognition dawned across Norman's face. 'Oh, with Fuzzy. Yeah, I remember vaguely.' He pushed his sleeves up over his wiry brown arms. 'What you've got to understand about me is I'm not a statistician,' he says. 'I remember things but I don't remember them in detail because there's things that you need to put out of your head. So I put 'em out of my head. Because I don't think it's necessary to have all that stuff in there all the time. One of my greatest strengths is my mind – always has been. I can remember chipping out sideways on seventeen and hitting a shot in there about ten or six feet and making the putt. I can remember the eighteenth hole. I can remember the first hole of the play-off. And that's it, really.'

1984 was the year that Ballesteros called Winged Foot and the US Open 'the toughest golf course I have ever played and the toughest tournament to win'. The USGA had taken care not to make it as cruel as it was when Hale Irwin won in 1974, but it was cruel enough. After two 68s, Irwin was the leader once again, with Fuzzy Zoeller and Norman contending, and a 69 helped him hold on for the third successive day. Zoeller was a stroke behind on 206, with Norman on 207.

On the final day, the atmosphere was tense and electric. The gallery ran amok, breaking through flimsy barriers and rushing down fairways as the thirty-nine-year-old Irwin collapsed with an outward 40 and inward 39, leaving Norman and Zoeller battling head to head. Bloodcurdling roars split the air at inopportune moments. Age wasn't the only thing affecting players' nerves. The Australian, who hit fifty-three greens in seventy-two holes at Winged Foot, the most of any man in the field, chose the closing holes to miss them, his loose iron shots wandering away from their targets at the fifteenth, six-teenth and seventeenth. And every single time he made a miracle save.

'Anyone who thinks Greg Norman's a choker only has to watch the last three holes at Winged Foot,' says Mike Clayton. 'That was un-believable golf.'

At the eighteenth hole, Norman, his hair snowy-white in the light, took out a six-iron. He swallowed hard. For the first time in his life, he was petrified of hitting a shot, scared stiff that he couldn't pull it off, scared stiff of the consequences. 'It was as if that final green was a dark room and I was a little boy, afraid to open the door,' he con-fessed later. He made an uncertain backswing and blocked the ball straight right into a grandstand set well back from the green. His heart in his mouth, he stared after it. He had spent half his young life preparing for this moment, and now that it was here he felt he was choking. 'I have never choked on a shot since then,' he said in 1987. With Zoeller putting out on the seventeenth, he needed a birdie to be sure of winning or forcing a play-off, and now that chance was gone. The best he could hope for was a par. Norman dropped without penalty and lofted the ball towards the gallery banked behind the green. It flew across the putting surface and came to rest in the thick collar on the far side, 40 feet from the pin.

In 1929, Bobby Jones had faced almost the same line on the rolling glassy surface of Winged Foot's final green. The 12-footer he holed, a curling clutch putt that forced a tie with Al Espinosa and then victory in the play-off, became a landmark in American golf history, such was its importance and degree of difficulty. Now Norman had a similar putt, only a good deal longer. He selected a small, worn patch midway to the hole and aimed five feet left. He struck the putt per-fectly. In the charged silence, he held his breath as the ball trundled across the green, crossed the brown patch, struck the flagstick and popped in the hole.

In years to come, that 40-foot putt and all that it implied will be held up alongside Watson's chip at Pebble Beach as one of the most precious US Open moments, and Norman felt the full impact of it. He rushed around the green in paroxysms of delight, leaping and laughing and holding his putter high.

Zoeller, standing on the fairway, mistakenly thought he had made a birdie. Reaching into his orange bag, he took out a white towel and, in one of the finest acts of sportsmanship golf has seen, waved it in gracious surrender. 'I said to my caddie, "This guy's going to beat us," ' he recalls. Gamely, he held on for a tie.

Norman grinned at him sheepishly when he came off the course. 'I said to him, "What are you trying to do to me – give me grey hairs?" ' Zoeller says, with a laugh. 'But what a great putt under the circumstances, oh, what a great putt. TV doesn't do him justice because it doesn't show the slope of that green.'

Norman was so emotional he could hardly speak. 'I could not put into words the feeling I had when I made that putt at the last,' he managed. He had trailed Zoeller by four shots after six holes and three after twelve. 'One of the greatest feelings in the world. Golf is very hard to explain. I could feel it in my hands. I knew I was going to make it . . . I just knew.'

Back home in Australia, they were stopping the presses to record his brilliant 69. 'Fearless Greg Forces Play-Off,' cried the Adelaide paper *The News*. After so many disappointments, the Shark's time had finally come.


On Monday morning, Norman, Hughes Norton and Laura drove up to the clubhouse for the play-off. Workmen spilled through the trees, tanned and sweaty, tearing down tents, grandstands and signs, dismantling the fairground paraphernalia of tournament golf. Norton watched worriedly as Norman climbed listlessly out of the car. 'I feel like I'm going to a pro-am,' he said slowly.

'There was a sense of let-down,' Norton recalls. 'It's like there wasn't the excitement of Sunday and a bit of the magic was gone.'

Norman remembers almost nothing about the last day, except 'waking up Monday morning with nothing in me. Just flat. I've had that a couple of times in my career, where I've woken up the next day just dead. Nothing in you. You know, your emotion's gone, your adrenaline's gone, and boom. It's pretty hard to recoup it all and that's how I was that Monday morning . . . Fuzzy never slept a wink so he had his adrenaline to play with that day. I had a great night's sleep so my body went flat. We've all felt that way. It's just one of those things. Maybe I'd be able to do it differently nowadays but in those days I couldn't. I couldn't turn it back on.'

Zoeller waited on the first tee, whistling and wisecracking, as contented as a cat on a sun-lounger even though he had been awake until 3 a.m., chain-smoking. He plucked out a telephone when Norman walked up. 'Make your last call,' he said to the Shark, much to the delight of the gallery.

Norman smiled unhappily. He was pale and drained after the effort of Sunday. Like Norton, Charlie Earp felt a twinge of worry as he hoisted Norman's bag onto his shoulder and followed him up the fairway.

'He didn't get the breaks,' Earp says now. 'Fuzzy got the breaks early. He's hit it wide on the first tee at Winged Foot. Another six foot and he'd have been dead. Greg's hit a great drive and knocked it on. They both birdied. The second hole, we'd been hitting a one-iron all week, but he wanted to hit the driver. I said to him, "What the hell do you want to hit a driver for?" But that's what Greg wanted to do. He felt confident about it. And he blocked it. Got it behind a tree. Fuzzy hit it down the middle and knocked it on the green, well past the hole. Greg was on in three and Fuzzy knocked it in from 65 feet. I said to him, "What did you do that for?" He said: "I was only trying to hit it close." Greg took six. On the third hole, Fuzzy's had a big block, Greg's knocked it on the front edge and taken three to get down. And that's how the round went from then on.'

After six holes, it was as good as over. 'Let's go, Shark,' a fan cried encouragingly.

Norman gave him a bleak stare. 'Where are we going?' he asked.

'Everybody says the long putt on two was the turning point . . .' Zoeller says, remembering that they managed to chat and share a few laughs on the way round. 'But really I think the turning point was number eight. I had a three-shot lead and I hit it in to about 10 feet. Greg made another bogey and that gave me an extra two shots. It was all downhill from there.'

After nine holes, Zoeller was five strokes ahead, after sixteen, the gap was nine. Twice they were slowed down, once for twenty minutes, to ensure that television, which only came on at three o'clock, managed to catch the closing holes. On the eighteenth, Norman took out a white towel and waved it in surrender, just as his opponent had the previous day. He scored a 75 against Zoeller's superb 67, handing the easy-going American the biggest margin of victory ever recorded in an eighteen-hole major play-off. They walked off the green arm in arm. 'Fuzzy, Fuzzy, Fuzzy,' chanted the fans.

'He had one of those days when nothing went well,' Zoeller says of Norman. He put it down to the ebb and flow of momentum. 'It wouldn't have made any difference who I was playing that week. I was on. I really had no fear at all. I was just out to do my job and I felt comfortable on that golf course, and that was a big plus.'

That fact that Norman has blocked the experiences of the 1984 US Open from his mind so completely that he cannot remember a single detail of the tournament, beyond the empty feeling with which he woke on Monday morning, says a lot about the suffering it caused him, and yet he bounced back with the resilience that was to become his trademark. Two weeks after leaving Winged Foot, he won the Canadian Open, shooting a 67 for a 10 under par total that left him two shots ahead of Jack Nicklaus.

'This was special because my wife called me this morning to remind me it was our wedding anniversary.' Norman grinned. 'She said the trophy would be just fine for a present, so that was my goal for the day.'

When Norman lost a play-off for the Western Open, was sixth in the Open at St Andrews and won the Australian PGA championship by eight strokes to end the year in third place on the world rankings, *Golf Digest* ran an article under the headline, 'Will Greg Norman Reach Superstardom?' In it, Peter Dobereiner was prepared to wager that Norman would win at least one major but beyond that, he preferred to hedge his bets. 'Those who know him best are equally ambivalent about his potential . . . Peter Thomson . . . has serious reservations about Greg Norman's capacity to go all the way in golf.

Jack Newton refers to him as "The Great White Fishfinger". Graham Marsh, on the other hand, believes that Norman will improve further and become a truly dominant figure ... It is enough to know of the rich rewards to be had watching Norman's progress, win or lose.'

# CHAPTER SEVEN

---

# THE SATURDAY SLAM

'Life isn't fair but golf is ridiculous.'

JIM MURRAY ON NORMAN'S YEAR, 1986

WHEN THE DRIVER OF the boat reached Norman, sweeping round in a frantic curl of foam, he thought he had broken his neck. The Shark floated limply in his life-vest, his head at an unnatural angle. His face looked as if it had been savaged by wild boars.

Not ten minutes earlier, Laura Norman had been sitting peacefully in a chair looking down their Orlando garden at the scene that followed the christening of Gregory Michael, their three-week-old son. The sun was setting and a few couples still lingered over their champagne. Out on the lake, Norman and Laura's brothers, Richard and Jay Junior, were water-skiing. Clinging to the back of a banana boat, a kind of long rubber tube, they bounded over the rippled jade surface. When the boat began to flip, Norman instinctively let go of the rope. Jay didn't. He smashed into Norman, his foot connecting with the Australian's face and knocking him unconscious.

'I was hysterical,' Laura says, remembering them carrying her husband, dripping with blood, more dead than alive, into the tranquil christening scene. 'He kept saying to everybody, "Calm her down, calm her down!" But he had this towel up against his face and every time he took the towel away there were no teeth and it was all bloody and it was awful . . . That's the most afraid I've ever been for Greg.'

Richard Andrassy, chief paediatric surgeon at the Children's Hospital in Houston, rushed Norman to casualty, where he underwent a four-hour operation, received some thirty stitches and lost three teeth. Splinters of the teeth were impacted into his jawbone.

On 17 October, less than three weeks later, Norman teed up in the inaugural Dunhill Cup at St Andrews. Tom Ramsey, the golf writer, had telephoned his house days before the event and found him full of the joys of spring. 'I tell you, I'll come out of this looking better than ever,' joked Norman, who was having plastic surgery the following morning. 'It just hurts like hell to laugh. I look like Muhammad Ali hit me six times in the mouth.'

David Graham, one of his Australian team-mates in the event, hoped that the accident might knock a little sense into Norman. 'He indulges in dangerous hobbies that could end a million-dollar career,' Graham said.

'Rubbish,' Norman said dismissively. 'This wasn't my fault.'

Nor was the headline that greeted his return: 'Norman Enters Golf Feud'. To be fair, he was only a bystander in a blazing row between his team-mates. Graham Marsh had publicly condemned David Graham for accepting what he considered to be excessive appearance money to play in the Queensland Open. 'Fortunately, this competition pits individual golfers against each other, head to head, and we will be playing separately and not strictly as a team,' Norman said. 'Otherwise, well, I don't know what would have happened.'

'Graham Marsh may be hearing from my lawyer,' David Graham told the *Edinburgh Evening News* on the eve of the match.

'I believe David Graham is looking for me,' Marsh snarled. 'All I can say is that it's a good job we're playing as individuals this week, not as partners.'

Five days later, Australia beat the United States 3–0 in the final.

By 1986, Norman's relish for danger, both on and off the course, was seen as a contributing factor in one of the game's biggest mysteries:

the glaring hole in his record. The man who had everything – the perfect family, the perfect house, the perfect swing, the perfect image – did not have a major victory, the universal yardstick for separating the legends from the also-rans. If, in the case of Norman, there was added pressure, it was the price-tag of his association with Nicklaus, and of his own larger-than-life persona and giant-killing game. 'I am very conscious that I have never won a major title . . .' he had said in 1983, 'and until I do I will not believe that I have successfully brought together the ingredients for greatness . . .'

Nowadays, Norman claims that he wasn't remotely surprised when year after year went by without a major victory. 'There's times when you've got to realize that you're not the only pearl in the oyster shell,' he says. 'There's a lot of good oysters out there with even better pearls. It's not a given.' But a glance at his record in the Masters shows that he probably cared too much. After finishing fourth in 1981 with outstanding scores for an Augusta rookie – 69, 70, 72, 72 – he returned the next year and shot 73, 75, 73, 79 to tie for thirty-sixth place. In 1983, another closing 79 relegated him to thirtieth place, in 1984 he was twenty-fifth and in 1985 he sank to forty-seventh spot after finishing 75, 78.

Peter Thomson believes that his problems were twofold: his swing was flawed, and he was weighed down by the burden of expectation. 'Clearly, he hit a couple of hurdles with his game. It was disappointing because I think he got on the wrong trail for a while with his technique, which is the modern thing that befalls all these young players, and that held him back for a long time. I think the expectations and the "troubles", if you want to call them that, came after he got all these endorsements for all sorts of wild money on the promise that he was going to win a major. He was sold by James Marshall and then after that by IMG on what he was *going* to win. Well, logically, when he wasn't actually winning, there were queries: "Will he fulfil his promise?" et cetera. That's when the expectations came.'

Few men have worked harder or longer to live up to those expectations, but nothing Norman did was ever enough. Year after year, he scooped up half the prizes on offer in Australia, and yet when he had a relatively poor season, he was mocked.

Jack Newton believed that Norman's biggest weakness was his

short-iron play. 'When he was really firing, I genuinely thought he had ten to fifteen per cent improvement left in him. For a great player, his eight-iron, nine-iron and wedge were pretty ordinary. I mean, he could miss a green with a wedge.'

Hughes Norton admits to growing more and more bewildered as the years passed without his client winning a major. 'I literally thought he would win a major a year. People talk about Augusta being made for Tiger [Woods]. You know, it's a sixty-eight-par golf course for him and he's four under par on the first tee. That's what people always said was true with Greg. I thought he would win Augusta multiple times. Because of his heritage in Europe, I thought he would win the British Open multiple times. I felt strongest about those two, but even the US Open and the PGA . . . If you had asked me to write it down, I would have said . . . he could be the fifth guy to win them all.'

When Norman turned off Washington Road into Augusta that spring, he believed it himself. After a year in the shadow of what he thought was an Asiatic virus, with pneumonia-like symptoms, but which actually turned out to be an allergy to certain grasses, he felt as good as he had felt for as long as he could remember, strong, vital and in control of his game. After a first-round 70, his best opening score since 1981, he felt even better. He followed it with a solid 72 and then a sweet 68 gave him the third-round lead on 210. Nick Price, who had broken the course record with a 63 on Saturday, Bernhard Langer, Seve Ballesteros, Donnie Hammond, Tom Watson, Tom Kite and Tommy Nakajima were all within two shots of him, and Nicklaus was four strokes back. Confident and excited, Norman drove off into the night to prepare himself for another dance with destiny.

'You still have to respect the old girl,' he had said of Augusta National in the interview room. 'When the pressure's on, you still have to be careful.'

It's the noise that people remember, the wall of sound ricocheting around the scarlet amphitheatre of dogwood in Amen Corner and rising like an anthem above the Cathedral in the Pines. It was the sound of Nicklaus charging. The Golden Bear, roused from a long, dispirited sleep by a newspaper article that said he was washed up at forty-six, had come to rain on Norman's parade.

Examined in hindsight, almost all majors have a sense of inevitability. Form, desire and luck become a potent alchemy that seems to come to one player's aid more frequently than the rest when the tournament is viewed as a whole. Not until the final hole on Sunday did it become clear that Nicklaus was the chosen one at Augusta. Like Norman, Ballesteros had thought it was to be him. · After eagling twice, he was leading the tournament standing on the fifteenth fairway, absorbed in the honourable purpose of fulfilling a deathbed promise to his father. On the hole ahead, he heard the gallery roar as Nicklaus almost holed-in-one. Rattled, he put a short, ugly swing on a four-iron. He watched the ball tip towards the water. He stood stunned on the fairway as a spreading ring of ripples sent a knife into his heart.

Norman had suffered a similar nightmare at the tenth, where he double-bogeyed. He had four-putted there on Friday. Afterwards he would say it was the only hole he disliked at the Masters. 'I'm infatuated with this course,' he admitted. 'But every good-looking woman has a blemish, and in the case of Augusta it's the tenth.'

That morning, Steve, Nicklaus's son, had called his father and asked him what he thought it would take to win. 'Well,' said the Bear, 'sixty-six will tie and sixty-five will win.' Steve told him to go ahead and do it. But Nicklaus started slowly. He was five strokes behind when a birdie putt dropped on the ninth, and four behind when his 25-foot birdie at the tenth was bettered by the eagles of Kite and Ballesteros. Then Nicklaus made the bogey on the twelfth that really kick-started his round. He birdied the thirteenth and eagled the fifteenth with a 298-yard drive. When he hit it to three feet on the short sixteenth, he was blinking back the tears.

Norman heard the roar. The cacophony that day made the 1984 US Open at Winged Foot 'feel like playing through a graveyard' in comparison. 'I remember I was on the fourteenth hole with Nicky Price and we had maybe fifty people behind the fourteenth green,' Norman recalls. 'We looked at each other and said, "Let's show these people we're not out of the tournament yet." And I proceeded to birdie four holes in a row.'

Inside the clubhouse, Nicklaus waited with his other son Jackie, his caddie. He was still one up when Kite missed a 12-footer on the last and Norman hooked his drive on the seventeenth. The ball rolled under two tall pines near the seventh green. Faced with a 160-yard shot under the branches and onto the glassy green, Norman decided to play what he described as a 'low-percentage, super-aggressive' punch with a nine-iron. It bounded onto the green and ran to 15 feet for an incredible birdie three. 'I was sitting watching on TV as Norman kept making birdies,' said Nicklaus, who had come home in 30, 'so when I came to the last putt I said, "Maybe I'll stand up." '

'I was really excited for him,' recalls Price, who had played steadily without making any real gains.

Norman was walking to the last telling himself, 'One more birdie and you're the Masters Champion.' On the tee, he reached for the driver. Pete Bender, his new caddie, stopped him. 'Take the three-wood and put it in a good position,' he told Norman, 'then we'll attack.' What Bender didn't count on was that, having hit a sensible three-wood up the fairway, Norman would not follow that strategy to completion by going for par and hoping for a three, but would be more obsessed than ever with getting a birdie. Looking up at the colourful crescent of spectators behind the green, Norman had only one thought in his mind and it was not the par that would tie him with Nicklaus. He took out his four-iron. It was the four-iron that had contributed handsomely to the double-bogey on the tenth, veering off into the crowd from beneath a pine tree.

'There are certain situations that you get into,' says Price, 'where you might, for example, not be hitting your sand-wedge that well. You might have hit one all day and you've duffed it. And you'll try like hell to avoid using it again. That's not a choke, it's just that you're not comfortable with it. But invariably you end up needing it, and it always seems to come at inopportune moments, under pressure.'

Unfortunately for Norman, the inopportune time was the seventy-second hole of the Masters. 'I should have hit a hard five,' Norman says in retrospect. 'I think I had a hundred and eighty-seven yards, if my memory's right, up the hill.'

He never made it up the hill. Instead, he spun out on it, slicing it

50 yards right into the gallery and making bogey to hand Nicklaus a sixth green jacket. 'I was trying to hit it too hard,' Norman said ruefully. 'I was going for the flag. I was going for the birdie and the win. It was the first time all week I let my ego get the best of me.'

'Greg wanted five straight birdies,' Bender said sourly. 'He wanted to make history. He wasn't going to go for the middle of the green.'

'He was on such a high after the birdies,' Price says, 'and you normally do hit a bad shot after a string of birdies. His just came at the wrong time. I really believe that. And he just put a bad swing on it, a little quick maybe, or over-aggressive. He was so fired up. There's no way in a million years that that was a choke like people wrote. I don't think anybody was more disappointed than he was. He could have been more conservative, but that's not his nature, and that's what people find appealing about him, like they did with Arnold Palmer. That's why they want to watch him, because they know he's going to give it his all. That's just the state of the union with Greg. I think it would be a mistake for him to try to change.' He firmly believes that it was the double-bogey at the tenth, rather than the four-iron shot at the eighteenth on which everyone focused, that cost Norman the title.

'The one criticism I've always had of Greg's game is his course management,' Jack Newton says. 'I think he's without a doubt the best player in the world . . . He's an aggressive bloke and he plays aggressively but the one thing he hasn't learned to do, in the Masters, for example, is find the line [between aggression] and undue risk. Playing very low-percentage shots under the gun you might play and get away with in the first three rounds, but in the last round of a major that ain't gonna work.

'I always compare him to Nicklaus because I played a lot with Jack,' says Newton, who was runner-up to Tom Watson in the 1975 Open at Carnoustie. 'I'm sure that Greg hits the ball as well as Jack, maybe even better. I think Greg's the best driver I've ever seen – the longest and the straightest. But Jack's mental approach and his course management are just incredible. I've seen Greg do things and I'd think to myself, Jack would never do that. Comparing him to the greatest player that ever lived is maybe unfair, but when you've played a lot with a guy like [Greg] and you see what he does and how he approaches a tournament like that, under the gun, in the later stages, Nicklaus is a mile in front.'

In *Shark Attack!* Norman describes Nicklaus as 'the best strategist I've ever seen', but adds that 'his overall game management is a shade on the conservative side'. Norman is the opposite. He also talks a lot about 'ego golf' and admits that he occasionally hits an ego shot or two himself. 'But those are bad shots,' Norman tells his readers sternly, 'even when they are played perfectly . . . Everyone makes an ego mistake once in a while, but only a foolish player does it often. Such a golfer bases his shots not on wise course management but on self-delusion and wishful thinking.'

In the press room, Norman shrugged off the single shot that separated him from his cherished ambition, shrugged off his flawed decision-making on the final hole and graciously acknowledged Nicklaus's triumph. 'Maybe he deserved it after what Watson did to him,' he said, referring to Tom Watson's miracle chip from the rough on the penultimate hole at Pebble Beach in the 1982 US Open. 'What can you say?' he added. 'He owns this place, basically . . . But one of these days I'm going to break his record of six Masters anyway.'

Years later, Norman told *Golf Digest* that he had learned sportsmanship from Nicklaus – 'I guess when you follow somebody's career, which I have really done, you learn a bit of his trade. But I have never been a sore loser. I never pouted even when I was a kid if I got beaten. I get frustrated with myself when I hit a bad shot, but if somebody else beats me, he deserves to win. I've seen the way Jack handles defeat and I've thought to myself many times, What would Jack have done if he were in my body right now? It can be very difficult to walk out and put your arm around a guy and say, "Hey, you know, what the heck, you beat me." But it doesn't do you any harm at all and you don't want your kids to hear that their dad was a real pain in the neck.'

But while Norman was outwardly sanguine, inside he was gutted. Laura, who was accustomed to seeing him throw off defeats as if they were nothing, saw the pain etched into his face. 'But after the tournament was finished, he was over it,' she said. 'That night, we had some friends come by our house and we had a great time.'

'I guess what makes me maddest is that everybody remembers my bogey at the last and not the four birdies to get there,' Norman said. He couldn't understand why he should be the one singled out for criticism when it was Ballesteros who effectively threw away the tournament at the fifteenth.

'People forget all that, you see,' he told the Golf Channel in 1997. 'People target one individual and they think everything happened to him.'

But in the end Norman, the heir apparent to Nicklaus – the most perfect golfer on earth, the consummate athlete who won one out of every five tournaments he entered worldwide and twenty out of a possible ninety-six majors – was held up alongside the Golden Bear and found wanting. Ballesteros had pull-hooked his ball into the water and Norman 'slid that four-iron into the customers on eighteen,' as Jim Murray put it in the *LA Times*. 'You never used to see Jack Nicklaus do that,' Murray said. 'At least, none of us ever remember it . . . You had to beat Jack Nicklaus. He didn't do it for you.'

Something was driving Norman forward, forcing him to reach deeper and deeper, work harder and harder. It was a feeling he had, intangible at first, but then so close he could almost touch it with his fingertips. He could sense it long before he won the Las Vegas Invitational in May, shooting 73, 63, 68, 64 (65) to leave the field trailing by seven shots, and even before he won the Kemper Open at Congressional in June, beating Larry Mize, an unassuming journeyman from Georgia, on the sixth hole of a play-off. Three weeks later, a third-round 62 helped him into second place in the Canadian Open. He had also come close to attaining golf's dream score, 59, at Bay Hill, lipping out for birdies at each of the last four holes.

'When it is my time to win [a major] I will win one,' he told his mother. 'I know I'm going to win.'

Away from the course, he was blissfully content. In February the previous year, he and Laura had packed a bottle of Dom Perignon in a picnic basket and carried it down to the water's edge in Orlando to celebrate their purchase of a gorgeous piece of land. Originally owned by a property-developer friend of Norman, it was set on a peninsula across from Arnold Palmer's Bay Hill Club. That day, the

Normans sketched their dream house in the sand, a wedge-shaped building that would make the most of the view while protecting their privacy.

Initially, Laura had been dead set against them living on the water. 'I had to fight him about it,' she remembered. 'Greg grew up on the water in Australia, so he was used to it. I had nightmares about my children drowning in the lakes. I know I was just paranoid so we talked it over. Finally, I gave in and I'm happy now that I did.'

When the house was completed, it was a 7,200-foot, two-storey building, with a glass front overlooking the lake and the boathouse, and a virtually windowless back. They named it Oak Pointe after the beautiful old tree Laura refused to have removed from the garden, and hung the US and Australian flags on two flagpoles. Norman's office and workshop, where he tinkered with his clubs and cars, played pool and conducted business, faced the swimming-pool.

'He calls it business,' Laura told *Golf* with a laugh, 'but mostly he talks to people all over the world about cars. Actually, Greg's office is where we spend most of our time when he's home. I take the children and a few of their toys in there and we watch TV and watch people ride by on the lake or just enjoy one another when he's not sitting there behind the desk with the phone in one ear.'

Norman had taken to fatherhood with an ease and enjoyment that astounded his friends. At Bay Hill, he made a point of rising early every morning he was home and eating breakfast with Laura and Morgan-Leigh, walking his golden retriever puppy and then taking his daughter down to the range with him. 'He's been great with the kids,' Bill Longmuir says. In his free time, he went fishing and diving with Nick Price, who lived near by. 'That's when our friendship really strengthened,' Price says.

Chris Hodenfield, who spent a week at Norman's home in 1987 for a magazine piece, remembers him as 'a hearty glad-hander in all public situations. He paid for every beer in sight. The rocketing trajectory of the early 1980s seemed to be all his, and he walked through them as if he was basking in a sunlit ticker-tape parade.'

Norman's biggest joy remained his cars. In the garage, he kept a Rolls-Royce Corniche convertible and a Ferrari, with Aussi 2 and Shark 1 on the plates, while the Jeep, and the jet-ski he'd bought on an impulse and already pulled a shoulder muscle using, lived outside. All his cars were fitted with radar-detectors. 'I've always been a car perv.' Norman grinned. 'I always had an ambition to have cars that stick out. The first car I ever had I had to make flash. Guess I've always been that way, although I wish I wasn't because I spend so much money on cars. It makes me happy. OK, so I might spend sixty to seventy thousand dollars on a car, but I never lose money.'

For the most part, his relationship with America was a profitable and harmonious one. His pop-star status was such that magazines carried little lists of his likes and dislikes. Shark favourites included Japanese food, Clint Eastwood, Eddie Murphy, beer, the author Robert Ludlum, watching NFL football on TV, a variety of music from Mozart to Lionel Richie, Nicklaus and playing Royal Melbourne and Augusta. He liked the US because, 'if you're a winner here, you can earn a hundred and fifty thousand dollars in a week. Win two like that and you've got three hundred thousand dollars. I can live on that.'

At the start of the 1984 season, Norman had engaged Pete Bender, a young Californian, to caddie for him. Bender had caddied for Frank Beard, Jerry Heard and Lanny Wadkins, but he was with Nicklaus when Norman met him during a practice round at the Masters the previous year. Norman had him doubled up with laughter that day, and when he offered the caddie a job later that season – an employment tactic that would become a habit – Bender left Nicklaus.

At first, Bender wondered if he had made a mistake. Nicklaus won the Masters and Norman shared second place with Tom Kite. But by the time they reached the US Open at Shinnecock Hills in Long Island, New York, Norman was playing the golf of his life. Bender remembers that he was 'driving superbly, hitting good irons, chipping well and his putting was great. I didn't think we could go wrong.'

In the early years of Norman's career, he was a streaky putter. As a boy, he had spent so much time hitting balls that his putting was neglected and left a void in his game when he turned pro. 'He was such a great driver, so far ahead of everyone in those days,' Scotty Gilmour remembers, 'but he was a very bad putter when he

106

was young. The game seemed to come easy to him, but he had to work on his putting.'

'I had to play a little bit of a catch-up game,' Norman concedes.

On the lightning greens of the US Open, Norman showed how well he had succeeded. 'I've never seen a guy play so well,' Nicklaus said admiringly, after a practice round. 'If Greg doesn't win this tournament, then there's something wrong.'

Shinnecock Hills, flanked by the Atlantic and the sparkling waters of Peconic Bay, is the nearest America comes to a traditional links course. Created in stages, first by Willie Davis, then by Willie Dunn, then polished, extended and transformed into a masterpiece by Bill Flynn, its grey-green fairways wound through scrubland, mounds and clumps of blackberry bushes, toughened by gusting sea winds.

Those sea winds, whipping cold and salty through the tournament at 20 or 30 m.p.h., combined with rain and temperatures as low as 40 Fahrenheit to turn Shinnecock into a brute on the first day of play. Of the 156 players who started, only forty-seven shot 75 or better, while forty-five scored 80 or worse. Bob Tway, a tall, athletic Oklahoman who had won the previous week at Westchester, led by one from Norman on 70, an exceptional score in the conditions. Tway hit eight greens all day. Norman hit just seven. No player broke par.

'This is the most difficult day I have ever seen in American championship golf,' Nicklaus said, after a 77.

In the second round, the wind eased and blue sky showed through thin clouds, and the scores improved accordingly. Norman went out in 31, stumbled a little coming home, but managed a 68 to lead the tournament by three strokes on 139. Trevino and Dennis Watson were next, with Tway, Tom Watson and Floyd on 143. Norman was brimming with confidence. After twelve holes of the third round, he was still three shots clear, playing with Trevino, and he was certain his time had come.

On the thirteenth hole, an imaginative par four where the angle of the drive has the effect of narrowing an already narrow fairway, Norman pushed his tee shot into thick rough. Trevino almost holed his approach, but Norman sent his second sailing over the green and into the jungle-like undergrowth that bordered a car-park. His backswing restricted, he then attempted to punch a shot up the bank.

It took off over the bank, across the green and into the rough on the other side. He chalked up a six for his trouble. When Trevino holed from two feet for a three, they were level.

When they reached the fourteenth, play had backed up and Norman, arms folded across his chest, stood steaming on the fairway with Trevino and waited for Floyd and Watson to putt out. All day, the gallery had been noisy and excitable, rushing across the fairways and moving off while the partners of players they were supporting were still trying to line up putts. Now, one raised his voice above the mutterings and murmurs, and called out, 'Norman, you're choking.'

Norman stiffened. His lip curled in an expression of amused contempt and he looked over at the heckler. Then he stared stonily ahead until the green cleared, and played an iron shot to the heart of the green. Trevino was starting to walk up the fairway when, without warning, Norman marched over to the gallery, poked a finger at the man, and snarled, 'If you want to say something to me, say it to me after this round when I can do something about it.'

The heckler and his accomplices blustered and stammered, but they never took the Shark up on his offer. Norman, on the other hand, felt much better for the outburst. It appeared to release his pent-up anger, and he settled down and played flawless golf for a 71. At the end of the round, he held a narrow lead on 210. Trevino and Hal Sutton were on 211. Tway was on 212, with Floyd and four others on 213.

For the third time in his life, Norman was in control of a major but he didn't seem to feel he was. Most mornings, he could tell on the practice range whether he would be sharp or flat that day and on Sunday at Shinnecock he tended towards the latter. It was a clear, bright morning with a fresh swirling wind, and even standing on the first tee with Sutton, he seemed tentative and unsure of himself. Trevino had just birdied the first and Sutton followed. Norman parred and they were tied for the lead.

Very quickly, a pattern emerged. So testing were the conditions that every player within shouting distance of the lead took one step forward and two steps back. Ben Crenshaw, Lanny Wadkins, Chip Beck and Payne Stewart all came and went. Unnoticed, Floyd began to climb the leaderboard. A week before, he had entered the last round of the Westchester Classic tied with Tway and collapsed to a 77. Distraught, he spent three hours riding round in a car with his wife Maria, trying to work out what had gone wrong. Now he put the results of that analysis to work, firing perfect shots at the flag with his flat, ugly swing.

Norman was on his way to a 75. After a birdie at the seventh, he had bogeyed five of the next eight holes to virtually eliminate himself from contention. While Floyd played precision golf for a 66, becoming, at forty-three, the oldest man to win the US Open, Norman was limping quietly to a share of twelfth place.

The hecklers had achieved their aim. Pete Bender felt that the incident with the crowd had upset Norman and cost him his momentum and, 'when you've lost momentum in this game, you've lost everything'.

Norman always says that when he loses a tournament, he holds a private conference with himself about his performance, holding up a microscope to the errors in his round and trying to decide whether they were mistakes of judgement or execution. These post-mortems marry uneasily with his assertion that he puts defeat out of his mind the second he leaves the course, but Laura insists that that's the case. 'After the US Open, riding back into New York City, everything was fine,' she said.

Tom Crow, vice-chairman of Cobra and a long-time friend of Norman, concurs. 'In my opinion, Greg has always had a great ability to switch off and relax,' he says. 'He's very driven, very focused and a perfectionist on the course. Off the course, he's still focused, but he's got a sense of fun. He doesn't think about golf.'

'Losing doesn't eat at him,' Charlie Earp said to *Time*. 'No, sir. It makes him more determined. He says it's only a game, what are you going to do about it? Play again tomorrow. He says you bloody beat me this time, but you won't beat me next time. He isn't going to go home and lose sleep over it.'

'We don't talk a whole lot about golf at home,' Laura told the *Daily Mail*. 'But when those horrible situations happen, like the Masters, it's nice to know that you can come back home to someone who is still going to love you, still think you're wonderful, and not be disappointed in you. Greg knows better than anybody what he's done wrong and why he's done it. He doesn't need to hear it from me. He doesn't need me to start on him because he feels bad enough.'

Away from home, the pressure mounted daily. Norman's close shaves had upped the ante. 'I wasn't the only one who wondered where he would end if he continued on the trend he was on,' says Peter Thomson. 'He was clearly standing still and people were going past him, and I didn't want to see that happen. Nobody here in Australia would wish that on him.'

---

# CHAPTER EIGHT

# OPEN SEASON

'I'd like to win the British Open first. It is *the* tournament in the world. It has the tradition. One day I believe I'll be the Open champion.'

GREG NORMAN, MARCH 1983

IT WAS MIDNIGHT WHEN Norman, drunk on happiness as much as champagne, walked down to the eighteenth green at Turnberry, accompanied by Laura, Hughes Norton, the photographer Lawrence Levy and his friend Howie Baws. Levy was wearing Laura's underwear, not having managed to find a clean pair of his own. They sat on the velvety surface where, hours before, a par had been sufficient for Norman to win the 115th Open Championship by five strokes. Norman gazed up at the little black star that highlighted his name on the great yellow leaderboard. 'Wouldn't it be great if I had that star to take home?' he said wistfully.

Baws jumped up. 'I'll get it for you,' he said, and departed to climb the grandstand. Hearing their laughter, eight policemen arrived with dogs, but not even they could bring themselves to detract from the most magical moment of Norman's career. They turned a blind eye to the champagne bottle upended in the cup, and hid their smiles as Baws clambered back down the stands, triumphantly bearing the

111

yellow placard emblazened with Norman's name and the black star denoting him Open Champion.

Just over a week earlier, Norman had been staring unseeingly out of the window of Concorde. He was on his way to the Ayrshire coast of Scotland for the Open and he was thinking about golf's cruelty versus its rewards, about how badly he wanted to bring home the claret jug and about destiny. 'He felt it inside,' Laura said. 'He told me on the plane coming over, "I'd like to lead for four rounds and win it going away." '

Days later, standing waist deep in the worst rough since Doug Sanders refused to leave the clubhouse at the 1966 Open on the grounds that 'there might be Apaches out there', Norman's primary concern was not breaking his wrists. Grimacing, he wriggled down into the wet grass at the par three sixth, his face red with cold and his trousers flapping like crazy in the gale and prepared to hack his way out. The ball careened across the fairway and plopped into the hay on the other side. Turnberry's landmarks, the proud white lighthouse and the eerie volcanic outcrop of Ailsa Craig, rose out of the gloom like the twin points of a smuggler's run. When he eventually managed to hit the green, Norman three-putted for a six.

'The Survival Open,' Nicklaus called it. Nine years after his epic 'duel in the sun' with Tom Watson, over a links so benign that questions were raised about its place on the Open rota, Turnberry had turned spiteful. On the eve of the championship, dark clouds moved in and icy winds gusted. 'Everybody is going to drive into the rough and make bogeys,' Norman said reasonably. 'The secret is to take nothing more than a bogey. Level par will win because it will be hard to make more birdies than bogeys.'

It was only when the gun went off that the full fury of the storm was unleashed. Spectators cowered beneath bucking umbrellas, and players and caddies leaned like suicidal lemmings into the rain. Norman opened with two birdies in the first three holes, before reality returned with a triple-bogey at the 222-yard sixth. Despite problems at the eleventh and a three-putt at the twelfth, however, he returned an eminently respectable 74. Of the 153 players who started the round, forty-nine failed to break 80, and the scoring average was

78.19. Collectively, the field was 1,251 shots over par. A pint-sized Welshman named Ian Woosnam scored 70, and Nick Faldo, Gordon J. Brand, Robert Lee and Anders Forsbrand were a stroke behind. Nicklaus and Floyd took 78, and Gary Koch was the best of the Americans on 73.

In the worst of the weather, the fourteenth, a 440-yard trip through a wind tunnel, was just one of eighteen nightmares. Only thirty-three players made par there and only Woosnam – hitting the best one-iron of his life – reached it in two. 'In the situation,' said Floyd, who lost a ball there, 'these are the hardest conditions I have ever played in.' Faldo called it 'the toughest course I have known'. Ballesteros was less complimentary.

'That was the toughest ever, no question,' said Norman. 'You can throw in all your US Opens. That was as tough as golf could be.'

There were times during the day when he had felt humiliated by the elements, reduced to a nonentity, 'hacking along, trying not to take more than five at a par four'. The rough was so savage that injury was a real possibility, and he and Floyd had discussed whether a player could sue the R & A for damages if he strained or broke a wrist trying to extricate himself. The fairways were ludicrously narrow. Watson paced them off and found that not one was more than 23 yards across.

In 1977, when Watson overcame the Bear, they shattered the Open aggregate so spectacularly that Hubert Green, who finished eleven strokes behind Watson, said, 'I won the Open – those two were playing some other tournament.' That was the year when the little-known Mark Hayes clocked up a second-round 63. Subsequently Turnberry had acquired a reputation as a low-scoring venue, a reputation that the first round in 1986 only briefly dispelled. By the second day, the wind had eased considerably and there was a dramatic drop in the scores.

Norman had arrived at Turnberry fresh from a two-week vacation and been assured by Bruce Devlin that his game was in perfect order. He exuded confidence in his pre-tournament press conferences. In practice rounds, Pete Bender had worked overtime getting him to relax, joking and teasing and tossing balls into bunkers and betting him a Coke he couldn't get up and down.

On his way to the first tee in the second round, Norman repeated to himself like a mantra, 'Blue skies and 65s,' the phrase he liked to use to get himself going. It worked like a charm and he made three successive birdies from the second. At the fifth, he came up short of the green and three-putted from 35 feet, but he bounced back almost immediately with an eagle at the seventh, hitting driver, one-iron to 20 feet and rattling in the putt. His mouth, white with Chapstick, was stretched into an uninhibited grin, his hair was as platinum as Barbie's. He was a lot happier than he had been the previous afternoon when a local paper had photographed him sitting with his head in his hands and captioned it, 'Don't cry, Greg.' Afterwards, he said, 'Everything seemed to flow. The ball was coming off the middle of the club and I felt really confident and comfortable with my swing. I liked the speed of the greens. That suited me. There were no distractions. I was totally involved in each shot. Everything seemed just right.'

He went out in 32, and hit a six-iron to five feet at the tenth and a nine-iron stone dead at the eleventh for two more birdies, causing the gallery to erupt. 'The crowd got me going,' he said. 'They really pumped me up. For the last four or five holes, there must have been fifteen thousand of them willing me on. It was difficult to keep my emotions in check.' At the fourteenth, the monster of the first round, Norman hit a three-iron to three feet, then sank a six-footer at the sixteenth to be 7 under for the day. An eagle putt slipped past the hole at the seventeenth and he needed a par at the last for a record 62. With the sound of the crowd ringing in his ears, Norman hit a seven-iron to 35 feet on the eighteenth.

Bender tended the flag for him. 'Pete, I want this one,' Norman said urgently. 'I want a sixty-one.' But he misread the speed of the green, rushing his first putt by and then pulling the return for a 63. 'With four holes to go, I honestly felt I might break sixty,' Norman said later. 'I mean, fifty-nine looked like a real possibility.'

'It would be tough to say he was disappointed with his round, but there's no doubt the last hole left a bitter taste in his mouth,' Bender said.

Watson was awestruck, describing Norman's 63 as 'the greatest round ever played in a tournament in which I was a competitor'. It

114

gave the Australian a two-stroke lead on 141. Gordon Brand was next, with Tommy Nakajima and Nick Faldo on 141.

'In the US Masters, I was beaten by the brilliance of Jack Nicklaus,' said Norman, who had nine single putts and used his driver nine times to equal both the course record and the major scoring record. 'In the US Open, I beat myself. But I have learned enough from those experiences to believe that this time I won't let it slip.'

Dan Jenkins, author of such classics as *The Dogged Victims of Inexorable Fate*, saw Norman's 63 as proof that Turnberry was a pushover. 'All of this by a player who is still trying to learn how to golf his ball, as they say,' he wrote. 'Norman's feet move on almost every swing, he addresses his putts on the toe of the clubhead, he sprays his shots woefully to the right or left when he does bad, and he is always making you wonder about his judgement. Despite these things, his power can be awesome and his touch at times can be likened to a brain surgeon. If he learns to keep it all together for a spell, everybody else can forget golf and go play polo with Prince Charles.'

In 1973, a virtual tempest had flattened Turnberry, blasting through the John Player Classic and turning tents and tee boxes into kindling. The 1986 Open saw nothing to equal that, but the third round rivalled any event on the globe for sheer nastiness. Norman, trussed like a supermarket fowl in a blue rainsuit, struggled manfully through the wind and rain, his hands slipping on the club. He extended his lead to five after the eighth, and then proceeded to make six bogeys coming home for an inward 40. He needed two drivers at the twelfth, was in the rough again at the fourteenth and in the bunker at the sixteenth. 'Four hundred and nine yards of terror,' said Peter Alliss.

'The difficulty of the rain was that you could not see,' said Norman, whose demeanour was, for the most part, remarkably cheerful. 'Every time I looked up to see where I was going, it hit me in the face and stung. At the ninth and tenth I pulled the trigger too soon.'

He used his driver from the rough at the last and smiled ruefully as he landed short of the green in the soaking grass. This time there was no applause as he finished a stroke ahead of Nakajima on 211; the gallery had long since abandoned him to sit by their firesides at home. Woosnam and Brand shared third place on 214, and Gary Koch was the lone representative of a defeated American contingent. It was the worst Open for US players since Royal Lytham in 1969.

Bruce Devlin rang Norman as he was getting into bed. 'You *can* do it this time,' he told him. Fuzzy Zoeller, John Mahaffey and Ken Green all lent their support, and when he phoned home to talk to Morgan-Leigh she said to him, 'Good luck, Shark.' But it was the encouragement of his boyhood idol that Norman cherished most. Earlier that evening, he had been eating dinner in the restaurant at the Turnberry Hotel when he was hit by the realization that everything he had dreamed of was once more within his reach. 'Though chatting pleasantly, Norman had the aura of a man who was to be hanged in the morning,' Rick Reilly said in *Sports Illustrated*. Through the mist that was threatening to descend on him, Norman heard Nicklaus asking if he could pull up a chair.

'Jack said there was nobody in the world he wanted more to win the tournament than me,' Norman recalled. 'I got a little choked up.'

'You deserve to win,' Nicklaus said sincerely, advising him, 'just concentrate on the pressure of your grip. That will orchestrate your tempo.'

Back in his room, Norman spent a fitful night clock-watching and fretting. He couldn't stomach much breakfast. When he made his way down to the range, it helped that the sun was shining and there was no breeze to speak of, but he was 'nervous as hell . . . I kept saying to myself, "All right, let's not do another Shinnecock here." ' Finally, he decided that it was better to be nervous than over-confident.

'We're just going to win a golf tournament today,' Pete Bender said soothingly. 'We've won plenty of tournaments. What's the difference between those tournaments and this one? They're all just tournaments.'

On the first tee, Norman took out a one-iron. Nakajima, the bespectacled Japanese golfer best known for the 13 he took at

Augusta's thirteenth, and the nine he took on the Road Hole at St Andrews, was his main threat. He had won ten events in Asia in the past eighteen months. But Nakajima was feeling a little jittery himself. He missed the green and three-putted from five feet to hand Norman a three-shot lead after one hole.

At the third hole, it came home to Bender that Norman was not capable of regarding the Open as just another tournament. His heart sank as he watched the Australian wrench his second shot into a big bunker, some 70 feet from the pin. But Norman's club flashed and the ball rose steadily into the wind, took one bounce and vanished into the hole to give him a four-stroke lead. Excitedly, Bender took his club, confident that Norman would now settle down. Instead, he bogeyed the fifth with a poor approach, and hit a low snap-hook off the seventh tee.

'Right then, I knew something was wrong,' Bender recalled in *How We Won the Open*. 'With having all those years' experience, I know when a player is nervous or choking or whatever people want to call it. His ball had gone into deep rough and I noticed he was walking toward it much faster than usual and he was talking to me faster. I said to myself, "Oh, boy, it's getting to him. He's feeling the pressure." '

Norman, wearing a patterned yellow sweater and a curiously ill-fitting pair of grey trousers, was in the rough with grass up to his knees, but he had a good enough lie to hack out onto the fairway, put his third on the green and save par. Walking to the next hole, Bender said gently, 'Greg, do me a favour. You're playing too fast right now. You're real nervous and you need to slow down a little. You're the best player here and you'll win this golf tournament, but you've got to take your time and enjoy it.'

The words glanced off Norman's tense frame and dissipated into the sunshine. He strode away as if Bender had not uttered a syllable. Bender grabbed his sweater from behind. 'Whoa!' he cried. 'Slow down and walk my pace. Let's talk and have fun.' He cracked a joke and Norman laughed and appeared to relax. 'Pete, you're absolutely right,' he told his caddie. 'I've got this won. Why try to pressurize myself into losing it?' At the eighth, he hit a four-iron to eight feet for birdie.

From that point on, Norman enjoyed himself. He was still edgy but he began to believe that he might win. At the fourteenth, he played the shot that effectively won the Open – a seven-iron from the rough that hit the flagstick and dropped beside the cup to give him a five-shot lead. Nakajima had fallen to pieces and Bernhard Langer, the only player to present any real danger, putted himself out of contention when he missed a five-foot birdie at the fourteenth and then yipped the two-foot return.

Otherwise, Norman's only real threat was himself. He was so shaky when he hit his third shot to three feet at the seventeenth that he said to Bender, 'Pete, I'm so damned nervous I can't see the hole. You'd better tell me where to hit it and how hard.' On the green, Bender lined up the putt for him and said, 'Inside right lip and soft, on the toe.' Norman, who could hardly hold the putter, knocked it three feet by and somehow made the return. Bender breathed a sigh of relief.

At the last, Norman wanted to take his driver, but Bender talked him into hitting a one-iron short of the bunker and a four-iron to the green. Hardly had the ball left the clubhead than the gallery broke through the barriers and swarmed across the fairway, engulfing Norman and bowling over Bender. Breaking free, Norman, hair ruffled, hands raised to acknowledge the crowd's ovation, was choking back the tears. 'I was so close to crying, it was ridiculous,' he said afterwards. He putted out shakily for a 69 to win by five shots from Gordon Brand with an aggregate of 280. He was the first Australian to win the Open since Peter Thomson in 1965.

'Apart from my wife and my caddie, Jack was the first person to congratulate me at the eighteenth,' says Norman, who was sprayed with champagne as he hugged Laura. 'He was under the bleachers waiting for me. Which I thought was very special.'

Norman sent two crates of champagne into the press tent, and followed them in with the claret jug wrapped in his arms, his face radiant with happiness. 'Everybody knows how much I wanted to win a major,' he said emotionally. 'The media is always writing, "Why can't he win here? Why not there?" and everybody's always saying, "Come on, Greggy, you can do it," and even if you know you can, it starts to get you down. You get a monkey on your back.'

'With a major, it will all be easier for him now,' Langer said.

Afterwards, Norman, bubbling with joy, kidded around with the bagpipers, and Mark McCormack hosted a celebration dinner for him at the Turnberry Hotel. 'I've never seen anyone enjoy a victory as much as he did,' remembers Bev Norwood, an IMG vice-president. Norman stayed up until 3 a.m. with Laura, Hughes Norton, Lawrence Levy and Howie Baws. Later, he would describe their party on the eighteenth green as a 'magic little interlude'.

He gave a press conference in the morning nursing a giant hangover, and was planning to while away the flight home working out how much his win was worth. 'I couldn't tell you how much I earned off the course in a year, but if you multiply my golf winnings by four, you'd get pretty close.' He smiled, adding, 'Winning the Open was the greatest moment of my life but I promise you this – it won't change me.'

His next target was the US money list. Along with his £70,000 first prize, he had already won $547,779 in America. 'I appreciate everything golf has given me and I like to show it,' said Norman, who was planning to buy an Aston Martin. 'I like to spend money and I'm lucky enough to have it to spend.'

The celebrations continued back in Orlando and then in LA the following weekend, where one of Norman's friends was getting married. At the reception, Levy pointed out to Norman that it was exactly one week and one hour since he won the Open. Norman laughed. 'And we've been partying ever since,' he said.

'He's such a nice guy,' said Bender, who had helped Norman to ten top tens in eighteen events. 'Would you believe he took the Open trophy to a New York jeweller's and had an exact copy made up for me? It's the proudest possession in my house.'

Toini and Merv were overjoyed. So many people told Norman that his mother won the ladies' club championship at Royal Queensland within hours of his Open victory that when he phoned her, he said teasingly, 'Hey, you're stealing my thunder.'

It didn't, as Bernhard Langer had predicted, suddenly become easier for Norman after he won his first major. Rather than diminishing, the burden of expectation increased. It was as though the Shark, having shaken his major hex, would now be unstoppable. He felt that way, too. In the weeks that followed his Open victory, he was carried along on a floodtide of pleasure and relief. When he teed up in the US PGA Championship at Inverness in Toledo, Ohio, it seemed perfectly natural that he should shoot a course record 65 to lead by two strokes from Craig Stadler and Phil Blackmar, and perfectly right and proper that he should follow it with a 68 to move four strokes ahead of Payne Stewart and Mike Thorpe on Friday. And what could be more appropriate than for Norman, so long denied, to put together a 69 in the third round, including a 60-foot par-saving chip, to maintain a four-shot lead over the fresh-faced Bob Tway on 202. 'Is this a soap opera or what?' Norman joked, as he posed for his zillionth photograph.

Then the first black cloud came scudding over the horizon. Sunday's play was washed out and the final round was delayed until the following day. But Norman didn't anticipate any problems. 'I'm in a good frame of mind and it won't go away overnight,' Norman said, declaring himself comfortable and ready to attack. 'There's no psychological problem. It's not like a sudden-death play-off. Everybody will come back and hit range balls, there'll be a gallery – it's all the same.'

For ten holes of the final round, it was the same. Norman, just as charismatic and talented as ever, was four shots ahead of the field and in control standing on the eleventh tee. Now, looking back at the calamity that followed, he says defensively, 'I didn't have two good holes, that's what it was. It was eleven and eighteen. That was it. The tide turned for me when I hit a perfect one-iron off the eleventh tee and I drove it into a half-filled divot and I couldn't get the back of the ball. I hit it real fat and I buried it in the front bunker about 40 yards short of the green. And that was it. My tide turned there.

'There wasn't anything much I could do after that. It was just one of those things, when you look back on it and you pinpoint the exact moment when it all started. Hit the perfect tee shot and I'm walking up there thinking I had a pitching wedge to the green. And that was it . . . I bogeyed eighteen because I was trying to make a chip shot. Eight out of ten times I'd get it up and down from that chip, because it was an easy chip . . . Why does that stuff happen? Are you a fatalist? Do you believe in destiny?'

Norman did. At the fifteenth, Tway conjured up a par after driving into the rough and hitting his second into the gallery. At the seventeenth, where he should by all rights have dropped a shot, he played an unbelievable pitch out of deep rough to within three feet to save par. Norman had bogeyed the fourteenth and they came to the last neck and neck.

At the eighteenth, Tway drove into the rough and then put his recovery into a bunker on the right of the green. Norman had played a fine approach and watched in annoyance as it spun back into the thick fringe, 25 feet away. He wasn't unduly concerned. Tway was in the front bunker, anchoring his feet in the sand. He was looking back and forth from the ball to the flag. Norman watched him with one eye as he considered his own shot. He saw Tway's club go back and the ball emerge in a pale flurry of sand, and then he saw Tway burst from the bunker like a jack-in-the-box, shouting with pure, unadulterated joy as the ball vanished into the hole.

'Oh, shit!' Norman said. He ran his own chip 10 feet past the flag.

Later he recalled that, 'Even when he chipped it in, I still thought I was going to chip it in! 'Cause I'll be damned if I was going to lose that championship.'

Tway could hardly contain himself. 'For something like that to happen on the eighteenth hole, it's just indescribable,' he said tearfully. 'I may never hit a shot again like that in my whole life. It was unbelievable. I just remember jumping up and down.'

'You can't get much unluckier than that,' Jim Murray said, of Norman's misfortune. 'That's like getting run over by your own car.'

'A lot of people have said to me my last-round seventy-six was a bad day,' Norman says. 'But I say, "I hit the ball as good as I hit it the first day. It's just that nothing happened." Like at eleven . . . An inch either way, I win the golf tournament, simple as that.' At the time he conceded graciously, 'I did the wrong things at the wrong time and Bob did the right things at the right time. Today he was the better guy.'

Tway's victory left Norman with the distinction of being the first man since Ben Hogan to have led all four majors going into the final round, but, unlike Hogan who won the Grand Slam, Norman only

121

won one. It was labelled 'The Saturday Slam', or, as Dan Jenkins cynically put it, 'The Choker's Slam'.

Only Ballesteros, who had lost the Masters in harrowing circumstances, thought that there was nothing surprising about squandering three third-round leads. 'To win one out of four in those circumstances is not bad, it's about normal,' he said.

'Bob Tway should never have been in the situation of holing a bunker shot to win,' says Rodger Davis. 'Everybody talks about how unlucky [Norman] was against Tway. Well, I looked at the scorecard and I saw him back in forty. Now that's not a good finish. It's just like match play. If someone keeps presenting you with things, then you start feeling really good and peppering the flag, and it's amazing how many times you can chip in or stiff an eight-iron because the other guy is giving you that opportunity.'

'The PGA was kinda tough because he played so well,' Hughes Norton recalls. 'But in 'eighty-six, particularly at Inverness, he was spinning the ball enormous distances backwards, and it certainly cost him. It was sad to see what he did on the back nine there.'

Steve Williams, the New Zealander who caddied for Norman in some Australasian and Japanese events until 1988, also believed that the Shark's ball held him back. 'He was playing a Tour Edition golf ball that spun more than any other ball.'

'Norman's problem is technique,' Mike Clayton says. 'People say he's a choker because he hits a four-iron eighty yards right of the last green at Augusta. That's not because you're choking, that's because your club is coming from the wrong place. His technique's killed him a lot of times. It's a measure of his talent that he's been able to play great golf with so many different methods, and he's never really stumbled.'

Asked in his post-Inverness press conference if he felt that the monkey – the burden of not having the right ratio of majors to talent – was back, Norman snapped angrily, 'What do you guys want? You guys are never satisfied. Face it: you know I did a hell of a job today. I don't understand you guys. Don't go saying the monkey's back on my back. I'll probably win next week and the week following that.'

He strode from the interview room, jaw set, studiously avoiding looking at Tway who was still regaling reporters with details of his miracle shot.

Norman didn't win the next week or the week following that, but when he did start winning in September it was to embark on a Byron Nelson-type streak. At the European Open at Sunningdale, he scooped the biggest first prize in the history of British golf. 'I haven't felt as excited as this on a golf course since the US Masters at Augusta,' Norman enthused afterwards, a strange statement given that he had won the Open Championship, a supposed lifetime ambition, in between. 'I was ready to play and I wanted to win. I felt I was ahead all the time.'

At the end of October, *Time* magazine did a feature on the Norman phenomenon. Merv and Toini had been up until 3 a.m. two days in a row watching their son in the World Match Play. Before overcoming Sandy Lyle in the final, Norman had gone head to head with Nicklaus in the semi-finals. They were level after thirty-four holes when Norman drained a 60-footer for an eagle and the eventual win. 'Well, you know, it was tough playing Jack,' Norman said. 'I love the man as a person and for what he's done, and I made that putt. I know he wanted to win, he wanted to prove that the older person is still as good as anybody – and he is still as good as anybody in the world. And I just wanted us to finish even: play all night and finish square and say, "Guys, flip the coin. Heads he wins, tails he loses." I really didn't want to see a result and when that putt went in he just gave me one of those Jack smiles and a wink.'

He was slightly less genial when he beat Lyle 2 and 1 in the final at Wentworth, marching off the course and declaring that he would never play in the World Match Play again. He accused the crowd of extreme partisanship, and claimed that they had deliberately tried to put him off by making loud noises on his backswing and cheering when he missed crucial putts. 'It didn't work,' he said. 'It made me concentrate even harder and be more determined to win. But if that's the way they want it, I'll stay away in future. I hope my feelings change before next year, but at the moment I am very annoyed. Of the thousands who were following us, I reckon only ten per cent were good. The other ninety per cent were bad.'

Back home in Aspley, Brisbane, his parents found it hard to

explain their emotions when they watched their son win another title. 'One didn't ever think that he would be number one in the world,' Toini said. 'I sort of expected him to win a few tournaments, but not the number that he's won.'

'Happy,' Merv said, 'proud. You sort of stand back and think, Well, there he is, walking the world stage.'

# CHAPTER NINE

---

# GREEN JACKET BLUES

'I *am* going to win the Masters one day, there is no question about it.'

GREG NORMAN, MARCH 1988

FOR NORMAN 1986 WAS, arguably, the best season any player had had since Arnold Palmer hitched up his trousers and kicked professional golf into the modern era. Between the European Open in September, where he beat Ken Brown on the first extra hole of a play-off, and the Australian PGA, he won seven times, including the Dunhill Cup at St Andrews (Australia beat Japan 3–0), the World Match Play, the Queensland Open (won by six shots) the New South Wales Open (by five), the South Australian Open (by three) and the Western Australian Open (by one) – the greatest run of form any golfer had enjoyed since Byron Nelson embarked on his eleven-victory streak in 1945. He won the US and Australasian money lists, became the first player to earn more than $1 million in a season and was the world number one. 'It's incredible,' Laura told reporters Down Under. 'We've almost forgotten how to lose.'

'I'm just over the moon about it, really,' Norman beamed.

To Dan Jenkins and others, 'The year became a haze . . . of

Norman winning eight or ten dozen tournaments in various corners of the world, and almost winning eight or ten dozen others, or so it seemed. It got so bad that when Greg did *not* win a tournament, fans felt cheated. And if a newspaper didn't have at least three headlines a week that said, "Norman Conquest", you figured there was no tournament that week.'

It wasn't until 1995 that Norman revealed that, throughout the year, he had been driven by something far greater than the fear of never winning a major. 'You've got to be so careful because somebody can get into your business and destroy you so quickly and take everything . . .' he told *Men's Journal*. 'It happened to me in the eighties. In 1986 when I won the British Open, I didn't have a penny to my name.'

He refused to divulge any details, but went on to say that his recovery strategy had been to play the best golf he could. 'One of Nicklaus's best years was when he won the Masters at forty-six. Why? It's not private information: he was having trouble financially. When a strong-minded person has his back to the wall, he comes out fighting. Nobody's going to stop the Bear when he's in a mood to get aggressive. Same [thing] with me. I was backed into a corner and the only way I could get out was to play hard, be dedicated, focus. I had to pick myself back up from scratch.'

Hughes Norton, who was not only Norman's agent during this period but one of his dearest friends, was rendered almost speechless by this claim. 'Absolutely ludicrous!' he snapped, his voice shaking slightly. 'It's just the weirdest thing I've ever heard. Now, several years before that he had to make a settlement with Marshall, which was costly, but by the end of 'eighty-three that was certainly over. In 'eighty-six, his income stream was fabulous. He's re-creating history. Why, I don't know. I'm amazed. I guess I shouldn't be, but I am.'

'It was a very temporary thing,' Frank Williams, who took over from Norton, says hastily. 'I think the severance with Marshall was very harsh and tough and he was forced to pay out a lot of money and I think there was a period of time when he was in financial trouble. But it was only very briefly and it probably wasn't as bad as Greg thought it was.'

Questioned about his *Men's Journal* comments two years on,

Norman is adamant that the situation was very bad indeed. 'In 1986, I probably couldn't have written you a cheque for a thousand dollars,' he insists. 'People warn you but you don't think it will happen to you. And yet it happens to everybody. You can go down the list – Nicklaus, Palmer, Muhammad Ali, Sugar Ray Leonard – in every area of sport. That's why, when my contract expired with IMG, I went looking for other things, to protect myself.'

'That's pretty amazing,' says Norton, who maintains that Norman was 'thriving' and buying houses and cars all over the place. Indeed, a cursory glance over the Australian's purchases between 1983 when he left Marshall and the end of the 1986 season turns up Ferraris, Jeeps, twenty-year-old Aston Martins, Jaguar sports convertibles, Rolls-Royces, countless journeys on Concorde, and a dream house in one of the most exclusive areas of Orlando. 'I had just negotiated the Spalding contract at Turnberry,' Norton continues, 'which was the largest deal ever signed by a golfer. We were setting records for appearance money. That Spalding deal alone was so far from penniless on the spectrum I can't tell you. If he was penniless and he had just won the British Open, he would have fired IMG on the spot. He *should* have fired IMG if it was true.'

But Norman didn't fire IMG – not that year at any rate. Why would he have? If the claims of his agents and the calculations of the press bore any relation to reality, he made £10 million in endorsements in the year following his victory at Turnberry, including a £1 million deal over three years to be a roving ambassador for Swan and Castlemaine XXXX Australian lagers; a £2 million deal with a Japanese hotel and leisure company; and up to £7 million over three years to promote Hertz rental cars, wear Reebok clothes and Niblick shoes, fly Qantas, conduct golf clinics at a club in Florida, and sport a calorie-injected McDonald's M on his sleeve.

But, as the wealthy always say, there's more to life than money. Norman drew on the golden residue of the previous season and took what he could into 1987. He won the Australian Masters by nine strokes and immediately flew to Brisbane for a lesson with Charlie Earp, telling reporters there was room for 20 per cent improvement. Then he tied for fourth place at the Players Championship in March.

But his main, if not his only, focus was Augusta. 'From the last day of the 1986 tournament, when I hit that second shot and missed the putt for par, from that very moment, and for the next year, twenty-four hours a day, I thought about the Masters,' he admitted. 'Every day it was in my mind. More than anything else in my life I wanted to win that one.'

That obsession, a complex alloy of passion and desperation, was what forced Norman through two lacklustre opening rounds to a third-day 66 on the astroturf fairways of Augusta. It's what kept him clinging on when he went out in 37 on Sunday, bogeyed the tenth and double-bogeyed the eleventh to lie one over par. It's what helped him claw his way back and sink a 35-foot putt on the penultimate hole to recover a dropped shot at the water-rimmed sixteenth.

That morning, hours before he teed off, a group of writers, one of whom was Tom Callahan, golf's most eloquent chronicler, had encountered Norman in the locker room. 'He was in there reading the papers,' Callahan remembers. 'Bob Verdi of the *Chicago Tribune* told him we'd all been in Australia for the Australias Cup. Instead of saying, "Did you like it?" he just went, "Hmmm." Then Dave Anderson said, "We played Royal Melbourne," and instead of going, "What did you think?" he just went, "Mmm." Then, foolishly, I dropped the third shoe. I said, "Yeah, we all bought one of those Akubra hats." Well, he looked at me and said, "Good, that's money in my pocket." And somebody there – it wasn't me – put a curse on that hat and said, "As long as he wears it, he's not going to [win another major]." Well, he gets chipped in there, and then he wins the 'ninety-three British Open [without a hat]. So among us, we kid that what he doesn't know is if he just took that hat off, he'd be all right.'

With his hat firmly on his head, Norman arrived at the last, needing a birdie for outright victory. Seve Ballesteros and Larry Mize watched his progress on television. They had tied on 285 after Mize, a gentle, mousy-haired local who had spent much of his childhood standing dreamily outside Augusta's exclusive gates, hoping and praying for a chance to compete there, holed a six-footer for birdie on the eighteenth.

Out on the course, Norman watched a 22-footer that would have given him the Masters slide past the hole. 'I don't know how it stayed out,' he said disbelievingly. 'A foot and a half from the hole, I could just feel it going in.'

'When Greg's putt just missed, Seve and I both looked at each other like, "We just dodged a bullet," ' Mize remembers.

With the momentum in Norman's favour, the three men walked to the tenth for the play-off. The sun was sinking slowly below the pines, and the fairway, dropping away into the valley far below, was bottle-green and criss-crossed with dark shadows. Between the Latin intensity of Ballesteros and Norman's presence and athleticism, Mize made a bizarre extra. At twenty-eight, he was pale and slender with only one win, four years earlier, to his name. Yet it was Mize who out-drove the stars on the first play-off hole. He was still bubbling over with the excitement of the birdie that had given him a tie at the eighteenth, so happy he could hardly contain himself. He hit a seven-iron up to the tenth, Norman was 20 feet away and Ballesteros putted up from the fringe.

'With Mize and Norman both having birdie chances, I gave it a little extra,' Ballesteros remembered, 'running it three and a half feet past. The sun was directly in my eyes on the return . . . I don't think I did anything wrong but I must have aimed left.'

With tears streaming down his face, Ballesteros began the long, lonely walk back to the clubhouse, as the other players made their pars. Even before he reached the top of the hill, history was being made on the eleventh. Mize had hit his five-iron second shot right, finishing some 140 yards away on a little rise near the twelfth tee. He went worriedly over to inspect it while Norman studied his long putt on the green.

' "Pete, I think if we just cosy this little son down to within two feet of the hole, we'll have a two-footer to win the golf tournament," ' Norman remembers telling Bender. 'That was my thinking, looking at the putt. It was a good fifty, fifty-five feet. I had hit it exactly where I wanted to hit it. Maybe it was six feet too far, because you'd rather have it hole-high than a downhill putt, but I was happy with it. Everything I did on that hole, I felt I executed right.'

Norman looked over at Mize, who was preparing to chip. Thousands of miles away, in the pro shop at Royal Queensland, Earp 'felt a cold shiver' pass through him as he watched the American set up over the ball on television. 'My wife will tell you. I said, "Mize is going to chip this in." My hair went all funny.'

The clubface flashed briefly and then the ball came bouncing gaily down the slope, took a quick skip across the green and dived into the hole. For a split second, nobody moved. The gallery stood aghast. Then Mize erupted, his purple-striped shirt flying upwards. 'It's just something that you dream about happening. I was so excited and thrilled, I'm running around screaming like an idiot. It was great.'

Norman sank slowly to his haunches, the blood draining from his face. 'I couldn't believe my eyes,' he said afterwards. 'I just couldn't believe it was going in.'

His own putt drifted away from the hole. 'It was almost like somebody ripped that jacket right off his back,' Laura remembers.

'I felt for Greg a little bit at the end,' Mize says. 'You're kind of not human if you don't.'

Back in the press centre, Norman described that day as the most demoralizing of his career. 'I'm just glad I'm playing for the next four weeks because if I went home right now I might be throwing things against the wall for the next five days,' he said with a laugh. But he was as sporting as ever. He cracked jokes, toasted Mize with a beer and said smilingly, 'I didn't think Larry would get down in two from there, and I was right. He got down in one.'

As he walked out, his four-year-old daughter put her hand in his. 'Daddy,' she said, 'I know you didn't win today, but can we still have a party?'

In the hours and even months that followed Mize's chip-in, there was no outward sign that this defeat was different from the rest, that it was, as Tom Weiskopf called it, a 'stake in the heart' – the kind of blow that Watson inflicted on Nicklaus at Pebble Beach, or Lee Trevino delivered when he chipped in to finish Tony Jacklin's career on the seventy-first hole of the 1972 Open at Muirfield. That evening, Norman flew back to Orlando with some friends on a chartered plane. They drank champagne and laughed so hard that when Laura looked at photos of the trip later, she said, 'Is this after we lost?'

Back in Britain, Ballesteros told *Golf World* that Norman made a mistake by going for the centre of the green rather than the pin on the eleventh, because it allowed Mize to believe he still had a chance. This ticked Norman off royally. 'Seve is so detrimental to his name right now,' he said. 'He can't shut his mouth up, because he keeps chastising other players for what they've done . . . I don't understand the guy, I really don't. I thought I got to know him the years I played in Europe, but now I'm totally lost with him . . . If he's going to throw stones at a glass house, he [should] never have three-putted the tenth . . . If he was in exactly the same position I was, I promise you, Seve Ballesteros would've hit it to the middle-right of the green.'

The media expressed Norman's own incredulity that he could be beaten twice in successive majors by a miracle shot. 'Ever seen a Great White Shark eaten by an anchovy? Twice?' Rick Reilly of *Sports Illustrated* asked, adding, 'Another catastrophe and you can look for Norman on the cover of *Psychology Today*.'

'Greg Norman will lose the next US Open when Joe Bob Zilch holes out a wedge from the top of a eucalyptus tree on the third extra hole in San Francisco,' Dan Jenkins intoned. 'Norman will lose the British Open when Sam Sausage holes out a wedge from ten fathoms beneath the Firth of Forth on the fifth extra hole at Muirfield. Norman will lose the PGA Championship in Palm Beach when Rex Shank holes out a wedge from inside a jewellery store on the seventh extra hole. Norman will then retire and autograph strait-jackets for a living.'

Outwardly, Norman was philosophical, admitting that it hurt but not saying how much. Charlie Earp thought that nothing in his life had hit him harder. 'But he would not admit that. Greg says, "Just forget it." '

'Inside,' Laura says, 'he was dying.'

It was not until 1991 that Norman admitted that it had taken him four years, not the four months he claimed at the time, to get over it. He hadn't wanted to tell people that, after Mize chipped in, he sat on the beach at three o'clock in the morning and cried. 'I was kind of, "Ohhhhh, what have I done wrong?" I sat down in front of my house and just listened to the surf come in.'

'I think the Larry Mize one was the most devastating loss for Greg,' Laura says. 'He tried to brush it under the carpet. He tried to pretend that it didn't hurt him and that he was just going to go on. But he had to deal with it eventually. It took a long time and it kind of got deeper inside of him the longer he let it go.'

A decade on, Norman is still trying to come to terms with the fact that the Mize defeat, still the most painful of his career, came so soon after Tway. 'In all honesty, I didn't do anything wrong in either of those majors,' he says.

Reminded that he came home in 40 at Inverness, he says, 'Uhhh, yeah . . .' before moving on smoothly. 'So people had to do something dramatic. Anyway, Larry Mize was the hardest one of the lot. I can deal with it when I screw up myself, but it's pretty hard when it happens back to back. People say, "Well, it's never been done before," and you start analysing it and you think, Shit, it's true. I did lose back to back majors with somebody holing miracle shots. I could have been on my way to a Grand Slam, but no. And then you sit back and look at all the people who holed shots against me – you can go down the list. My life, my career, has been so much better than theirs. I kept on winning. Larry Mize hasn't won.'

'If you actually look at Greg's failures, if you want to call them that, if you actually analyse them, it isn't just that he's been unlucky and lost,' James Marshall says. 'To me, that's the easy way out. People have been able to parlay that around and say, "Poor guy! Larry Mize chipped in or Bob Tway came out of a bunker." But people forget that he dropped four or five shots, so he didn't lose to Bob Tway, he let him in. So I think he's been cushioned by that over the years.'

'They were all his fault, except the Larry Mize one,' says Mike Clayton. 'I mean, that was outrageous. But he shot forty on the back nine at Inverness. He made a double-bogey at the eleventh with a pitching wedge. He was in a divot, sure, but he made a double-bogey. He played so well for three and a half days and then he shot forty. Bob Tway was never in it. Sure, the guy made a bunker shot, but when was the last time you saw someone shoot forty on the back nine of a major and win?'

One of the guiding principles of Norman's life has always been that of rewarding himself for his hard work. Since he had worked hard for seventy-four holes of the Masters, he rewarded himself with a

$118,000 Ferrari Testarossa, a trip to the Indy 500 to hang out with Roger Penske in the pit, and a $3 million ocean-front house in Lost Tree Village, North Palm Beach, close to Jack and Barbara Nicklaus. The Normans had not been happy with the standard of education in Orlando, and the Nicklauses had convinced them of the advantages of sending their children to the exclusive Benjamin schools in Palm Beach, which all the Nicklaus children had attended.

To Pete Coleman, this typified Norman's penchant for befriending the rich and famous. 'He's a showbiz man,' he says. 'He moved to Bay Hill and was playing with Arnold Palmer when Arnold Palmer was still a bit of a name, then he went to North Palm Beach where Jack Nicklaus lived and was always flying and playing golf with Jack Nicklaus. He's promoted himself very well by being seen with the right people all the time . . . and when you're doing that, people talk about you in the same breath. They say, "Jack or Greg or Arnold." And if he'd come and play a practice round, it was mostly with Jack or Arnold or Nick Price. It was always a name. He's completely different from somebody like Bernhard who'll roll up and go out and play with Joe Bloggs or Jack Smith or anybody who wants to play. But I think Greg was a guy who wanted to promote himself.'

'Greg makes a lot of money; he flaunts it and that pisses people off . . .' said former Masters champion Cary Middlecoff, who was living at Lost Tree at the time. 'He is very popular, but that's the reason he is not more popular.'

But, according to Frank Williams, the opposite was true, and in fact the Normans had moved away to Jupiter Island in Hobe Sound, Florida, within three years. 'They hated it,' he says. 'It was too snobby for them, for want of a better word.'

When Laura first saw the North Palm Beach property, she called Norman in Australia. 'Should I spend a million dollars without you seeing it?' she asked.

'Do you like it?' Greg asked.

'I love it,' said Laura.

'Well, go ahead and get it,' he told her.

The existing house was then levelled and replaced with a six-bedroom French-style villa with a fountain and lots of arches. The dining room could seat a hundred or more, and the trophy room housed the billiard table used in the 1932 world championships.

'I feel that my place is do to anything and everything to help Greg's success,' Laura told April Tod of the *Daily Mail*, 'and that means keeping a low profile and helping with all the trivial background stuff . . . There are times when we are forced apart because of all of Greg's golfing commitments, and I know there are women out there who love to follow him because of who he is. But I don't think I've ever been jealous of those attractive girls who follow golfers. Greg is smart enough never to risk anything.'

The anxiety of watching Norman play often caused her to shed pounds in weight, and she felt physically ill after his Mize defeat. Asked whether she was concerned that Norman would be felled by another miracle shot at the forthcoming US Open, she cried, 'No, no, no! It just couldn't happen again. In fact, I really feel more of a relief now. It's all over. And you know what? I have a feeling that this time Greg is going to pull one of those miracles on somebody else.'

But there were to be no spectacular feats from Norman in the majors that year. Quite the reverse. He tied for fifty-first in the US Open and was thirty-fifth at Muirfield, the year Faldo won the Open in horrific conditions with eighteen straight pars. Afterwards, Norman stood in the cold in a garden illuminated by car headlights, giving a lesson to the head chef of Greywalls Hotel, Andrew Mitchell. Having torn a strip off Mitchell at the start of the week for underfeeding him with half a lobster, an entire Dover sole, vegetables and dessert, Norman was so pleased when the chef responded with giant portions of roast pork, duck, lamb, apple strudel and raspberries that he offered to give him a thirty-minute lesson rather than the five minutes he had cheekily asked for.

Only the hotel manager was not amused. 'I shudder to think what would have happened had the club secretary caught my chef and Norman on the course,' she said.

Norman's own game had gone into decline. After the Masters he had tinkered with his fundamentals in an effort to eliminate from his game the blocked shot he sometimes hit. As a consequence, he had begun hooking the ball. 'At the British Open, I hit a couple of iron shots that I really didn't like so I said, "Screw that, forget it." I've gone back to my old left-to-right method and I've stuck with it.'

At the US PGA, where Norman trailed in seventieth, a row brewed when the *Orlando Sentinel* published remarks Paul Azinger had made during a friendly round of golf, to the effect that a lot of people Norman had beaten in his time had been only mediocre players. He was responding to comments Norman had made about the foreign players being more dominant than the Americans at that time – comments that echoed those of Mark McCormack, who called the US pros a bunch of pampered prima donnas. 'They can't face up to the fact that they aren't the best in the world any more,' McCormack said scornfully.

'He confronted me with [the article],' Azinger remembers, 'and said, "What is this? Why have I whipped you into a frenzy?" I said, "That's trash, man, you never whipped me into a frenzy." I mean, I'm sorry, it was nothing. The press made such an issue of it, like Greg and I had this big falling-out. It was nothing like that.'

'We had a discussion,' was the way Norman phrased it to *Golf Digest*. 'One thing I've always believed in is that you never mention another player's name in a derogatory fashion ... because it will always backfire on you. Always.'

He conveniently forgot about the forty or so character assassinations he had performed in his autobiography, or his criticisms of Ballesteros and even Mize the previous November when poor Mize was chosen by his fellow pros as the player with the least intestinal fortitude. 'I almost hate to say it, but Larry just doesn't show that special look at any time,' Norman told *Sports International*. 'He never seems to say, "Hey, I've got a chance to make a birdie here . . ." I've played with him a couple of times and I've never seen that. He pulls that shoot-to-the-centre-of-the-green routine way too often.'

The day before Thanksgiving, Norman sacked Pete Bender from his car-phone in Australia. 'He just said, "It's time to change," ' Bender recalled. 'I said, "Give me one reason why you're firing me. What's your excuse?" He said, "I don't have an excuse." '

Bender told *Golf* magazine that Norman fired him for no reason, but the feeling among some of the caddies was that he had grown too cocky and boastful. He was nicknamed 'The Million-Dollar Caddie'.

However, Bender's friend Andy Martinez, Tom Lehman's highly regarded caddie, says that no caddie worked harder. 'I think it had to do with some of the flaws Greg has, like maybe finding a scapegoat. I don't know. With Greg, it seems like he's tried a lot of different realities.'

To Martinez, in the three-year period Bender had caddied for the Australian, Norman had changed from being fun, one of the boys and 'loose', to being 'wound so tight all the time'. Martinez, who carried Norman's bag for a day at the 1987 International when Bender was sick, actually experienced the effects of this change first hand. 'I tell you, in that one round, I saw the whole gamut of emotions. I even had to give him a pep talk. He was having one of those days, and he was forcing shots, and putts were lipping out. I said, "After the year you had last year, this should be a piece of cake. What you did last year, it's in the history books. You've got nothing to prove." But it seems like he always feels like he's got something to prove, every week.'

'Greg intimidates caddies, too,' Bender said. 'You're afraid to say stuff to him, even if you're right, because you don't want to be fired for it.'

It was almost the last controversy of the year, but not quite. On 29 November, the fourth round of the Australian Open had to be abandoned when Norman and Sandy Lyle led a walk-off in protest at the third green at Royal Melbourne. Players and reporters crowded into the locker room after officials refused to do anything about the farcical position of the cup, cut into a slope on a triple-cut, quick-silver green in a howling gale. Rodger Davis, who was in the first group out, thought that the decision to down tools was entirely reasonable. 'Guys were eight-putting and penalizing themselves for all sorts of stuff. It was on a hill. You putted up, it rolled back fifteen feet. Sandy Lyle was the one who refused to putt. Greg found out and walked off. Fair enough. I mean, it was absolutely stupid. You can't have a shot at him for doing that. And then they blame some fifty-year-old greenkeeper when at the end of the day the AGU didn't go round and check all the pins.'

When the tournament resumed the next day, Norman won by ten shots.

*

The story of Jamie Hutton and the Heritage Classic is an integral part of the 1988 season. Shortly before the tournament, Norman had been contacted by a charity called Thursday's Child, which helped to fulfil the wishes of children suffering from extended or terminal illnesses. Jamie, a small, slightly built seventeen-year-old from Wisconsin, had suffered from Crohn's disease since he was seven and in February had discovered he also had leukaemia. He idolized Norman. Like the Shark, he was a Boston Celtics fan, and his dream was to watch Norman play a tournament and win.

Norman willingly agreed to meet the boy and promised to do what he could about victory. Jamie was so excited about meeting his hero that, when he reached Hilton Head on Thursday night, he phoned Norman at eleven o'clock and woke him up. They arranged to have breakfast together. 'I couldn't believe he eats cornflakes,' Jamie said. 'He was like a normal person.' Norman, in his own way, was equally overwhelmed. After breakfast, he had taken Jamie down to the Atlantic. The boy stopped and stared. 'My God, it's so big,' he told Norman, who realized with a shock that Hutton had never seen the ocean before.

That afternoon, Norman, who had opened with a 65 to share the lead with Azinger, introduced Jamie to some of the stars. By coincidence, Curtis Strange was also looking after a young boy with leukaemia. After Saturday's round, Norman was four strokes off the lead. Out on the course, he was conscious that Jamie was willing him to win. When he found out that Jamie would have to leave before the final round on Sunday, he and Lawrence Levy chartered a plane to take Jamie and his mother to Madison for bone-marrow transplant tests on Monday.

'He's very generous,' Laura says. 'He has no problem giving or doing things for other people. He does a lot for sick kids and kids who don't have anything.'

Norman had arrived at Hilton Head filled with more confidence than he had had in months. A tip from neighbour Nicklaus, to quicken his hands and be more aggressive through the ball, had helped win a succession of early-season events in Australia, including the ESP Open at Royal Canberra, where he opened with a course record of 62 and left the field trailing by seven shots. When he read in a Sunday paper that the other Australians felt they were playing for second place at the Australian TPC, he took them at their word. 'I had those guys beaten even before I walked onto the first tee,' he said, with typical modesty. 'No guts, no glory.'

In America, he had battled to a final-round 64 for a share of fifth place at Augusta the previous week. Had it not been for opening scores of 77 and 73, the outcome might have been very different. 'The old saying is that you don't go out to shoot sixty-fours, they just happen,' Ken Venturi, who had allowed three Masters titles to get away, told *Golf Digest*. 'Norman has to let it happen. He's tried to make it happen. His first rounds have been horrendous because he puts so much pressure on himself to live up to expectations.'

On the final day of the Heritage Classic, Norman struggled to concentrate, distracted by the 'freedom of expression' with which Jamie talked about the illness that made him measure his life in months. When he stood over a six-footer at the eighteenth with a chance to win, he said to himself, 'This one is for Jamie.' He holed it for a 66 and victory. 'That was probably more pressure than I have ever put on myself – because I knew I would break the boy's heart if I missed it,' he recalled later.

It could have ended there, but it didn't. Norman, who presented the boy with his trophy, kept in constant touch and sent him clubs inscribed, 'To Jamie from Greg'. Honoured for what he had done for Jamie at a New York golf writers' dinner in June, the same month Jamie underwent his bone-marrow transplant, Norman stepped up to the microphone and broke down. Tears poured down his face. 'Pardon me,' he said. 'I've never done this before. Please excuse me.' When he could finally speak, he said unevenly, 'I don't think that many people know what goes on with a sick child. Heck, they haven't reached one quarter of their life. They don't have a chance.'

He received a standing ovation.

If the Jamie Hutton story represented one side of Norman's character – warm, compassionate and infinitely generous – the Italian Open in Milan represented the profligate, flamboyant and overbearing aspect. He arrived there with Laura from the Monaco Grand Prix in May, followed by a taxi transporting the luggage that hadn't fitted into the boot of their car. 'It cost around eleven hundred dollars – the guy ripped us off,' Norman said, with a laugh. 'He just took advantage of a couple of foreigners.'

By the end of the week, he had paid for it with a £60,000 appearance fee and the £35,000 winner's cheque. In between, he found time to criticize the world ranking system, Seve Ballesteros, and Ian Woosnam's decision to change his clubs, which he said was 'like cutting off the hand that feeds you'. He also ordered a £200,000 Ferrari F40.

Norman was addicted to high-octane activities. People unlucky enough to find themselves in a vehicle with him experienced near-heart failure and sudden-ageing after handbrake turns at 80 m.p.h., although Norman claimed that he had received just four speeding tickets since he first moved to Florida in 1982.

'It used to bother me,' Laura once said. 'Anything dangerous he likes.' Once when they were in Britain and she was pregnant, Norman started rocketing through the country lanes until the fields were a dizzy blur. The last time she had the courage to look at the speedometer, it was 140 m.p.h. 'Please, Greg, slow down,' she whispered.

'It's OK,' Norman said, foot to the floor.

'He's just that way,' Laura told *Golf Digest*. 'People used to tell me he'd change. But he never will. I've learned to live with it.' She admits that, 'When he dives, I'll still watch the bubbles and I'm always thinking about what could happen. But I'm not afraid, I'm just over-cautious. He's always fine.'

Norman's passion for speed led to his friendship with Nigel Mansell, the British Formula One driver. They had met the previous year in a pro-am and had formed a 'brotherly' relationship based on a mutual love of golf and cars. 'We have the same chemistry,' Norman said. 'He loves to be a winner, so do I. When you feel comfortable with a friend you can get a lot off your chest. It makes you feel relaxed.'

Norman had watched Mansell win the British Grand Prix at Silverstone in July 1987, and Mansell had visited him at the European Open at Walton Heath a few months later. 'He was in his helicopter and I had a Jag,' Norman told *Golf World*. 'I was staying at a hotel near Gatwick, normally about thirty-five minutes' drive round the M25 and so – I guess I was crazy doing this – I bet him dinner that I could beat him back. He had to give me ten minutes' start before he could even start the engines. Typically, because he didn't want to get beaten, he only waited five minutes. I had the car off the clock all the way and he landed at the same time as I pulled into the hotel. That's how we are – both very competitive.'

He'd probably scare some people who don't know about automobiles,' Steve Williams says, 'but he knows how to drive a car.'

For Norman, the Italian Open turned out to be the high point of the season. In June, he lost a play-off to Ballesteros for the Westchester Classic, and damaged the ligaments in his left wrist when his club hit a rock on the ninth hole of the US Open. Golf writer Melanie Hauser remembers Norman flying into the locker room 'half hysterical. He was on the phone to his doctor and just going crazy. You could tell he was scared to death that he had ripped up everything in his wrist. He said something to the effect of, "This is my career and I need to be seen now!" '

Norman was out for eight weeks. By the time he realized he might be fit enough to play the Open, it was too late to re-enter, and he was desperately disappointed to find that he would miss that too. A top ten in the US PGA provided little consolation.

By then, he was embroiled in two new controversies. Not only had the PGA of Australia decided to pick Peter Senior and Roger Mackay, leaders of their 1987 Order of Merit, over Norman and Ian Baker-Finch, the highest Australians on the Sony World Rankings, to represent them in the World Cup, but Norman's inability to play the obligatory fifteen tournaments required to maintain membership on the US Tour had provoked a storm of protest. There was still plenty of time for him to play all fifteen, but he was committed to events in Australia and the Far East.

'I can't believe that Greg would challenge the rules,' cried Curtis Strange, the US Open champion and, until that point, a close friend of Norman.

'Why should Greg be different?' demanded Doug Tewell. 'The rules are the same for everybody.'

Ballesteros was angrier still. Two years earlier, he had fallen out with the US Tour commissioner Deane Beman when Beman had stripped him of his membership after his father died and he did not complete the requisite number of events. 'If Norman breaks the rules, he should be suspended just as I was,' Ballesteros said.

But Beman was in fact sympathetic to Norman's cause. 'Deane told me there was no problem,' Norman said defiantly. 'I don't want to get into a slanging match with other players. I've supported and stuck up for this Tour.'

CHAPTER TEN

# LONE SHARK

'With the glory goes the pressure.'

JACK NICKLAUS ON GREG NORMAN, 1989

THE SEASON ROLLED OUT from under the new year, heavy as lead. 'Is Greg Norman overrated?' That seemed to be the burning question. Or as one magazine put it: 'Is Norman overanxious? Overwrought? Overdue? *Overrated?*'

There was no escaping the endless analysis and speculation. Norman had won fifty-two titles around the world but everywhere he turned he was competing with ghosts: his own and the paragons of history. Jack Nicklaus said the Australian worked harder than he had ever done on his own game – 'He's on the practice tee at eight in the morning' – and let it be known that he thought Norman and Ballesteros were head and shoulders above anybody else in golf. 'I think Greg is a better shotmaker than Seve,' he said. 'It's just that Seve has greater imagination and a short game that is out of sight.' But it was not enough, not for the media and not for Norman. Norman might have been number one on the world rankings for the best part of three years, he might have an estimated annual income of

£10 million, and he might, says Nick Seitz said, be a 'tall, powerful Australian with the meat-cleaver features and the regal bearing of a Degas stallion', but at thirty-four he had just one major and five US Tour wins to his name. At the same age, Nicklaus had won twelve professional majors. Even Ballesteros had won five.

'He has the ability to be the finest player in the sport, but his record in the States has not been that outstanding,' Johnny Miller told *Golf Digest*. 'There's a close correlation between Greg Norman and Tom Weiskopf. Tom should have been the best golfer in the world but he never was.'

'I don't think Greg will ever win a lot of tournaments because he's big business,' Curtis Strange said disparagingly. 'He could quit today and spend a lot of money.'

For the first time ever Norman admitted that burn-out, the extinguishing of desire by off-course pressures, was a distinct possibility if he continued at his current pace. Reebok, McDonald's, Akubra (he was reportedly paid £40–60,000 to wear his trademark hat) and other sponsors all demanded their pound of flesh; and his obligations to two Tours – the Australian PGA were rumoured to be forking out £500,000 over five years in appearance money – meant that he flew back and forth to Australia as frequently as most Wall Street bankers commuted to their day jobs.

'I have been overloading my schedule,' conceded Norman, blaming himself rather than IMG for his reluctance to turn down appearance fees averaging £75,000. He planned to take things easier. 'The bottom line is that I've tried to please other people ahead of myself and my family. I thought I could go charging around, playing all over the world, and I've enjoyed doing it, but it's been affecting the way I am as an individual and it's been affecting my game,' Norman said. 'I'm mature enough to say no. From now on the majors will be more important than making money.'

But in reality slowing down was not an option. Driven by his fear of failure, poverty or anonymity – sometimes it was hard to know which – Norman confronted his demons at Augusta in the spring of 1989. A sense of urgency inhabited his game. A naturally quick player, he seemed to fidget and deliberate more over shots, executing a series of careful waggles and then launching himself at the ball.

Lacklustre rounds of 74 and 75 left him eight strokes behind Faldo and Trevino at the halfway stage.

As seemed to happen so often, Norman was at his best when coming from behind. He shot 68 in the third round and, on the back nine on Sunday, caught fire. He made birdies at the tenth, thirteenth, fifteenth, sixteenth and seventeenth holes, before a five-iron shot to the final green fell short of it like a pricked balloon and cost him a bogey. His 67 left him a shot out of the Faldo/Scott Hoch play-off.

As twilight cloaked the pines of Augusta, Norman pasted a smile on his face and joined Mark O'Meara and Payne Stewart in the clubhouse for a beer. 'I may not show it,' said Norman, who had declined to be interviewed, 'but I'm incredibly disappointed, incredibly down.'

'You will win the Masters sooner or later,' a bystander promised.

'Sooner or later?' Norman replied, smiling as if his life depended on it. 'How much *later* is it going to be?'

For all Norman's macho image, Weiskopf, among others, wondered whether he was too soft to win as many majors as he should, whether he lacked a killer instinct. 'He wants to be the best, no doubt about it, and I wish it to him,' the former Open champion told Bob Verdi. 'But to be the best, you have to be a motivated, selfish, egotistical, demanding perfectionist. But I give him lower marks on selfishness and ego, as far as golf is concerned. In life, Greg's a great guy, a man's man, who cares about friends and spends a lot of quality time with them and his family. He might not be mean enough to be the best in a cut-throat business, which is OK as far as I'm concerned. That was never a priority of mine, to be the best golfer in the world at all costs. I don't know about Greg. He's not a phoney. He's a whole person who enjoys having a beer with friends and fishing with his kids. Is that bad? You tell me.'

'Well,' Norman said, 'I do want to be the best golfer in the world, very much so. But I am a nice guy, and I also want to be that. You know, when I don't win, I feel worse for the people who root for me than for myself. I feel as though I've let them down. But I don't want people to feel sorry for me. I came from very little and I've done remarkably well, surrounded by great people, starting with Laura . . . I'm not comfortable, though. I'm driven to win.'

Norman told Verdi that he didn't think he could be meaner if he wanted to. 'I give one hundred and ten per cent on the course, but I also sleep at night. Where I was brought up, you give it your best, and if somebody beats you fair and square, you congratulate him for it and move on. Keep trying. Try harder. Too hard? Perhaps.'

None the less, the ticking of the clock wore on Norman's nerves like water torture. Privately, Nicklaus thought that Norman allowed himself to be discouraged by too many encounters with players with hot putters, but Norman felt there was more to it than that. He prayed there was more to it. 'When I won the British Open, I wasn't ready to win a bunch of majors,' he admitted. 'I feel ready now, but first I've got to get the next one, and I'm very aware of wanting it too much. If I try too hard, I could lose. I also know that if I reach thirty-nine and haven't done it, it might be too late. I don't want to be remembered as the poor fellow who was there for those two chip-ins. I've got to believe there will be a day . . .'

Norman stood nervously on the first tee at Royal Troon in the Open Championship play-off, with Bruce Edwards at his side. A veteran caddie, with the weathered, slightly hard aspect of a range rider in a Western, Edwards had spent sixteen years working for Tom Watson, but when Watson cut back his schedule to watch his children grow up, Edwards took up Norman on his oft-repeated offer of employment. Their first tournament together had been the Westchester Classic in June.

'I thought he'd be fun to work for,' Edwards recalls. 'I thought, having worked for Tom and seen how he won, how he became a champion, maybe I could bring that to Greg. So, the first two years I worked for him, we got along great.'

Right at this moment, Edwards was having all the fun he could have wished for. It was blazing hot for starters. Frog-bellied Brits waded in the muddy-blue shallows of the sea, and Troon was dry and dusty and not a fraction as vicious as usual.

'People say the field is bunched because of the benign conditions,' Watson had said. 'But even if the wind doesn't blow, that'll probably change on Sunday because of the choke factor, the pressure factor . . . You've got to have bottle.'

Wayne Grady, the gentle Australian, Tom Watson, looking like a contestant in *One Man and his Dog*, and the entertaining Payne Stewart were respectively on 204, 205 and 206 when Norman teed off on the final morning. He was seven shots off the lead, with only the remotest possible chance of winning the title, and yet he felt good about life. He rolled in a birdie putt on the first and his grin broadened. He rattled in another at the second and laughed. By the time he reached the third, he was in heaven. Six straight birdies brought him to within a stroke of Grady. At the sixteenth, he narrowly missed an eagle. At the par three seventeenth, he holed his chip to save par. At the last, he used his putter from the thin rough skirting the green and almost birdied again. His 64 was a new course record, and set a clubhouse target of 13 under. When Mark Calcavecchia hit an eight-iron to five feet at the last for a birdie soon afterwards, and Grady bogeyed the fourteenth and seventeenth, they were tied.

Standing on the first tee of the play-off on that golden evening, Edwards felt confident that the tournament was theirs. There were lots of laughs. Calcavecchia, with his red and white banded shirt and mischievous face, looked like an irreverent high-school footballer. He kept asking the R & A officials if it really was a four-hole play-off. 'You're sure now? After one hole nothing changes, right?'

Norman and Grady were more tense, their smiles a little strained. Even when Norman birdied the first to gain an early advantage, he didn't seem to relax. At the second, he hit his approach to about 15 feet and birdied. The American followed him in from the back fringe to be a shot behind him. Grady trailed on level par.

At the seventeenth, Norman hit a four-iron through the back of the green. He contemplated his lie in the pale grass. Grady was busy making bogey from a bunker, and Calcavecchia was waving his putter jauntily, laughing at some private joke. Norman took out a putter. 'What I remember most vividly', Edwards says, 'is that there was a long piece of grass, like kind of a straw, and as he took the putter back it was kind of catching it. But he still liked that play. The ball was just through the green on the fringe. I wanted him to putt it.'

Edwards shouldered the bag and prepared to move back.

'Don't go away,' Norman ordered, 'I might chip it.'

'I thought, Oh man,' Edwards remembers. 'I've always felt, as a caddie, that you never say anything around the green. I mean, it becomes a touch shot. I really don't think a caddie should tell a guy, "Don't putt it, chip it," or "Don't chip it, putt it." So I didn't. I don't know what he was thinking but when he hit the chip I knew it was too hard. At that point we didn't need a birdie, all we needed was a three, and we would have had a one-shot lead going into the last hole. And it went about 10 feet by and he missed the putt. I felt right then that we had thrown a shot away due to him being too aggressive.'

Grady thought it was bizarre. 'He used about an eight-iron, which is probably not the right sort of club in that situation. I would have used a sand-wedge.'

'He could have putted it, hit it with a seven-iron, anything,' Jack Newton said. 'Instead, he tries to hit a fancy spinning chip. Seven years later he tried to hit the same fancy chip at the tenth hole in the final round at Augusta. He still wants to play the low-percentage shot he'd play in the first round and that isn't the way to win majors.'

Drake Oddy, Calcavecchia's caddie, said that the American had also been surprised. 'There didn't seem that much between him and the green that would cause him trouble,' he told Norman Dabell in *How We Won the Open*.

Norman's mouth tightened when he missed the putt. 'It didn't go left,' he told Edwards, with a scowl, as they walked to the eighteenth tee.

Whenever the 1989 play-off appears on the list of Norman's perceived failures, the chip on the penultimate hole is rarely mentioned. It is his tee shot at the last that is held up as symbolic of the over-zealous approach that has cost him so dearly in the majors. Yet not one of the five who stood with him on tee will condemn him for it.

Calcavecchia drove first, careening the ball off the metal railings way out to the right and rebounding into the rough. Norman considered his options. He had taken a driver off the last in all four rounds and, with Edwards in complete agreement, he was quite comfortable using it again. In the television commentary box, Nicklaus gave a little gasp of surprise. 'I can't imagine what Greg is thinking taking out a driver here,' he said. 'The only thing he can do by hitting a driver is bring the bunker into play, which is the one place out there he wants to avoid.'

Standing on the tee, Norman and Edwards didn't see it that way at all. 'I really didn't feel like that far bunker was in play for him,' the caddie says, 'and as well as he was hitting it, I didn't see it going anywhere but right down the middle. Which basically is where it started out. It hit a little mound and it kicked a little right and just fell into the bunker. *Dead*.'

'People said I shouldn't have hit a driver,' Norman said later. 'But if I'd hit it three yards to the left, they would've said I hit the greatest drive ever.'

Grady, whose own tee shot skated along the bone-dry fairway to within 10 yards of that fatal bunker – 'about twenty yards closer than I'd been all week' – thought that Norman's choice of club was entirely appropriate. 'It was one of those shots where, as soon as he'd hit it, he bent straight down to pick up his tee, thinking it was perfect, and I thought it was perfect and bent down and teed up my ball,' Grady says. 'Then we heard the oohs and aahs as it went into the bunker.' In his opinion, Norman hit a flawless fade and was cruelly punished by a bad bounce. He refuses to accept that Norman took the wrong club. 'It might have been the adrenaline or something, but at no stage did any of us think that that ball was going to reach the bunker. Somehow it got there, and I don't think he deserves the criticism that he's received on that tee shot. It was just one of those things that happened.'

Norman's position in the bunker was about as bad as it could be. He stood in the sand with his hands on his hips and his eyes empty. The sod-face of the pot bunker, just three feet high and about 120 yards from the green, was as insurmountable as any obstacle in golf in those circumstances. He looked over at the American. Calcavecchia, his freckled, roguish face aglow, was swinging at his ball with a five-iron. 'It's a shot I'll never forget,' the American said later. 'I watched it and I said, "I don't care where it ends because that's the best shot I've ever hit." '

The ball flew 205 yards to the heart of the green and ran to six feet. Grady, who needed to hole his approach shot, put his best swing on it and got it to four feet.

'Is that close?' Norman asked Edwards, knowing the answer.

Yeah, it's close,' his caddie replied.

Norman frowned at his ball. 'What do you think?' he asked Edwards.

In the commentary box, Nicklaus tutted. 'What he has to do now', he opined to the viewers, 'is play a wedge of some kind safely onto the fairway and hope he can pitch the ball close enough from there to make par. If he goes for the green from that lie, the best he'll do is knock it in the bunker in front of the green. If he does that, he's in serious trouble.'

Edwards, meanwhile, was telling Norman that if he thought he could get the ball over the lip and onto the green, he had to try. Norman agreed. He took an eight-iron and gave it everything he had. The ball caught the lip and dropped like a stone into the trap near the green. Behind him, the crowds broke across the fairway like surf, pouring through the barriers and rushing towards the green in an uneven wave.

Trying to escape the second trap, Norman caught the ball thin. It emerged from the sand as if it were rocket-propelled, airmailed the green and disappeared out of bounds. His score on that hole was X, just like an amateur hacker. 'I just walked away, thinking, God, we should have won this thing,' Edwards says. 'And I felt for him. I really felt sorry for him. But that's the nature of the game. That stuff happens.'

Norman was crushed. To shoot 8 under par, birdie the first two holes of the play-off and not win was hard to take, and yet when a roar of applause greeted Calcavecchia's final putt, Norman was the second person to congratulate him, smiling warmly and sincerely at the lucky American. 'He didn't moan and groan about it, which I liked,' Edwards says of Norman's reaction, 'but he was hurt. That hurt.'

Wayne Grady was gutted. 'Don't you feel sorry for Greg?' someone asked him. Grady stared at him in disbelief. 'I thought, With all due respect, no. I mean, I did, but I had the tournament there for two and a half days and I lost.'

In the press centre, a wall of black-eyed lenses and cynical journalists waited to hear Norman's explanation for the latest black mark in his chequered career. 'Destiny has a funny way of saying, "Hey, this is the way it's got to be," ' Norman said, gazing steadily and courageously back at his interrogators. 'But we all accept fate. It's what keeps us coming back hoping. You've got to keep thinking positively. I have to believe my time will come soon.'

Asked if he felt destiny owed him a major, he gave a dry laugh. 'Shit,' he said, 'it owes me four.'

Later, when he read the papers and had had time to think about what had gone down, Norman found Nicklaus's remarks almost as hard to deal with as defeat. Laura was upset on his behalf. 'It's easy when you're sitting in a chair to make a guess, but what Jack Nicklaus would do or Johnny Miller would do is not what Greg would do, and that's all you can go by, what you feel at the time. I don't think Greg to this day would tell you he made a mistake there. It was a bad bounce, it went into the bunker . . . When we got off the aeroplane in Washington, they never once said, "You know, he made it so exciting in the last round." There were guys leading and they never mentioned that those guys lost the tournament. They talk about Greg. Well, Greg came from seven shots behind to get there.'

To Norman, held accountable once again for failing to live up to history, that was life. 'Sometimes you play bad golf and win. Sometimes you play good golf and lose,' he told *Esquire*. 'Because of the way things ended up, people forget what I had created that day. I had painted this beautiful picture, and I didn't win.'

Typically, Norman used defeat as a springboard to victory. Nicklaus had described the US as the Shark's last frontier and in the second half of the year he conquered it, winning the International at Castle Pines and the Greater Milwaukee Open and finishing fourth in the World Series. In Australia, he won the Tournament Players Championship at the Riverside Oaks. 'I hate failure,' he growled at a reporter from the *Sunday Express Magazine*. 'The idea of failure is, I think, my driving force.'

For Norman, still smarting from the disappointments of the previous season, 1990 could hardly have started better. Not only did it involve a spot of deep-sea fishing, but it carried the threat of danger and, as Steve Starling, who recorded both for *Modern Fishing*, observed,

Norman is 'an unabashed adrenaline junkie'. A promoter had combined golfers and anglers in a worldwide fish tagging and fairway contest, involving, among others, Curtis Strange, Jumbo Ozaki and Nick Faldo, and the Shark was required to face a Great White through the bars of a steel cage.

On the due day, Norman donned a heavy cold-water wetsuit, mask and oxygen tank in Spencer Gulf, Australia. The film crew were as slow and laborious as film crews always are, and the Shark quickly grew frustrated. 'He bristled at each delay and openly resented the director's instructions,' Starling reported. Finally, it was time to enter the water, and Norman splashed into the cage then surfaced in a cloud of bubbles. He was handed a beer, and was swigging it back and grinning and giving a thumbs-up to the crew when a deckhand shouted, 'Here she comes. Get that bloody cage closed.' In an instant, Norman snapped his mask on and retreated into the blue-green depths. A bucket of minced tuna was tossed in after him.

The silver outline of a shark came curving slowly out of the darkness and slammed against the steel bars. 'Greg Norman had a ringside seat to the show of his life and all the adrenaline rush any mortal man could desire,' Starling wrote. Afterwards, the human Shark, who had hand-fed the Great White with a salmon and punched it playfully on the snout, was 'wide-eyed and pumped up . . . As his American minders surrounded him and slapped his back in congratulations, a steely glint entered Greg's expression. "Man," he exclaimed, "I gotta get one of those suckers! There's a twenty-five-foot feature wall in my house back in Palm Beach that's just waiting to have that mother hanging on it." '

The next day, Norman returned with the cameras to attempt to catch a world-record shark, which would then be tagged and released. After maiming and losing one 1,600-pound shark in a four-and-a-half-hour struggle with a rod and line, Norman and his friends managed to land a 1,000-pound Great White. Sadly, as he was reeling it in, it became tangled in the wire trace at the end of the line and died horribly.

Across Australia, environmentalists rose in outrage. 'Sad Trophy Boosts Golfer's Ego' was one headline; 'Great White Golfer Savaged Over Shark' was another, and Norman was depicted beaming proudly beside the bloody carcass. Ian Gordon, Australia's top authority on sharks, said that there were probably fewer than fifty Great Whites in the country's southern waters, and declared that the shark had been 'sacrificed for the sake of publicity . . . This creature died while the cameras rolled.'

When 'bloody [Jacques] Cousteau', as Norman referred to the man who had been his childhood hero, added his voice to the litany of complaints a month later, Norman said it was because he thought mistakenly that two sharks had been killed. 'Things are said without the facts,' Norman told *Esquire*, choosing to overlook the fact that the maimed shark would probably have died or suffered immeasurably after the injuries inflicted upon it. '[For example,] people say I hit the wrong chip at the British Open. But I was the only one who could see the lie.' His only regret was that the maimed shark had escaped. 'We had that big sucker in the boat twice,' he said frustratedly. 'Twice we had our hands on him. And he got away.'

When it comes to hobbies, professional golfers are almost universally drawn to four things: televised sport, fast cars, gardening and hunting. Angelic, sweet-natured men like Davis Love III and Tim Simpson shoot at all manner of creatures with bows and arrows, others just use guns, and one smiling, cuddly legend is reported to have slaughtered elephant with a machine-gun from a helicopter.

'I guess it's the challenge,' Norman said lamely, when asked what appealed to him about hunting, before resorting to the age-old hunter's defence. 'Where I go hunting, it's culling. I don't go out and indiscriminately shoot. I've never done that. Where I go hunting in Australia, they ask you to go out because they have problems with the pigs. Where I go hunting in America, you have to buy a licence and *then* you're only allowed one animal.'

The trip to South Australia was one of the first major excursions Gary Stuve took with Norman in his capacity as the Shark's boat captain. Originally, he had been Nicklaus's boat captain, working with the Bear from 1967 to 1977 and from 1984 to 1989, and had met Norman when Nicklaus and Norman went into partnership together to build a boat. 'I thought he was kind of a fancy dresser,' remembers

152

Stuve, 'and he had a fancy car. To my style, he was overdressed for the occasion.'

Stuve was more down-to-earth, but he and the Australian hit it off quickly because they shared a love of sportfishing and, since Nicklaus was using his boat less and less as his businesses expanded, they often went out together. The custom-made boat was a two-year project, but midway through Norman decided he could afford a similar boat of his own and he offered either to buy out Nicklaus or sell his share. The Bear kept the 58-foot boat and Norman ordered a 65-foot one of his own.

'It seemed like one was always trying to get a bigger boat than the other,' Stuve said. 'It was a kind of one-upmanship, was how I saw it. Jack bought an eighty-foot boat, then Greg bought an eighty-seven-foot boat and that's where they stand now.'

The problem was that Norman then went a step further and hired Stuve. Nicklaus hit the roof. 'There was conflict because basically they each wanted me for themselves,' Stuve explains. 'There was resentment on Jack's part because even though they're friends, they're competitors on the golf course, and any time you take an employee away . . . Jack was a little annoyed about it, and it wasn't an easy decision for me to make because Jack had done a lot for me. But I saw a better future with Greg.'

To Edwards, there was a pattern to Norman's recruitment strategy that started when the Australian lured Pete Coleman away from Ballesteros and Pete Bender away from Nicklaus. 'He hired Jack Nicklaus's boat captain away from Jack, he hired Jack Nicklaus's helicopter pilot away from Jack and he hired me away from Tom Watson. He wants the best he can afford. He wants to surround himself with top people.'

Between 1989 and September 1996, Stuve went on hundreds of trips with Norman, spearfishing and scuba-diving in places like Mexico, Belize and the Bahamas, sometimes accompanied by Laura and the kids, sometimes with Nick Price and sometimes with just Norman. 'He was a really fun guy,' Stuve said. 'He was really regular, liked to hang out with the crew and get drunk and party. Jack was a good person but he was a little more reserved. He was always with his family. Greg would like to get away, to be one of the guys and hang out and drink beers.'

Flash, the first mate on Norman's $4.8 million sportfishing yacht, *Aussi Rules*, told *Sports Illustrated*, 'Here's a vacation with Greg. Get up early, wolf down breakfast, dive, come up, fish, then a quick lunch, bottom-fish, dive, troll for sailfish, then dinner, sleep and start again the next day.'

'He likes to be busy,' laughs Nick Price. 'I can put my feet up and relax and watch the world go by for half a day. Greg can't relax for an eighth of that time.'

*Aussie Rules* had been designed to Norman's own specifications and included two staterooms finished in Australian Silky Oak for his children, both keen anglers. According to *Motor Boating and Sailing*, the list of TVs, videos, CD players and other appliances ran to two pages. A cushion in the plush master bedroom read: 'I love my wife but OH that boat.' Norman felt he needed more space. 'In a few years, we may look at a mother ship and maybe take off for two or three years to really have a look at the world,' he said.

But as the years passed Norman spent less and less time on his boats and according to Stuve they became more of a business than a pleasure. 'I think he thinks that just because he puts his name on it, people are going to rush out and buy it. People in boating couldn't care less about Greg Norman.' Stuve adds, 'He knows a lot about boats but he doesn't know as much as he thinks he does and that was probably the cause of the friction that we had. I'd make a rec-ommendation that he shouldn't buy a boat, and he'd buy it anyway and lose money on it or not like it.'

Stuve felt that they gradually grew apart. Norman was perpetually buying larger and larger boats, while simultaneously trying to down-size his crew, and Stuve, who was a sportfishing captain at heart, quit. 'I think the sport he is in, boating, is a very expensive hobby. You don't get any return from it. They're not investments, you're just throwing money away. I think Greg was OK with that, but his wife wasn't into it – she gets seasick and she's not really into fishing – and she was always trying to get him not to spend so much money on it. He was torn between trying to keep her happy and keep the crew happy and in the end you've got to stick with your family.'

*

Norman was 5,000 feet above the earth, fighting with the joystick of his helicopter. Black rain battered the doors and drowned the engines, and a gale-force wind tossed the craft like a paper plane. His passengers said their prayers and reached for the sick bags. They were on their way back to West Palm Beach after the third round of the Doral Ryder Open, and it was beginning to look as if they might not make it. Miserably, one man raised his head to see how Norman was coping. His steely eyes were on the controls, his hands gripping the joystick. He was laughing.

The next morning, the Shark returned to Miami in the same helicopter. He teed up on Doral's notorious Blue Monster course seven shots off the lead. 'This year will be different,' he had said. 'I'm young enough, I'm strong enough. This is the year I start turning those negatives into positives.' He planned to try Nicklaus's approach to course management – visualizing holes in reverse, from green to tee. 'In other words, where do I have to hit the ball on the tee shot to have it in the right spot for the approach shot to have it in the spot where I want to reach the green.'

At Doral, Norman chiselled steadily away at the leaderboard. At 7,000 yards, the Blue Monster is one of the longest, most brutal layouts in America, and its tree-lined fairways and yawning water hazards have been the final resting place of a million golf balls, but Norman had a feeling it was going to be his week. He birdied the 514-yard first with a drive and a two-iron, and hit eight-iron shots to four feet at the third, and five feet at the seventh. At the eighth, he holed a sand-wedge.

It was a mesmerizing performance. His bottom lip caught between his teeth, his hair shining snowy-white, he lashed from the tees as if there were no tomorrow. He took twelve putts out and twelve putts back for eight birdies, an eagle and a 62.

The most hair-raising moment came at the eighteenth, where Norman insisted on cutting a seven-iron into the water-lined green after Edwards tried in vain to persuade him to hit a relatively safe eight-iron. 'I feel comfortable with it,' he assured Edwards. The ball bounced off the hill and trickled dangerously near to the water.

'We get down there,' Edwards recalls, 'and I thought, Well, Tom would take out a sand-wedge and lob it up there. Greg takes a nine-iron and tries to bump it into the hill. It goes thirty feet past the hole and he makes the putt for par.'

As fate would have it, Norman met Mark Calcavecchia in the four-man play-off, and redressed the past by holing an eagle chip for victory on the first hole to end one of the most impressive rounds of golf ever played in ordinary competition.

'We won, we won, we won!' cried Nigel Mansell, leaping up and down beside the green, his arms around his wife Roseanne and Laura, who was crying with joy.

In a practice round the following week, Edwards asked Norman whether, if he had the shot at the eighteenth again, he would hit an eight-iron instead of a seven. 'No,' Norman said stubbornly. 'I'd hit the same shot again.'

'I thought, Well, there you have it,' Edwards says. ' "You just don't get it. You don't understand what we're trying to do here." ' Five years on, Norman hit a six-iron into the water on the same hole at Doral to lose to Nick Faldo.

Norman, meanwhile, credited his caddie with guiding him to one of his finest victories. 'He tells me a lot of the things that Tom used to do, and so in getting Bruce as a caddie I'm also getting Watson's knowledge,' he said. 'Bruce is very positive. Just before I played the chip on the play-off hole, he told me to chip it in. He said I was due one. That helps. The reason I'm playing so well now is that I'm getting the ball in the right place and doing the right things. I'm not as brash as I used to be. That means I can be aggressive when I want to. As Bruce says, I'm painting beautiful pictures now.'

Three weeks later, Robert Gamez, a bright, fearless rookie from Las Vegas, holed a seven-iron from 176 yards for eagle on the seventy-second hole at Bay Hill to beat Norman by a stroke in the Nestlé Invitational.

For a man who had already been tried to the limits of endurance by the wicked machinations of fate, it was a cruel blow. Norman's nerves were still frayed a month later when an incident took place at the USF&G Classic in New Orleans that could well have affected the outcome of the tournament. Walking off the ninth green after a bogey in the final round, Norman was infuriated when an ignorant spectator approached him. 'The guy was wrong to ask him for an autograph,'

Edwards says, 'and Greg stormed by him. The guy said, "Well, I hope you bogey the next hole too," and with that he stopped, wheeled and went right back in this guy's face and confronted him. I just kept on walking. I thought, I'm not going to go back and separate this. Greg ought to know better.'

There was more. Edwards claims that, in a darkly comedic scene, Norman had accidentally driven over a security guard's foot at the golf-club entrance that morning. 'Greg doesn't show credentials because he's supposed to be so recognized,' Edwards says. 'The guy wouldn't let him in.'

The net result was that, through divine intervention or plain old bad luck, lightning struck Norman a second time. David Frost, a South African living in Dallas, holed a 50-foot bunker shot on the seventy-second hole of the tournament to beat him by a stroke. Numb with despair, Norman hardly knew what to say. It was no great surprise when he missed the cut at the masters, surrendering the green jacket to Faldo for the second successive season. As Norman said, 'The law of averages says you win fifty per cent of the time, not lose a hundred per cent of the time.'

At Christmas, Norman had stood for an hour in Nicklaus's drive-way, communing with the Bear. Absorbed in conversation, he had no idea that it was raining until Barbara, Nicklaus's wife, came out fussing that they were getting wet. They were discussing the Tway incident and other factors that had prevented Norman from winning more majors. 'Greg, you just have to understand that when you're a certain type of player, people want to beat you, whether it's holing a shot or playing a phenomenal round to catch you, whatever,' Norman recalls Nicklaus telling him. 'You're going to have to learn to accept that, because you are one of those players people want to beat. And you should take it as a compliment. I know, because that happened to me a lot.'

'The things that have happened to him are extraordinary, to say the least,' says Nick Price. 'What would you call it? Is it fate? Is it luck? If I was Greg, I'd feel a little picked on . . . But, as Trevino said, God never gave golfers everything, he always held something back. Jack didn't get a sand-wedge and Greg didn't get any luck.'

Hughes Norton, who was closer to Norman than anyone apart

from Laura, despaired on his client's behalf. 'He's certainly carried on as well as anybody who's had the disappointments that he's had,' he says now, 'but we're all human. I think that those were wounds that hurt him – the multiplicity of them was something that was tough for him. I think he thought about that a lot more than he let on. It seemed to be a situation where, every time that he lost, not only in the majors but at Bay Hill or New Orleans, someone rose to the occasion. It was absolutely uncanny. The other side of that is that people say, "Look at his back nines of those tournaments." OK, fine, but still there was always this conspiratorial situation, and you really felt for the guy because he's really a good guy. I think he gets in his own way sometimes and is maybe misunderstood, but he's a good person. And you hate to see that happen to any great player.'

# CHAPTER ELEVEN

# FLIRTING WITH DISASTER

'Golf to me is a battle within yourself, it's the struggle to understand yourself. There's no doubt about it, golf could drive you crazy.'

BOB TWAY, 1993 US PGA CHAMPIONSHIP

NORMAN WAS FLIRTING WITH disaster again. His favourite quotation – Teddy Roosevelt's assertion that it is better to 'know the agony and the ecstasy of defeat and victory than live for ever in the twilight of never having felt either one' – had become a one-line script in the play of his life. 'Greg Norman reminds me of the movies,' said Rick Reilly. 'Every time you think he's going to get the girl and ride off into the sunset, his horse breaks a leg.'

The ecstasy part had come early in the week at the Open at St Andrews in the summer of 1990. Norman had taken a ride in a 111 Squadron Phantom, flying, along with two other jets from the RAF base at Leuchars, at 550 knots and pulling three Gs. 'It was a great thrill and something you really can't describe,' he said. 'The nearest thing to the feeling is seeing your baby born or walking down the eighteenth at Turnberry.'

His happiness was complete when he shot a 66 to share the lead in the opening round, and then he tied with Nick Faldo on 132 in the second. When they were drawn together on the third day many saw it as a showdown between the two best players in the world. A kind of day of reckoning between the giants of the game.

To David Leadbetter, who had coached Faldo to three major victories by then, Norman's relish for the dramatic had cost him dearly in the race for golf's greatest titles. 'The fact is, it's not always about being the most aggressive and hitting the most startling golf shots. It's about getting from A to B. And Nick's a master of that. Greg tends to try to take the course by the scruff of the neck and as a result it can be an all-or-nothing sort of experience. Nick is a very methodical, workmanlike player, and majors require that sort of game to a large extent.'

Analysing the rivalry between the two players in his *World of Professional Golf,* Mark McCormack calculated that, on the thirty-two occasions they had gone head to head in the previous three years, Norman had come out in front nineteen times to Faldo's eleven. Each had won three times when the other was in the field, but all Faldo's victories were majors.

When morning came, Norman stood on the first tee in front of the Royal & Ancient clubhouse, gripped by the peculiar flatness that had dogged him in the Winged Foot play-off. The sun was blazing down, the historic grey town was etched against the skyline and the sea was a cornflower blue, but Norman felt no rush of enthusiasm or adrenaline. When Faldo holed from outside of him for a birdie at the first, Norman was unable to respond. 'You have to feel invincible to be invincible, especially with putting,' he said later.

The agony began there and never let up. Norman three-putted three times in the first ten holes. 'I lost my rhythm with my putter,' he said sadly. 'The putt I missed on the second was a very makeable putt, but I just hit it too hard and hit it through the break. The next putt I missed, I hit too soft. So now I'm second-guessing myself on the line and speed, and as time goes by I'm getting worse and worse in a hole about my putting. Then I hit a good drive on twelve which I thought was perfect and it trickles into the bunker, and I hit a drive on thirteen which I thought was perfect and it rolls into the bunker.' He felt that the twelfth, where Faldo made par from a gorse bush and Norman three-putted, was where he lost his momentum. 'Nick was making everything he looked at and he had a lot of confidence. And he kept the momentum going. So that's what happened: it was the ebb and flow of momentum.'

At the end of the day it added up to a 67 for Faldo, which helped him to a five-stroke victory the next day. Norman shot 76 and was shattered. Wiping sand out of his eyes after the bunker shot at the thirteenth, he looked on the verge of tears. But as hurt as he felt, he did not, as was wrongly reported, refuse to talk to the press.

'Greg feels the knocks but he forgives and forgets even though he's seething inside,' Charlie Earp said. 'He keeps his pain inside.'

'That third round killed me,' Norman conceded reluctantly.

It's hard to pinpoint the exact moment when Norman changed, or even why he changed, or to show when precisely he entered a slump so deep that at times it threatened to consume him. Was it, like everyone suspected, the humiliation of that third round at St Andrews, following as it did on the heels of Tway, Mize, Calcavecchia, Gamez and Frost? Was it the harsh treadmill of tournament golf? 'You wake up every morning and go through the same routine so it gets kind of monotonous and boring,' Norman admitted. 'Sometimes you just want to say, "I'd love to walk away from it for three months." But you can't.' Or was it the bittersweet side-effects of fame? 'Success is wonderful but it can also be very painful,' mused Norman, back at St Andrews for the Dunhill Cup in October. 'I've been pretty good with it, but in the last twelve months it's been a lot harder to take. People have been a lot more critical.'

It's ironic that, some eighteen months earlier, Norman had clashed with Jack Newton at the 1989 Australian Masters over the chief cause of that criticism: his propensity for opening his mouth and telling the truth as he saw it to anyone who would listen, regardless of the pain it might cause or the consequences to himself.

'You can't just open your mouth and blurt out the first thing that comes into your head,' Newton warned him.

'All I'm doing is being honest,' Norman protested.

'I said, "Well, you can't do that," ' Newton recalled recently. 'Now here we are seven or eight years later, where he hates the press, mistrusts the press, because he feels he's been hard done by.'

In spite of their differences, Newton liked Norman and felt he had a lot of good qualities which were worth salvaging. Having taken him to task over his misplaced candour, he added more gently, 'Look, Greg, you've lost your mates, you've lost your real roots. The guys here that you started out with, they all feel that you're unapproachable. Why won't you go and have a beer with them and sort of shoot the shit about what happened in the old days, just to get away from all the tension?'

Norman was stung but he had to concede that Newton was right. After some discussion, he went along quite enthusiastically with Newton's plan to round up his mates from the early days, men like Mike Ferguson, Payne Stewart's brother-in-law, Brian Jones and Stewart Ginn. They arranged to meet at a club on the outskirts of Sydney. 'We drove there to have dinner with him and there's a guy from IMG,' Newton remembers. 'It just put a dampener on the whole evening. So I guess you'd have to put some of the blame for that on Greg.'

It was true that the speed of Norman's ascent in golf and the staggering demands on his time had left most Australians behind from the day he won the West Lakes Classic. Even though he went out of his way to help other Australians, often financially, many felt that Norman moved in more élite circles, and they admired him from a distance. 'Wayne [Grady] and I respect Greg's privacy because he's always so busy,' said Ian Baker-Finch. 'But he's one of the guys and he's very generous.'

Norman's busyness was a constant refrain. 'He doesn't have time to go to dinner,' said Mike Clayton. 'The demands on his time are greater than on anyone else's.'

Newton thought that friendship was a two-way street. 'Some of the guys felt that he had got so big he was on another level and, from Greg's point of view, I think he probably expected them to call him . . . I can remember some of the guys who lived near him in Florida saying Greg had complained because they never called him about going fishing. But whenever they did, they always had to go on his boat, because it was bigger and faster and their boats weren't up to speed.'

The relationship between Norman and Australia has always been complex. In many ways, it was epitomized by the events of 1990 and 1991, when the media, variously labelling him the Great White Carp, the Great White Minnow and the Great White Fishfinger, savaged him for a 'pathetic performance' in the Australian Open and found reasons to condemn him for disqualifying himself from the Palm Meadows Cup after officials acted on a rules violation he'd made in the first round, shortly before he teed off in the third. He had shot a record-breaking 63 in the second round.

He could do nothing right. When Bob Hawke, the prime minister, offered Norman the position as Australia's ambassador of tourism without telling Paul 'Crocodile Dundee' Hogan, who had done the job for years and made Australianisms such as 'Toss another shrimp on the barbie' common currency, it caused a diplomatic incident. When Laura begged him to forego the Australian Open just once to spend Thanksgiving 1991 with his children, newspapers reported that the AGU were considering legal action because he was playing in a skins game at the same time. They were not and he was not. And there were tabloid reports that he and his entourage were thrown out of a nightclub, and that he had come within an inch of hitting a man who punched him in the shoulder and shouted abuse at him in a restaurant.

'I wanted to hit him back,' Norman said, 'but of course no one, let alone someone like myself, can go around doing things like that. We're just supposed to sit back and take it. But it's becoming pretty hard.'

Norman himself was not blameless. He had expended a huge amount of effort in trying to persuade the recalcitrant members of St Michael's, a windswept course near Sydney, to allow himself and his mate Kerry Packer, Australia's richest man, to turn their course into a $300 million resort aimed at Japanese tourists. When the members baulked, Norman said patronizingly to the *Australian*, 'I guess they didn't understand the document. You try to make them understand . . . you try to be rational with them. The crazy thing about it is that the golf course is in desperate need of attention. I mean, they can't even afford a mower out there.'

On the Gold Coast, his first course-design venture in Australia opened for just one day in July 1991 before the Japanese conglomerate behind it went bust. The Grand Golf Club became a dense, snake-filled jungle before a group of Australian businessmen bought it six years later and persuaded Norman to come back on board.

Then there was the ever-controversial issue of appearance money. James Erskine, head of IMG's Sydney office, said that anyone who ran a tournament in Australia or anywhere else without getting Norman to play in it needed to 'go see a doctor' because he generated 'an increased turnover in gate takings, world TV, sponsorship and the like of one point two million dollars'. But when Norman, fed up with being attacked over it, announced he was foregoing appearance money for three years from 1996, the sponsors rushed straight out and paid Tiger Woods record appearance fees.

'Appearance money is something that's always irked me, I've got to say,' Newton remarks. 'Not that he doesn't deserve it, but I've said to him lots of times, "Greg, I couldn't care if you want to go to Italy and get five million dollars and five Ferraris to play, but when you come back to Australia there's something ethically wrong with holding your hand out for huge sums of money." Now his answer to that would be, "Other blokes are getting it, why shouldn't I?" which is true, but you know, you've got to remember that he is a guy who gets ridiculous sums of money all because of IMG, who created all this, and now it's become a real cancer in the game. In [the old] days in Australia, fair enough, the prize money wasn't that good. Now he's sort of playing for a million dollars and instead of the appearance money going down, it's gone up.'

Peter Thomson agreed that appearance money lay at the heart of the anti-Norman feeling but felt that IMG should shoulder a lot of the blame. 'It was said he exploited our tournament scene here almost unmercifully. However, I even defend him on that score because, at first, when IMG did all the deals, they were getting part of the money. Once he knew how much money they were making out of the tournaments, it made him very angry. And he reckoned if they were going to make money out of it, so was he . . . That truth didn't come out. He got the rough end of the stick there, but perhaps he didn't handle it perfectly.'

When all was said and done, it had as much to do with the 'tall poppy syndrome', the natural antipathy of Australians towards people who appear to be too rich, too famous or too pleased with themselves, as anything else. 'The ambivalence is a result of uncertainty,' the Australian magazine *Inside Sport* reported. 'Ours. We're no longer sure if he's one of us: if he feels Australian any more. His staggering wealth . . . and seemingly insatiable thirst for more puts distance between us.'

'In the US, they see a big car and they want to get a car like that,' Norman said. 'In Australia, they run a key down the side of it. I don't understand that mentality.'

In 1990, Norman made a four-hour helicopter journey to the bedside of Sam Roberts, the desperately ill son of Australian television presenter, Sandy Roberts. He had visited and telephoned Sam, a haemophiliac who had contracted the AIDS virus, numerous times before. Later, when news of the boy's death reached Norman shortly before he teed off in the Australian Masters, he wore Sam's name on his hat and walked down the fairway with tears streaming down his face.

There were countless, unpublicized examples of his generosity. He and Laura gave freely, raising millions for children's cancer research, other charities and young Australian golfers through the Greg Norman Foundation and the Greg Norman Junior Golf Foundation. 'We both feel very fortunate, so we want to do what we can to help those who are not,' Laura says. 'It helps balance you. It makes you feel OK about what you have.' In his pocket, Norman carried a thank-you letter from the mother of a boy to whom he had spontaneously donated a putter. But none of it made up for what were perceived as 'ostentatious displays of wealth' and 'frequent ego trips'.

'The Australian philosophy has always been to build people up and chop 'em off at the kneecaps when they get too big for their boots,' Newton said. '*I* don't think that way about Greg, but I think that the average guy on the street likes to see his champions with a bit more humility. I don't really think that the average guy on the street gives a damn about how many Ferraris he's got.'

James Marshall agrees. 'Australia is a funny society,' he says. 'They like their sportsmen to be down-to-earth, and I don't think there's any question that Greg has succeeded in rubbing a lot of the sportsworld up the wrong way in Australia. That's self-evident. If you look at Seve or Faldo, they don't spend their time letting people know that they've just bought a new car or a new house or they've just made another couple of million . . . I think it's a great pity that Greg is not . . . well, he's not a humble person.'

But Peter Thomson, who has, over the years, been one of Norman's harshest critics, felt that behind the façade, Norman was 'very likeable. His public image doesn't match his private personality. I honestly think that under the guidance of a management structure an image is created in order to make everybody wealthy, and that doesn't necessarily reflect the real person. Some people throw it off. Sam Torrance, for instance, would never be anybody other than who he is. Peter Senior is another. You couldn't possibly invent an image for either one of them. But, in the case of Greg, I think he enjoyed the image-making. So there it was.'

All of these things – the on-course pressures and the off-course stresses – combined to shake Norman's hitherto unshakeable confidence. That October was only the second time in their long relationship that Norman had flown Charlie Earp to a tournament for an emergency session on his game. Even when he had won the Memorial he felt that he was playing 'horrible golf, probably the worst golf I've ever played'. Now his old friend had come to help him find a cure. For two hours they worked in driving grey rain, cold enough to chill a polar bear, and at the end of it they felt they had found the problem: Norman wasn't swinging down the line.

Back in his room, Norman, golden and larger than life, downed a beer, read a fan letter, bantered on the phone with Nigel Mansell and gave every impression of being a blissfully contented man. 'Sometimes I wish I wasn't as committed,' he remarked at a cocktail party, 'but when things are going well I don't pay any attention.'

On paper, the 1990 season was one of the best of his career, earning him the Australian Masters and, in the United States, two prestigious titles, eleven top tens, $1,165,477 and first place on the money list. But every day, Norman felt himself sliding closer to the abyss. 'This IMG mob is milking the cow dry,' Earp ranted to the *Australian* after Norman, who had not slowed down as he promised, finally reached overload on the Australian circuit. 'I mean, Greg

Norman is the greatest drawcard on earth. People would scramble over broken glass to watch him hit golf balls, and IMG's demands on his time mean that golf is third rate now to Greg. He's too bloody busy all the damn time. The person hasn't been born that can hit a ball like he can. And these people are roping him down and tying him up. But Greg can't see that. He says, "It's OK, Charlie, it's OK," but I can see it isn't. It damn well isn't.'

James Erskine, IMG's Australian kingpin, was not pleased. 'His words are childish and ill-informed,' he snapped. 'Greg Norman decides exactly what he wants to do himself . . . Charlie's argument is that because Larry Mize or Bob Tway chip in to rob Greg of a major tournament win, or he gets the yardage wrong on the last hole of the Masters, or loses the British Open in a play-off, then somehow it's IMG's fault. That's absolute bloody nonsense.'

Norman was forced to mediate. '[IMG] work for me not the other way around,' he insisted. 'Golf is my number-one priority.'

Earp was unconvinced. 'What Greg doesn't see is that people are using him,' he said. 'Do you really think the PM wanted Norman to leave the tournament in Melbourne, fly to Canberra for the night [to attend Bob Hawke's sixtieth birthday party], then fly back to Melbourne again for the last round because Hawke considers him a bosom pal? I doubt it. But Greg is blind to all that. He just can't seem to say no.'

It was years before Norman would admit that burn-out had been a large factor in his slump. Laura wanted him to take six months off; he wanted three; his schedule barely allowed for one. 'For five years I put my blood, sweat and tears into it, because I had to,' he said. 'I wanted to, but I had to. And I was just plain tired.'

He made one last attempt to put things right, consulting Mitchell Spearman, David Leadbetter's assistant, at Royal Melbourne. Spearman had written an article describing Faldo's technique as an 'iron swing', meaning that he hit down on the ball, and the Shark's as a 'driver swing', meaning that he tended to hit the ball a little on the upswing. 'His stance was too narrow and his left-hand grip was a little too much in the palm,' Spearman says. 'I remember him showing me how much he was wearing out his gloves. His swing was very upright at the time. He said he felt that he didn't have the control at the top of the swing. He was trying to get it a little flatter.'

When Norman returned to the States, they tried working together for a few months. 'Very strong character,' Spearman says. 'Has strong opinions, strong beliefs. Gives his word, sticks to it. Honourable. I confided in him a few years back on a business deal and he gave me some advice and told me his door was always open. It meant a lot to have someone like Greg Norman say that to someone like me.'

Unhappily, Spearman's advice effected no miracle transformation in Norman's game. When he missed the cut at Augusta for the second year running, Laura put him on a plane back to Australia for a couple of weeks. 'He was so down,' she said, knowing that, in spite of everything, Norman still loved and missed his homeland enough for a holiday there to be healing. 'That was the one time I've really seen him let down and relax. He saw his friends, saw his parents – no phones, no demands.'

It was there that Norman's simmering relationship with his father, his need to make Merv understand why he lived the life he did, to make Merv acknowledge that he had made something of himself after all, came to a head. 'Hold on a second, Dad,' Norman said, as Merv headed into the house one day. 'We argued, we discussed, I told him what I thought,' Norman told *Sports Illustrated*. 'He told me what he thought. It was good. We both needed it.'

Norman was riding the agony/ecstasy rollercoaster yet again. On the first Sunday of July, he found himself leading the Western Open by five shots, having played the first ten holes in 6 under par. Reams of joyous, 'comeback victory' copy was already rolling off the typewriters when Norman made his first bogey. He made another for good measure, then another and another, finally finishing with a flourish by bogeying five of the last six holes. Two balls homed in on deep bushes, one was unplayable, once Norman emerged from the woods with leaves and twigs in his hair, and once he found his ball under a woman's purse. The end result was that Russ Cochran, a left-hander, made up seven shots to beat him by two and achieve his first victory in nine years. Norman's misfortune was almost always someone else's good fortune.

'If somebody told me when I made the turn on Sunday, "In two hours' time, you aren't going to win this tournament," I would have called him a liar . . .' Norman said. 'But life's a humbling experience. I made a major blunder there, and I didn't win.'

'That collapse, it's added another chapter, hasn't it?' said Tom Weiskopf at the Open the following week, where Norman bounced back with a tie for ninth place. But he added, 'Thank God there is a Greg Norman. He's made a lot of people in golf happy. He's exciting, he's a great personality and he's a nice guy too, but one of these loners.'

Unfortunately, the constant dashing of his hopes and see-sawing of his emotions was having a detrimental effect on Norman's personality and his relationships with other people, in particular Bruce Edwards, who felt he was the cat to be kicked on the course.

'He really disappointed me,' says Edwards, his dark, strong face tense as he describes the events that led to him leaving what should have been the best job in golf. 'I found he was very fickle, I found he was very moody, I found that professionally on the golf course he had a hard time dealing with adversity – bad bounces, bad breaks – which is part of the game. I tried to bring him a calmer attitude, but in the end I felt that there was nothing I could do.'

According to Edwards, one of the PGA Tour's most respected caddies, his attempts to help Norman achieve a more relaxed approach on the course failed signally. 'At first, he didn't really blame me, but he would be so negative,' he says. 'There would be two balls in a bunker in our group. One would be buried, one wouldn't. He'd walk up and say, "Well, you know which one mine is." I'd say, "Come on, Greg. Prepare yourself. Even if it is the one that's buried, you've still got to play it. There's nothing you can do about it." I mean, Tom [Watson] had the ability to gut it up and carry on, and if that meant hitting it to thirty feet, if that was the best he could do, well, he'd go ahead and try to make the putt.

'Greg, it seemed to me, if he got in a bad mood or got really pissed off about the result of a shot, it would carry on for the next hour. I'd find myself wondering how we'd get through it. When he'd come off the eighteenth on Sunday, I'd think, Gee, if he'd just kept his wits about him back there on Friday or Thursday or whenever that one hour happened, we wouldn't be one behind. In other words, he threw shots away because his temper would get the best of him.'

Edwards's portrait of Norman contrasted sharply with Norman's view of himself. The Shark claimed that he had 'never been a negative individual. Never. Let's say I'm playing my bunker shots poorly. Instead of going out there and practising my bunker shots hour after hour, I'll go and chip or hit my five-iron, something I can be positive about. Then, after four or five days of not even touching my sand-wedge, I'll say, "OK, let's go to work." Boom! It comes back very quickly.'

To Edwards, Norman was the greatest talent he had ever seen, but when the special player/caddie teamwork crucial to success disappeared from their relationship, he began to find his job a struggle. He built a house on Norman's generosity, but he was always on edge, worrying that Norman might fly into a rage, make biting comments on his prowess as a caddie, send a club winging its way towards the bag, or criticize his yardages or his club selection.

'Maybe tomorrow we'll pull the right club,' Norman would snarl.

'Did you hit that fat?' Edwards would query.

'I hit it right on the screws,' Norman would snap back.

'I made him a bet in Australia one year,' grins Edwards. 'I said, "Greg, I'll buy you dinner anywhere in the world if you can go four days without moaning or groaning." And he agreed to it. And it was very funny because we got to Saturday and he hit this shot and it went left down the hill. He said, "You can have the goddamn dinner. Fuck the dinner." And exploded. I thought: You can't even go four days.'

Edwards had his own theories about the times Norman had snatched defeat from the jaws of victory and on several occasions he unwisely communicated them to his boss. 'I felt like his ego would get the best of him,' says Edwards, who was not without a degree or two of arrogance himself. 'Sometimes thirty feet right of the pin is an excellent play in the hunt. You don't always have to hit it in close. If Tom said to me, "Do you like a three-wood or a four-wood?" and we're playing a green where the pin's five feet on and there's a bunker in front, I'd say, "Well, do you mind being in the bunker?" In the same situation, Greg would say, "What do you think, three-wood or one-iron?" and I'd say, "Well, do you mind being in the front bunker?" He'd say, "I don't want to be in the bunker, I want to be by the pin." And I'd think, Greg, the game's not that easy. There's no guarantee that a certain club will get you pin-high every time. But that was his thinking.'

Gradually, his relationship with Norman broke down to the extent where they rarely spoke away from the course. He claims that the Shark would stride out of the locker room in the morning, slam down the bag and depart to the range without a word. Edwards felt that he was becoming a bad caddie because he was too afraid to say what he thought. 'I also felt that the novelty of him having me wore off and once that wore off, he was treating me like I'd heard he'd treated all his caddies in the past . . . It's sad because I truly liked him when I started working with him but I think he misread me and that's when he changed. I was no different from anybody else who gets chewed up and spit out and discarded.'

Edwards quit before he could be fired. 'Once you get on his bad side, that's it. Once you're on that four-letter list, once you cross that line in his mind, that's it, you're done. I saw that all the time.'

On a clear November day, Norman stood pounding balls at the TPC at The Woodlands. He had not won a tournament for eighteen months – the longest dry spell of his career – and, after two days of play, it was clear that he was not about to win the Houston Open. Instead he was headed for fifty-third place on the money list, his worst position since joining the US Tour, and he was ready to give Ballesteros lessons in how not to hit the fairway. When he set up to hit a fade, he came up with a hook; when he set up to hit a hook, he managed a banana slice. Hitting it straight was not on the menu.

The hip injury that had caused him to pull out after twenty-seven holes of the US Open was a nagging ache. That had been another black spot. Reporters and sundry officials had surrounded the fitness trailer at Hazeltine and refused to leave him alone until he explained himself. 'It was like somebody had died in the thing or something,' Norman said incredulously. 'These guys didn't realize the pain I was going through, and yet they wanted to rip me for withdrawing. I wanted to keep playing. My physiotherapist made me withdraw. But, God almighty, it was like something major, a catastrophe. It was ridiculous, total stupidity for that much attention to be thrown on the situation. I mean, I get *injured*, and I get nailed for it.'

Five months on, Norman felt about as desperate as he had ever been. He took a deep breath and went over to Steve Elkington, who had been urging him to talk to his coach, Claude 'Butch' Harmon, son of the 1948 Masters champion, and the pro at Lochinvar in Houston. Norman had wanted to try to work things out on his own.

'Elk,' Norman said hesitantly, not used to eating humble pie, 'do you think Butch would take a look at me?'

Harmon, now famous as Tiger Woods's coach, was a pragmatist with a flair for applying sound, traditional techniques without detracting from natural artistry. He had worked with Davis Love and Jeff Sluman as well as Elkington, universally regarded as having the most flawless swing in the game. He was stockier than Norman but they had the same super-confident, outgoing personalities and the same tanned, half-genial, half-cynical faces. He had known Norman since the late eighties when they had both participated in a tournament to raise money for a children's cancer hospital and over the years they had developed a mutual regard for one another. Harmon was a fan of Norman's intensity and ability with the driver. Watching him lose majors with iron shots that wandered right, he had always wished he could help. 'The funny part about it is I was totally prepared when he asked me. I'd studied so much film of his swing I knew exactly what avenue of approach I would take if I ever had the chance.'

On the range in Houston, Harmon watched Norman hit a few balls. 'You need to read your own book,' Harmon told him, referring to *Shark Attack!*'

Norman stared at him. 'You need to go back to basics,' Harmon said firmly. 'Your fundamentals are bad and you're not doing any of the things in your book.'

He remembers thinking how steep Norman's swing and how narrow his arc had become. 'His arms got trapped behind him on the way down. Most of the time he could square the club from that position with his hands, but sometimes, especially under extreme pressure, he wasn't able to. I wanted to put more rotation in his body and get him to where he wouldn't have to use his hands so much under pressure.'

He handed Norman a two-iron. 'Stand closer to the ball and swing as hard as you possibly can,' he ordered. Norman took the club uncertainly and swept the ball away. Harmon didn't say a word. Norman smashed another ball over the horizon, then another and another. Into his hands and his heart crept a feeling he had almost forgotten – a feeling of freedom, of standing young and strong and carefree on the fairways of West Lakes, smashing the ball into the blue. All of a sudden he remembered why he had always loved practising so much. Why nothing gave him as much pleasure as being out in all weather, exploring golf's nuances, hitting the full six hundred balls he believed a player should hit daily in order to groove his swing.

Harmon sent him right back to basics – altering his grip, improving his posture, shortening his swing slightly, encouraging him to use his lower body more and rotate his hips faster, and removing his famous slide. 'That was the first thing that went and that took the use of the hands out except where they should be,' Harmon says. 'He was relying on his hands for everything. That's not to say you can't play well from there, because he did play very well from those positions, but it just seemed that every time he got under the most extreme pressure, that swing failed him. I wanted to get that shot that he hit to the right out of there and we did a good job of doing that.'

'Butch just said the right words to me – positive words – at the right time,' says Norman. 'I could relate to what he was talking about.'

One morning, Norman caught sight of himself while he was shaving: sallow, discontented, unhealthy, verging on chubby. He had succumbed to burn-out, had allowed himself to take it easy. That summer, he had seriously contemplated packing it all in and buying a cattle ranch: 'I didn't need what was happening to me.' He had gone so far down that untrue rumours were circulating that he was on drugs. When he picked five-year-old Gregory up from school one afternoon, the little boy had been taunted by the other children and was in tears.

Laura had persuaded him to face up to the fact that Mize's chip-in had wounded him more than he realized. 'I learned that the longer you hold something inside, the worse you are going to react to it,' Norman said. 'You might find yourself at the pub having had a few cocktails and, if someone hits you the wrong way with something in conversation, you just pop. It makes you look like a jerk.'

And now his pride had begun to hurt.

'I had to look myself in the mirror and ask, "Do you want to do the work to get back on top again?" ' Norman told the author of *A Good Walk Spoiled*, John Feinstein. 'It would have been easy to walk away, but that would have been quitting and I've never thought of myself as a quitter. I knew climbing back up the mountain wouldn't be easy and it wouldn't happen fast, but I knew I wanted to do it. I missed Sunday afternoons. I missed that feeling of being back in the hunt. Even if you don't win, being there feels so great. I wanted that back again. But I knew it would be hard. I also knew if I did it, it would be the best feeling I've had in golf. That's what makes failure so great. You can't really appreciate success – I mean *really* appreciate it – until you've failed.'

CHAPTER TWELVE

# KING OF THE HILL

'It was like somebody put a coin in the juke box and the right song started playing.'

GREG NORMAN ON HIS CANADIAN OPEN VICTORY, 1992

IT WAS NORMAN'S EXPRESSION that was unforgettable. His fists were clenched and his hands were reaching to the sky in a triumphant celebration of his Canadian Open victory, his first in twenty-seven months, but it was his face – awash with joy and a profound, almost grateful, relief – that imprinted itself on the memory. 'I knew it was coming,' he said. 'I could feel the incline.'

It was September 1992. Two months earlier, playing the Open, Norman had felt the old hunger stir in him again, that once-familiar but long-forgotten feeling that had led him to compare golf with making love. While Nick Faldo stood on the eighteenth at Muirfield, kissing and cuddling the claret jug for photographers for the third time in his career, Norman indulged in an entirely new experience: that of savouring a top-twenty finish.

'I came off the seventy-second hole and said to my wife and Butch Harmon, "We're back." I said, "I've just put on a clinic out there for

175

seventy-two holes. Nobody'll know about it but I did." And that was it. Muirfield was the turning point.'

At the Canadian Open, Norman used a putter he'd first picked up at the age of seventeen to try out tips given to him by a club pro in Florida and a friend at Glen Abbey in Ontario. 'They just said to swing the putter, to feel the weight of the putter head. That's all putting is, but I guess I've been too confused about trying different positions.' The resulting rush of confidence helped him overcome Bruce Lietzke on the second extra hole of a play-off. 'That did more for me than winning by three or four shots,' Norman said afterwards. 'That told me I could play tough shots under a lot of pressure.'

Looking at her husband's proud, happy face as they jetted off to Japan, Laura experienced the same relief Norman did when the winning putt dropped. 'It's nice to have you back,' she told him gently. Lietzke had said exactly the same thing.

In the space of a season, Norman's life had undergone a quiet revolution. Thanks to Laura's Fit for Life diet, Harmon's coaching and Pete Draovitch's fitness expertise, his sallow face and hangdog body language had given way to hard, bright focus and the taut nut-brown physique of an athlete. He had lost fifteen pounds by giving up soft drinks and eating more fruit, and he no longer had headaches after a day of golf. 'And,' he told the *Australian*, 'you can still have as many beers as you like and wine at mealtimes.'

His bedside reading was *Zen of the Martial Arts*, a book he said he would probably read a thousand times before he died. His favourite lesson in it was the part where the Zen master tried to convince his student that he needed to start all over again. 'He takes a cup and starts pouring tea into it,' Norman told Feinstein. 'And just keeps pouring and pouring until the tea is all over the floor. The student says, "Master, the cup is too full, the tea is all over the floor." And the master says, "The cup is exactly like your mind – it is too full." And he takes the cup and empties it. "When your mind is empty, you can begin to refill it," he says. "But not until then." '

Having soothed his soul, Norman began to recondition his run-down body with the help of Draovitch, the physiotherapist who had healed his shoulder problem. Ten minutes with the Shark persuaded

Draovitch that 'he worked hard but not smart', so he designed five fitness programmes, ranging from postural training to explosive training with medicine balls, to boxing drills, that would improve Norman's health and help his aching back without adding to his stress. The weight-room programme, for example, involved thirty to forty minutes of cardiovascular work, plus stretching, medicine-ball training, abdominal and lower-back exercises, weight training and step-ups, all of which took around two hours. Since Norman lost four or five pounds when he played continuously for a month, Draovitch also advised him on nutrition.

He travelled with the Australian most weeks and found him easy-going and kind, likening the atmosphere on Norman's jet to being in a locker room. He had already been the butt of Norman's practical jokes, one of which involved a nurse with a twelve-inch hypodermic telling him he needed shots if he wanted to leave the plane in Johannesburg, South Africa. 'The unfortunate thing about Greg the golfer versus Greg the person, I think, is not a lot of people get to know Greg the person,' Draovitch says. 'And I think if they did, they would be a lot better to him.'

Draovitch's exercise plan for the Shark was so gruelling that Davis Love, reaching out to catch a medicine ball Norman had tossed him, was almost bowled over. 'It was like in cartoons, where the guy throws you the ball and it throws you through the wall,' he said. 'I knew Greg was in shape but I didn't really know just how strong he'd gotten.'

Financially, Norman had entered another stratosphere. If his slump had shown him anything it was that his passion for business and the adrenaline buzz that accompanied the successful conclusion of a high-risk deal was easily the equal of his passion for golf. In 1990, he had put his trust in Tom Crow and Cobra when he invested $2 million of his own money in a 12 per cent stake in the equipment company, becoming an equity partner. At more or less the same time, IMG negotiated a contract for him to represent Cobra and carry their bag.

Crow had known Norman since 1977 when he called up out of the blue and said, 'My name is Greg Norman. You don't know me, but I've seen a set of your mild steel clubs. Would you be prepared to make a set for me?'

'Actually,' said Crow, who had seen Norman win the West Lakes Classic, 'I do know you. And I'd be happy to.'

Norman loved the clubs so much that Crow made him a back-up set nine weeks later, but when Norman signed with IMG, they negotiated a deal with Spalding. 'I didn't have any business affiliation with Greg, so I respected that,' Crow said. 'He wanted a contract that paid him a lot of money. He needed money at that stage. In retrospect, I think the Spalding ball cost him two majors. But that's only a personal opinion.'

Norman, who learned to make his own woods and irons as part of his training under Charlie Earp, was actively involved in the club-making process. 'He has his own ideas of how a club should look' – Crow laughs – 'which are not necessarily the same as anyone else's, but he's got a great eye and an incredible feel for the weight and balance of a club.'

The exercise, the diet, the business and the Zen all helped revive Norman's zest for life, but it was the soundness of his swing that boosted his confidence. 'I now trust my swing totally under pressure,' he said. Aided by his new caddie Tony Navarro, a taciturn man with twenty years' experience, Norman was inching towards greatness again. There were runner-up spots in New Orleans and the Western Open and half a dozen top tens. In December, he shot a closing 63 at the Johnnie Walker World Championship in Jamaica to catch Nick Faldo, but lost on the first extra hole.

In March 1993, Norman blazed a fiery trail around Doral, tying his own course record with a 62 in the third round and ending with a 70 that spreadeagled the field. He had devised a secret seven-year pro-gramme of psychological and physiological improvement to carry him through to the year 2000, and this was its first reward.

'I played the best golf I think I've ever played and I lost by four shots,' said Paul Azinger, not sure whether to be annoyed or impressed.

'Mark it down, folks,' wrote Gary Van Sickle of *Golf World*. 'The sulking, frowning, irritable, sensitive Norman of the last two years is history. The often spectacular, fun-loving, outgoing, happy-go-lucky warrior, the Great White Shark who was a dominant force in the late eighties, is back.'

Norman was pretty emotional himself. 'For twenty months I was my own worst enemy,' he said. 'I got frustrated and down on myself. I re-evaluated what I wanted. I could have walked away, but I didn't want to. I wanted to get back to playing good golf. To do that, you have to practise hard. And to do that, you have to prioritize.'

Balanced like a gymnast about to execute a handspring, Norman stood on a tawny slope at the far end of the range at Royal St George's and clipped the ball off the turf above his feet. In practice rounds, his swing had not been on song. The steepness had crept back into it and Butch Harmon had just spent ninety minutes using the slope to help his pupil get the feel of a flatter plane. It was the best ninety minutes Norman ever spent.

'It was just that little bit of work that made everything fall into place,' Harmon says. 'It was funny because the R & A didn't like it. They were very upset that we went out of the driving range and hit the ball back over. They criticized him quite a bit for it, told him he couldn't do that again. But that hour and a half was all we needed.'

For Norman, who leaned heavily on adrenaline, inspiration and the pre-round preparation that would tell him how he would play that day, there were no signs that this Open would be any different from the rest. Quite the reverse. Nothing was going according to plan. At Augusta, he had opened with a 74. 'What is it that happens to me in the first round here?' he fumed to Laura. He scraped through the cut with a 68, but a last-round 77 left him thirty-first. At the US Open, he failed to qualify.

He dreaded performing as poorly at St George's. 'The strange thing is there are tournaments we've gone into that you just feel so sure this is going to be the week,' Laura says. 'We never felt that that week. Neither one of us. You never know, but things were not all on synch like they had been at other places.'

The first round was wet and changeable and Norman started in-auspiciously, carving his tee shot into the high rough to the right of the first tee and racking up a double-bogey six. He managed a birdie at the second. 'He was playing shit,' remembers Gary Evans, a young Englishman. The experience of partnering the Shark for the first two days at St George's left a strong impression on him. 'He attempts to intimidate you. Whether that's because he's such a good player, I don't know, but it didn't faze me at all.' He recalls Norman, usually a quick player, deliberating painstakingly over every shot. 'He made a few comments during the course of the first round which I thought were sort of peculiar. I mean, I laughed at them but . . .'

Evans started birdie, par, so it was Norman's honour when they stepped onto the third tee. 'He pulled a two-iron and nearly shanked it. It was such a bad shot. I had my hand on a three-iron. I was just pulling it out. He walked past me and he said to his caddie, "Jesus, Tony, I got all of that." I just thought: Why try and put me off the club I want to play? Anyway, we played on and we get round to twelve. I'm three under and he's one over. We've both got seventy-yard pitch shots. The pin is cut on the front shelf. He hit a lovely shot, pitched it about three foot past the flag and it ran away to about twenty-five feet. I pitched it about three feet short of the flag and stopped it a foot from the hole. And he made a comment along the lines of was my sand-wedge legal?

'Anyway, one of the biggest lessons I've ever learned was on the golf course that day. I was four under and he was one over after twelve  holes, and he made a good birdie at thirteen to go back to even. He hit driver, eight-iron to five feet. We get to fourteen, the long par five, and he hit it left into the crap, then he hit his second in the crap and then he left his third shot twenty yards short, right of the green. I've hit driver up the middle, three-wood up the middle, wedge to eight foot. He hit this pitch and it was too hard. It bounced twice, hit the flag about a foot up and dropped into the hole. And from walking around the golf course with his face on the floor, miserable as sin, playing very averagely, he's gone birdie, birdie, and all of a sudden he's bounced onto the fifteenth tee, hit driver, five-iron to three foot – in. Sixteenth tee, he hit a seven-iron to forty foot for birdie, then stood on the seventeenth tee, hit driver, six-iron to four foot – in, then parred the last. I shot sixty-seven and played great, and he shot sixty-six and played crap all the way round to thirteen. It taught me a big lesson. It doesn't matter how badly things are going, they can turn around. On the second day he played great and there was no stopping him.'

At the end of the first round, Norman shared the lead with fellow

After the agony, the ecstasy. Tears of joy stream down
Norman's face as he celebrates his second Open Championship
at Royal St George's in 1993. *Allsport*

LEFT: Norman, who has been called the greatest driver in the history of the game, powers his way to victory at the 1993 Open. *Phil Sheldon*

BOTTOM: Despair shows on Norman's face as another major gets away at Troon in 1989. *Phil Sheldon*

OPPOSITE LEFT: Arch-Rivals: Norman's body language speaks volumes as he crosses swords with Faldo in the third round of the 1990 Open at St Andrews. *Phil Sheldon*

OPPOSITE RIGHT: Watched by Olazábal and Woosnam, Norman high-fives his son Gregory. *Phil Sheldon*

OPPOSITE BOTTOM: Norman demonstrates the graciousness in defeat that is his most endearing trait after losing the 1995 US Open to Corey Pavin. *Matthew Harris*

Power Play: Norman and Laura discuss strategy with Bob Hawke, the former Australian Prime Minister, and his wife during the 1996 Presidents Cup. *Phil Sheldon*

Birds of a Feather: President Clinton shows Norman how to play the game at New South Wales Golf Club in Sydney, Australia. *Associated Press*

The steps Clinton made infamous lead the way to the Hobe Sound mansion the Normans call home. *Associated Press*

Norman tosses his putter skywards in disgust after a three-putt on the second play-off hole saw him hand the 1993 US PGA to Paul Azinger. *Phil Sheldon*

After a day in hell, Norman surrenders emotionally to Faldo's embrace at the 1996 Masters. 'It wasn't so much what he said,' he told one writer, 'it was the hug. I've never been hugged like that by a man.' *Phil Sheldon*

Norman and his erstwhile teacher Butch Harmon search for perfection. *Phil Sheldon*

The Shark tries to extract another Great White from the deep.
*Yours In Sport/Lawrence N. Levy*

Top Gun: Norman and his alter ego – the boy who dreamed of being a fighter pilot.
*Colorific/Robert Beek*

Jetsetter: the Shark and his entourage arrive at Augusta (Frank Williams is at his left shoulder). *Phil Sheldon*

Speed Merchant: Norman tests the horsepower on his beloved Harley Davidson. *Allsport*

World-weariness etches Norman's face as he turns to face his critics after missing the cut at the 1996 US Open. *Phil Sheldon*

A Prayer Before Dying: Norman collapses at the fifteenth green at the 1996 Masters after the chip he had pinned his hopes on skirts the hole in the final round. *Allsport*

Australian Peter Senior and two ghosts from his past, Fuzzy Zoeller and Mark Calcavecchia, over one of the toughest fields ever assembled at an Open. With the exception of Ronan Rafferty, Bruce Lietzke and Jumbo Ozaki, the top fifty players on the world rankings were competing, and the best of them were at the top of their games. Some forty-seven players delivered scores in the sixties, a first-day record, on the rain-softened course.

Norman, greeted the next morning by 'Jurassic Shark' headlines, had not allowed himself to be rattled by his opening six. 'I guess I had to eat humble pie on the first,' he said. 'As I walked off the green, I said to myself, there are seventy-one holes to go. Be patient. I was just thinking about getting a couple of birdies quickly.'

Ballesteros was full of smiles after a 68 that was vintage Seve, full of sensational drives and miracle shots. 'When you go under par you feel young,' he said.

Friday belonged to Faldo, the defending champion. On a blustery day with swirling cross-winds he made seven birdies in a course record 63, equalling the championship record. 'That's as good as it gets,' said Faldo, who, twelve months earlier, had used a second-round 64 as a springboard to victory at Muirfield. He holed a 50-yard pitch from the rough on the fourteenth from virtually the identical spot Norman had in the first round. The roar that greeted Faldo's effort was so loud that Norman, standing over a par putt on the seventeenth, backed off and then missed. He was now two shots in arrears and had to sink an eight-footer on the last to stay that way.

Told that the bookies had installed Faldo as 2–1 favourite to win the Open, Norman said curtly, 'What do they know about golf? I don't pay any attention to them.'

Norman is not a superstitious man, but when 15-knot winds toughened Sandwich on Saturday, he joked that he'd be taking his good-luck pills each morning. Tony Navarro already had his: his entry pass for the last two days was numbered 0001. Both men were helped by Norman's driving, which was superlative all week.

'Greg is the best driver of the last couple of decades, without a doubt,' Butch Harmon says. 'I think Tiger hits the ball further than Greg, but he's a little wilder than Greg and Tiger doesn't really yet have the command of his shots, the draws, fades, high, low that Greg has all the time. That was the thing that impressed me most about him.'

Norman, who uses a King Cobra metal driver with nine degrees of loft and a shaft flex of X400, puts down his prowess with it to his physical stature. 'I have small hips and a fairly good upper body from surfing and stuff. Look at Tiger Woods. He has a big upper body and a tiny lower body, so he gets that out of the way quicker.'

A third-round 69 left Norman a stroke behind Faldo and Corey Pavin on 7 under par. Langer shared third place and Price and Peter Senior were on 6 under. 'This', Norman said, 'is going to be one of the greatest British Opens ever.' He refused to accept that Faldo would be the main threat in the final round. 'He's not infallible,' Norman said sourly. 'If I admitted he was the number-one guy, it would be admitting he was better than me. I don't think that, ever. He's a great player but he can be beaten.'

On the final morning, Norman emerged in a cerise, black and blue shirt, not quite as flamboyant as a circus marquee. It looked like an acid trip or something a snake charmer would wear. All week, Norman's dress sense had provoked a mixture of amazement and despair. 'The striped shirt was fine,' said the *Guardian*'s Mike Selvey of one outfit, 'but the sleeveless jumper – a fluorescent punky pink with green trim on the front, and a back that might once have been white but looked as if he'd spent the night on a park bench without checking if the paint was dry – made him look like a cross between a particularly nasty migraine and Bertie Bassett on psychedelic drugs.'

Describing another creation, David Miller wrote, 'Tom Watson would not be seen dead in it: an ice hockey umpire's stripes at the back, a Mexican second division football shirt's peacock mauve at the front. Only money, surely, could persuade anyone to walk about in public in such a garment.'

On Sunday, Norman was not wearing the cursed hat and his face beneath his overlong hair looked chiselled and intent. When he strode onto the first tee, he was wearing a sweater with a black front, a blue back emblazoned with a multicoloured shark, and one black and white striped sleeve. It looked like an economy measure from Yoko Ono. But it was the last time anyone spared a thought for Norman's fashion crisis. Minutes later, his drive pierced the blue and the crowd roared. One of the greatest final rounds in Open Championship history had begun.

Norman and Langer quickly birdied the first to join Faldo and Pavin on 8 under. On the tee behind them, a raucous and enthusiastic crowd sang happy birthday to Faldo. Norman played as if he was cocooned in a heavenly bubble. Nothing entered it, not the colourful walls of spectators or Langer's immaculate iron play or Faldo creeping methodically up the leaderboard. At the third, he rattled in a 25-footer for birdie. At the par three sixth, he slipped his tee shot to 12 feet for another. At the ninth, he pitched a nine-iron to a foot to go out in 31.

'I remember watching him in that last round and he was just so calm,' Laura says, 'out there having a good time. Greg has such high expectations of himself, you know. I think he just played within himself that day. Sometimes he has a hard time doing that. He tries to play to please the people that expect him to win, and you can't do that because you put too much pressure on yourself. That day he just played for Greg.'

After ten holes, Norman led by two on 11 under from Faldo and Langer. At the eleventh, he saved par from seven feet and bounced back with a perfect sand-wedge at the twelfth. Pavin, Senior and Ernie Els, who would become the first man to break 70 in all four rounds of the Open, were lurking in the wings on 6 under.

Then came the dangerous fourteenth, the kind of hole where Norman, if the jinx was on him, would take out his driver and carve a completely unnecessary, over-aggressive tee shot out-of-bounds right. Langer, who had just birdied two holes to draw within two strokes of Norman, did that very thing, steered there by a left-to-right wind. A red flag signalled disaster in the distance. Norman took out his driver. He could not have been more confident of the outcome if it had been carved in stone beside the tee box. He was so focused that he never saw Langer go out-of-bounds.

After a textbook drive down the fairway, Norman fashioned a beautiful three-wood just short of the green, then pitched to 10 feet for another birdie. At the short sixteenth, he delivered a flawless tee shot to five feet and sank the putt to stay out of range of Faldo, who birdied the fourteenth, and Langer, who birdied the fifteenth and sixteenth. 'Well,' said a TV commentator in an awed tone, 'sometimes you just run out of superlatives.'

Throughout the day, there was the feeling that something magical, almost spiritual, was taking place, that the game of golf was being taken to a new level.

'It was chemistry,' Norman says. 'Every top player knew that the other players were at the peak of their games. Every player knew that if you made a bogey, you'd lost two shots, not one shot. We were so finely tuned, we were like violin strings. We were at the perfect pitch. And to come out of that beating all those guys – outside the West Lakes Classic that was my best feeling ever.'

On the seventeenth, Langer's three-wood approach hit the flagstick. 'This championship really does have a touch of the Steven Spielbergs about it,' the commentator breathed melodramatically. Norman looked at the leaderboard for the first time and immediately missed a 14-inch putt, making his only bogey of the day.

Millions of TV viewers swallowed hard collectively. Norman seemed unperturbed. 'My stomach fell, more from embarrassment than anything. But it was a blessing in disguise because it kicked me into gear . . .' Counselling himself to trust his swing, he launched a huge drive down the eighteenth fairway and strode majestically towards it, blond head held high. He hit a 198-yard four-iron to 18 feet to set up his eighth birdie chance of the day. As the roar of the gallery rose like thunder into the evening air, and Australian flags and inflatable sharks danced, Langer crossed the fairway and said to Norman, 'That's the greatest golf I've ever seen. You deserve to win.'

In the crackling silence, Norman holed out for a 64, the lowest final round ever scored by a champion, and the lowest aggregate score in Open history, 267. Afterwards, he sat stunned in the scorer's hut while his friends and family cried and hugged each other outside, afraid to believe that he had just played the greatest round of his life to win the Open. He didn't smile. He just sat stoically watching the television, waiting for Faldo, who had birdied the seventeenth, to do something marvellous to overtake him. It was not until Faldo holed out for a 67 and joint second place with Langer that Norman allowed himself to feel the heady rush of achievement.

'I'm not a man who tends to boast,' he told reporters, 'but I was in awe of myself. I have never ever gone around a course and not had a single mishit. Every drive and every iron was perfect. I only screwed up on that one little putt at the seventeenth, but that was probably the kick in the backside I needed. It was like playing a game of chess. I had an angle to every flag.'

Speaking at the prize-giving ceremony, ninety-one-year-old Gene Sarazen, winner of the 1932 Open at Sandwich, described Norman's performance as 'the most awesome display of golf I have ever seen'. Gary Player called it 'the best golf I ever saw played at the British Open', and Gary Evans, Norman's partner on the first two days, agreed. 'That last round was one of the best I have ever seen, no question,' he said.

'I think that the last round at Royal St George's is the best round of golf I've ever seen,' said Butch Harmon, who rates it above Tiger Woods's twelve-shot victory at the masters, 'when you consider the conditions, the wind blowing thirty or thirty-five miles an hour, when you consider that all the contenders played well – Faldo shot sixty-seven, Langer shot sixty-seven, Couples shot sixty-six. I mean, everyone who was there to win played fantastic, and Greg just played that much better and won the tournament. I still say it's the best round of golf I have ever seen in my life. He played as well as anybody can play. I don't think you could play a better golf tournament than he played that week.'

His arms wrapped around the silver claret jug, Norman told the cheering galleries, 'To say I've won the British Open, which is the Open championship of the world, the number-one championship major, the *best* major, to win it once was great, but to win it twice gives me twice as much pleasure.' His 64, as perfect a round of golf as has ever been played, would rank for ever among the greats: Ben Hogan's 67 at Oakland Hills, Arnold Palmer's 65 at Cherry Hills, Jack Nicklaus's 65 at Augusta, Johnny Miller's 63 at Oakmont. Only one player had ever finished under par at St George's in an Open – Bill Rogers in 1981 – and Norman demolished his record by nine shots.

On his way to the prize-giving ceremony, Norman was embraced in a bear hug by Faldo. 'Great job,' he said. 'Well done. You finally stuck your fingers up to them.'

Norman burst out laughing. 'Yeah,' he said. 'Fun golf, wasn't it?'

'Greg was always out of my range,' Faldo said. 'I needed every birdie but when you are staring at these opportunities in this kind of pressure, it's difficult to get the thing in the hole.'

Afterwards Norman, showered and relaxed in jeans and trainers and so happy he could have wept, climbed into a red Rolls-Royce with Laura and rode away into the sunset to a champagne party. 'This makes me feel so good,' he said. 'For myself, my friends, my family. They've seen what I've gone through, and they see what I want to achieve. I did it today.'

A month after his Open triumph, Norman was climbing out of his car on the final morning of the US PGA Championship when he was accosted by a well-meaning spectator. 'When you win today,' the man said, 'I want you to take your hat and throw it in that bunker. You throw it in the exact same spot where Tway made that shot.'

Norman smiled. Good idea, he thought. From the moment he signed his scorecard at Sandwich he had been thinking ahead to the US PGA, which was returning to Inverness, the scene of Tway's implausible bunker shot. 'I am ready for another major win,' Norman said confidently. 'My game is strong right now.' But even he couldn't ignore the possible implications of karma. 'It seems unbelievable that I'm going back to Inverness as Open champion,' Norman said, 'a flashback of 1986. That's a mind-boggling coincidence.'

Now, standing on the eighteenth tee at Inverness, minutes after he had ended the 1993 tournament tied with Paul Azinger, Norman was trying hard not to think about coincidences. He didn't want to picture Tway popping ecstatically out of the bunker, or see the surprised, elated faces of Mize or Calcavecchia or Frost or Gamez as fate handed them aces. And he certainly didn't want to dwell on the double-bogey he had chalked up by leaving his ball in the bunker at the sixth that afternoon, or the bogey at the seventh. After all, he'd recovered with four birdies that took him past Faldo, Vijay Singh and Tom Watson and left him tied with Azinger on 272. And his 69 made him the first man in history to shoot eight successive rounds in the sixties in majors.

Azinger was a nervous wreck. His sinewy forearms were tense, he was having trouble breathing and he was worried he might throw up. He was beginning to think that the 'best player in the world not to have won a major' was a tag that should never have been applied to him. Maybe there was a reason he had bogeyed the seventy-second hole of the 1987 Open to lose to Faldo, that his game went south on the back nine at majors.

Beside him was his caddie Mark Jimenez. Now that really was a coincidence. Jimenez was the man who had carried Tway's bag to victory at Inverness in 1986. Azinger breathed in deeply and hit his tee shot. Both men were on the green in two and the Australian had an 18-footer for birdie. Azinger watched as Norman, strong and charismatic, crouched down to inspect his lie.

For Norman and everyone who watched him, there was something fitting about the scene, almost as if destiny had come full circle. When the ball left his putter, it rolled unerringly towards the hole and tipped in, so that joy was surging across his face and his putter was thrusting upwards in anticipation of triumph when, defying every law of gravity and nature, the ball reappeared. The crowd gasped. Norman's putter flew into the air and his hand covered the shock and pain on his face.

'Two feet from the hole, there was no doubt in my mind that the putt was in,' Azinger said.

'That was as perfect a putt as I could have hit,' said Norman.

There was a palpable feeling of doom as they proceeded to the tenth. It was hard not to believe that some kind of hex was in operation and, not altogether unexpectedly, Norman hit his approach to 18 feet and three-putted, missing a five-footer that would have kept his hopes alive, to give the American his first major victory.

Head bowed, Norman ran the gauntlet of the gallery on his way back to the clubhouse. His son Gregory held his hand. 'I'm proud of you,' the boy told him.

'He was unlucky in that his ball ended up just in the rough,' Azinger says, 'and you know you're in a play-off and you've got to go at the flag . . . He had no chance, really . . . The first putt he had was nearly impossible. People say that the second putt was a three-footer. It was a four- or five-footer and it had a significant amount of break. But if he had hit [the first putt] hard enough to go three feet further, it might have reached the hole and then gone ten feet by. It was a hard putt.'

Norman wasn't the first player to achieve the ignominious distinction of losing play-offs in all four majors, but he was the second: Craig Wood managed it in the thirties. Norman had now finished runner-up six times in a major. 'Well,' Norman said, 'at least I was there.' He refused to accept that he might be jinxed and graciously acknowledged Azinger's achievement. 'It wasn't meant to be, it's as simple as that. I walk away from here with good feelings. I'm still proud that I've turned my career around in a phenomenal way this year. I'll have a couple of beers and I'll be fine.'

'That week was an incredible ball-striking week for me,' Azinger says. 'Statistically, I was first in greens in regulation, I was first in driving distance, and I was second in fairways hit. I didn't have a three-putt the whole tournament, and when I think about how good I hit it and the fact that Norman's putt could have lipped in on eighteen instead of lipped out, wow! I could still not have won a major. How much luck is there involved when you think about it?'

Jim Gallagher Jnr had just been the recipient of the largest dollop of good fortune he'd seen in ten years as a PGA Tour player, but he was uncertain whether to do cartwheels or apologize. For sixty-five holes, the Tour championship had belonged to Greg Norman. Serene and powerful, he had strolled the fairways as if every metre of San Francisco's Olympic Club, from the cypress trees to the $540,000 prize that would ensure he won the money list, was his by divine right. Then, inexplicably, he bogeyed four of the final seven holes to plummet into second place. 'Norman wasn't so much mishitting as misplaying – unnecessarily forcing the ball at the pin with efforts that were poorly conceived and inappropriate to the situation . . .' Jaime Diaz observed in *Sports International*. 'Norman went from being a tank rolling inexorably and triumphantly toward Olympic's stately clubhouse to a cable car careering down Hyde Street toward disaster.'

In rapid succession, Norman missed the twelfth green with a 131-yard nine-iron, hit a poor chip from behind the green at the thirteenth, plugged his ball in the bunker with an aggressive

60-degree wedge shot at the sixteenth, and hit an ill-advised eight-iron shot directly at a pin cut on a severe slope at the back of the eighteenth green.

'I didn't physically put on a bad performance, I just mentally put on a pathetic performance,' Norman said frankly. He was striding crossly from the recorder's hut when he bumped into Gallagher, the thirty-two-year-old who 'backed into' the third victory of his career, playing the last four holes in one over par. Caught on the hop, Gallagher was unsure what to say. 'Sorry about that, Greg,' he said sheepishly.

Norman was not exactly devastated; it had been too good a season for that. He had finished in the top ten seven times in fifteen appearances in the United States. But he was frustrated to have fallen at the last ditch and to have lost the chance to compete for Player of the Year honours. He had forgotten his own formula for playing Olympic – aim for the middle of the greens and forget the flags – and he had no-one to blame but himself.

'When you look at Greg Norman, his strengths and his weaknesses are almost one and the same,' says Butch Harmon. 'Greg Norman's strength is that he's not afraid to try any shot in any situation, and sometimes that's a weakness in that he gets too aggressive when he should maybe be a little more conservative. But then again, that's how Greg plays and he wouldn't be the great player that he is if he didn't play like that.'

In December 1993, Norman flew to Melbourne for the Australian Open, arriving pale, distressed and ill. Throughout the twenty-one-hour flight from Los Angeles via Hawaii and Pago Pago, he had been running a high fever and he had been ill several times. Norman suspected food-poisoning. Raymond Floyd, who had been with him, was convinced it was exhaustion. 'I think Greg is just run-down. He's been doing so many things in such a short period without time even to take a breath.'

There was plenty of evidence to support this assumption. Prior to the Tour championship, Norman had been in Japan. Having finished second in San Francisco, he flew to Cairns, Australia, for a fishing holiday, returned to Japan and holed an eagle putt to win the Taiheiyo

Masters, flew back to the States and won the Grand Slam of Golf, jetted to California to play in his own charity event, the Shark Shootout, and was on the plane to Melbourne for the Australian Open within an hour of finishing.

'If I'd been in America, I would have pulled out,' said a grey-faced Norman. 'But down here it would have hurt everybody, and I just figured I'd rather hurt myself.'

'How he is able to play golf at his level is beyond me,' said Frank Williams, IMG's man in Melbourne. 'He gets up at the crack of dawn and keeps going till he flops into bed at ten or eleven at night, and then he gets up and does the same thing again.'

It turned out that Williams, like Norman, was an incorrigible practical joker. At the Australian Skins earlier in the year, the Shark was autographing programmes and shirts for the television cameras when he was asked to sign a glove for Boris Yeltsin. 'Screw Yeltsin,' Norman said with a grin. He thought it was a joke.

Williams smiled quietly to himself. When Norman came off the course, worrying about his performance, Williams stopped him with a dark stare. 'Greg,' he said sternly, 'that's the least of our worries. We've had to close down the switchboard at Sanctuary Cove because of all the complaints. Why would you say, "Screw the Russian President"?'

'What are you talking about?' said Norman, alarmed.

'Look,' Williams said angrily, 'how many times have I told you that when you've got your mike on, you must put your hand over it if you don't want to be heard.'

Norman paled. 'Oh, my God!' he cried. 'What am I going to do?'

At first, Williams pretended to be unsympathetic but finally he relented and helped Norman concoct a story whereby Yeltsin was a boatbuilder from Detroit who was hassling him over the purchase of another yacht.

In the interview room, Tom Ramsey had been primed to ask the leading question. 'Greg,' he said, 'Rupert Murdoch has phoned me personally and he wants to know why you said fuck off to the Russian President.'

'You always believe what you want to believe,' Norman said. 'There is a boatbuilder in Detroit called Yeltsin . . .'

He stopped. The journalists were collapsing with laughter. He looked around for Williams. 'I'll get you,' he said. 'No matter what, I'll get you.'

A week later, Williams was holding a players' party at IMG's Melbourne office when five policemen came to the door. He apologized for the noise, but they ushered him into a quiet room. 'We've got a warrant for your arrest,' one told him.

Williams beamed. 'Oh, yes,' he said. 'Who's arresting me? Greg Norman?'

The policeman scowled. 'If you think we've got nothing better to do than come here on the whim of some adolescent golfer, you're very much mistaken,' he said, and handed Williams the warrant. Williams cast a glazed eye over the official emblem and list of charges, including tax evasion and illegal transference of money. He began to panic. 'I thought to myself, No, it's got to be Greg, but I can't see Greg anywhere to pounce on him. Then I look across and see my wife crying. I thought, Oh, my God, this could be for real.'

Before Williams could utter another syllable, the police were bundling him into the paddywagon. He was taken down to the station, finger-printed, read his rights and locked in a cell after having his belt and shoelaces removed. Jesus Christ, Williams thought as he sat on the bed with his head in his hands. My whole life is falling apart. With trembling fingers, he reached for the envelope he had been told would inform him of his legal position. There was a note inside. It read: 'Paybacks are hell, you asshole!!!!'

## CHAPTER THIRTEEN

# POWER STRUGGLE

'There's no doubt in my mind that Greg will end up a billionaire.'

FRANK WILLIAMS, JUNE 1997

IN A HOTEL SUITE IN downtown Sydney, Hughes Norton was staring goggle-eyed at Greg Norman, face grey and sweating, body paralysed with disbelief. In the space of five minutes, life as he knew it had ended. Divorce had been hard enough on him, but this caught him right in the solar plexus. Outside the sun was shining and the crowds were flocking to the fairways of the Greg Norman Holden Classic, but Norton felt chilled to the bone.

'The guy I'd done enormously wonderful things for, in the end, forgot it. I guess. It's the way life is in our business.'

It was still December 1993. Norman had summoned Hughes Norton, James Erskine, IMG's Sydney Head, and Frank Williams, the regional manager for IMG in Melbourne, to a meeting. There were no preliminaries. Norman simply stood up and said bluntly, 'As you all know, I've not been happy for some time, so I've decided that I'm now leaving. Frank has accepted a position with me and he will also be leaving.'

Norton and Erskine slumped in their chairs like stunned mullet. Norman had been without a contract at IMG for more than a year, during which time Williams had repeatedly warned the company that Norman hated being leveraged with other clients (packaged with lesser players to help boost their value) and did not feel he was getting the service he deserved, but somehow Norton didn't have the slightest inkling he might go. He either didn't see it, or did not want to see it.

'Let's make this friendly,' Norman said brightly.

'Hughes was devastated,' Williams recalls.

Depending on whom you talk to, Mark McCormack, Erskine and Norton are all variously blamed for Norman's decision to walk away from IMG, but his actual reasons were more specific. Williams believes that one of the most critical was Laura. 'He considers his wife and himself a partnership, and I think James made the mistake of not including his wife as part of the partnership. He never consulted with Laura *and* Greg. She's a very important factor in [Greg's] life. She's the single most important person in his life, along with his children. I think they deliberately tried to keep her out of the loop and I think Greg resented it.'

To Norton, who without prompting had described Laura as 'one of the greatest people I've ever known', this statement was extraordinary. 'That's the first I've ever heard of that,' he said. 'She was always around for discussions on important issues, so I'd be amazed if she thought she wasn't involved in decisions.'

Bev Norwood, a friend of both men, supported this view. 'Having seen the interaction between the two, I can tell you I have never to this day heard Laura Norman's name mentioned by anyone at IMG in a negative context.'

The whole split was traumatic. Norton considered himself to have been 'fired', a statement Norman views as 'extraordinarily rash. Hughes Norton was never fired. My contract expired with IMG, so I didn't fire anybody. Matter of fact, during the time of the contract running out, I'd asked for certain specific things to be done by IMG and they totally ignored them. They didn't recognize that I needed extra help because of the way my business was. It had nothing to do with Hughes Norton. It had a lot to do with IMG because they didn't fulfil the wishes of their client.'

Nick Price who, along with Faldo and a host of other top players, would soon leave IMG, totally supported Norman's decision. 'We spoke a lot about IMG over the years,' he says, 'especially on the golf course. At that stage, I felt that [leaving] was the best thing for him. Don't get me wrong: IMG is a good company. But it is archaic, to say the least. The company was structured in the sixties and it hasn't changed, and I think it's been to their detriment. They're going to have to change their tactics if they want to survive in the next decade, because sure as hell there is going to be somebody behind them that is going to challenge their position. I think Greg and myself and Faldo would still be with them if they had listened to us.'

The fall-out from Norman's departure was tremendous. Personally, it was as painful a blow as Norton had ever experienced; professionally, it cost him dearly. As a direct consequence of the Shark's departure, he was summarily demoted from head of IMG's golf division. Rightly or wrongly, he held Norman responsible, although the evidence suggests that the knives were already out within IMG.

Norton, who is liked as much as he is loathed, has few regrets. 'I could be wrong, but my feeling after the fact, analysing it, is if Greg had allowed or I had pushed more to have [people like Ian Todd, who runs the European operation, and Alastair Johnson, whom he thinks the world of ] involved, that we would still be together. As I say, that's not the way Greg wanted it and I didn't realize then, as I do now, how important that is. That would be my one regret. But, in terms of the job that I personally did or that IMG did, you know, we made this guy a hundred million dollars.'

'They wouldn't have made him a lot of money if Greg wasn't winning,' Laura said drily, 'and on top of that, they made money, too.'

Norton claims that the Australian pleaded with him for years to quit IMG and work for him. 'I would always say to him, "That's very flattering and it would be great for me, but it's not in your best interests" . . . But I always felt that he wanted loyalty and I gave him a hundred and ten per cent. He'd say, "You're not loyal because McCormack signs your cheques not me," and I'd tell him, "Yes, Greg, but you're doing much better with me at IMG than you would with me as your Great White Shark guy." '

The breakdown of the relationship between Norman and Norton had as its roots the Cobra deal. In September 1993, Norman, an equity shareholder in the company, had relinquished some of his shares in the first public offering. The second offering was a year later and then on 1 January 1996, when American Brands bought Cobra, Norman realized on his investment, earning some $44 million in total from his $2 million stake.

When Norton approached Norman around the time of the initial offering and asked him to pay him $1 million of that money, Norman was appalled. Was Norton really suggesting taking money due to his employer? If he was capable of that, what might he do to Norman?

Norton did not flinch when this allegation was put to him.

'Do you want to know the truth of the matter?' he asked. 'And it's never been said before. I did the Cobra deal with Greg and for Greg. Greg tried, at the end, to withhold commissions on the deal which we felt were very much due and proper. Greg's thing had been that he had enormous personal affection and respect and loyalty for me, but less for IMG the corporate entity, and at the end I felt that the only way to get for IMG what was duly ours was to appeal to him on a personal basis. And that's the absolute truth of that scenario. He chose not to do that either, so . . .'

Asked whether he thought that Norman might have gained the impression that Norton wanted the money for himself rather than his employer, he replied, 'Oh, I'm sure he did. Obviously. That's what he said.'

But according to Norman, 'IMG had nothing to do with the Cobra contract.' He smiled cynically. 'Very interesting, isn't it? I'll leave it at that.'

'IMG could never have been entitled to any of the Cobra money because they didn't make an investment,' Tom Crow says. 'It was Greg's name on the cheque, it was his money. Hughes Norton negotiated the representational deal, the deal for Greg to represent Cobra clubs and carry the bag. The other deal had nothing to do with Hughes Norton. Goddammit, he didn't put his name on the cheque. Without question, Hughes Norton has and had absolutely no entitlement to the money.'

Norton sticks to his story. 'I came up with the concept, I created

195

the value,' he says emotionally. 'And it's not the money, it's the principle. It's ethically, morally and logically wrong that he would not have paid me for the creative work of what turned out to be the *greatest* deal of his career.'

Since 1996, Norton has been more famous, or infamous, as Tiger Woods's manager. He avoids contact with the man who was once his closest friend. When Williams suggested that the three of them have a conversation about what had happened, Norton retorted, 'We just had it.'

'It was just like a lovers' quarrel or something,' Laura says. 'Hughes took it personally and it wasn't anything personal. It was simply business.'

Three years on, Norton still finds it distressing to discuss the matter. 'To yell and scream about loyalty and then do what he did to me on the Cobra deal alone is unconscionable,' he says shakily.

He admits he is saddened by the situation. 'We all have our flaws and Greg has his and I have mine, but he's basically, deep down, a really good, giving, caring person, and I miss that. But I'm also the sort of person, whether it's my divorce, or my divorce with Greg, I'm not a great one to chase him around after I've been fired and say, "Let's be buddy-buddy and hang out and be pals. I'm just not that way. I'm more of a black-and-white loyal person.'

Fuzzy Zoeller was waving the white towel again. In a tongue-in-cheek echo of Winged Foot, he took it out of his bag as he walked towards the eighteenth green at the 1994 Players Championship and raised it in admiration, causing Norman to burst out laughing and place his hat affectionately on Zoeller's head. For four days, Zoeller had ambled his way around the Stadium Course at Sawgrass and never once scored worse than 68. He had shot 20 under par on a course so wicked that Tom Weiskopf described it as 'Donkey Kong' golf, and lost by four shots. 'That's the best I've ever played and had absolutely no chance of winning,' Zoeller said wryly.

Instead, the honour went to Norman. He shot three 67s and a record-equalling 63 for a 24 under par aggregate of 264. His only bogey came when a leaf blew across his line as he prepared to hole a nine-footer at the thirteenth. It was his first for 66 holes, and the first for 92 if you included the Nestlé Invitational the previous week. 'I really wanted to go bogey-free,' said Norman. 'There are things you have an opportunity of doing in life maybe once or twice. And seventy-two holes without a bogey is rare.'

For once no carefree rookie recorded a double-eagle to beat him on the eighteenth, and for once Norman didn't beat himself. The only hint of his old lunatic bravado came at the narrow, water-logged sixteenth in the final round, where he decided he was swinging well enough to hit a sliding three-wood into the green. Tony Navarro clung to the club. 'Let's just lay up,' he pleaded, fear of failure moving him to say the four words Norman hated most in golf. Norman fumed and fretted and champed at the bit, but he saw reason. He laid up and made par. 'A play like that might help us out in the future,' Navarro said afterwards optimistically.

Since missing the cut at the 1993 US Open, Norman's finishes read 2, 1, 3, 2, T4, T7, 10, 2, 1, T18, T7, T6, 1, and yet he was about as far from being a happy man as it was possible to be. Sitting in the locker room after his first-round 63, picking irritably at his orange workout shorts, he responded with hurt and anger to a question on why he was no longer gregarious but world-weary and withdrawn. 'I'll tell you what happened,' he burst out. 'You become cynical. Why did Michael Jordan retire? Because of all the badgering. Why do athletes go into a shell after a period of time? Because of all the constant badgering. Unfortunately, that's the nature of the beast. We do it to ourselves and the media is such now that it focuses on whatever it can get its hands on. I was never a cynical person. Never have been. But I am now.'

Behind the scenes, Frank Williams had moved in as managing director of Norman's new company, Great White Shark Enterprises, amid a certain amount of sniping from IMG. When Norman dared to suggest that the Australian Masters had lost its magic, James Erskine snapped, 'What do you want? Gold loo paper?'

'That's the stuff you use, right, James?' Norman retaliated.

'Yes, Greg, I got it from your private jet,' Erskine said sarcastically.

The vilification heaped on him during his slump was a thorn in his side even the Open trophy hadn't soothed. It rankled that other players could make eleventh-hour cock-ups or offensive statements without being crucified the way he was. On the Monday of his Open defence at Turnberry, he stood on the edge of the putting green glowering at John Daly. 'What the hell could you have been thinking?' he burst out. Daly, who had thoughtlessly alleged to a British tabloid that some players took drugs, looked up in surprise. When Norman repeated the question, he became defensive and said he was tired of being portrayed as the only black sheep on the Tour.

'I was livid with the guy, absolutely livid,' said Norman, who was tempted to follow Daly into the locker room but didn't want to do something he regretted. 'How dare he say any of us are on drugs? I'm not the one who beat up my wife. I'm not the one who is an alcoholic. I'm not the one who tears up rooms . . . If I had done the things he's done, I'd have been ostracized so fast it would have been ridiculous.'

The needles were coming in again, and they were much deeper and more painful than Norman's worst nightmares could have led him to believe. Even Davis Love, the moon-faced, likeable former Players champion, was in on it. 'If he walked out here now, he'd get attacked,' he told *Golf Digest*, suggesting that the Shark needed to add a body-guard to his staff. 'Guys would pin him in a corner and scream at him.'

The cause of this outrage was the bombshell Norman had dropped at the Shark Shootout on 17 November when he announced the $25 million World Golf Tour, a series of eight $3 million super-events, featuring the top thirty players on the rankings and ten invitees.

The background to this was simplicity itself. The Montgomery brothers, John, from Executive Sports, and Scott, who ran the Doral-Ryder Open, approached Norman and asked if he would be prepared to put his name behind a World Tour in 1995. Norman, who had always been a big fan of the idea, said he would, but only if the difficulty of individual circuits protecting their power-bases could be overcome. The Montgomery brothers went away and came back with a plan whereby existing events, such as Norman's own Shark Shootout, could be used. Norman was convinced, Rupert Murdoch, the Australian media tycoon, weighed in with a $120 million offer from his Fox television network over five years, and it was decided that John Montgomery should announce it at a press conference at the Shark Shootout.

'John got up in front of the microphone and froze,' Williams recalls. 'So Greg stepped in and said, "This is the deal . . ." And the shit hit the fan.'

Nothing – not fame, not abuse, not wealth, not suffering – had prepared Norman for the scale of the fury that came his way as the news exploded around the golf world. 'Greg's Golf War,' declared the *Evening Standard* in London, amid reports that Tim Finchem, the US Tour commissioner, who was diplomatic and reasonable in the immediate aftermath, had hardened his stance considerably when his players rallied behind him. The US Federal Trade Commission was already investigating the Tour for possible restraint of trade, but, for the sake of protecting his $82 million circuit, Finchem was prepared to resist them, suspend any players who joined the rebel Tour, and fight all the way to Congress if necessary.

The player reaction was even more extreme. Arnold Palmer put his face inches from Norman's and warned, 'Greg, slow down,' and the *New York Times* ran a poll showing that not one of the top thirty players supported Norman's plan. To Norman, who had canvassed player support – starting with the major champions of 1994, Nick Price, Ernie Els and José Maria Olazábal – and believed he'd got it, it was devastating. 'Nick was the first guy I spoke to,' Norman said. 'If he didn't think the idea was any good, I wouldn't have proceeded.' But Price, like Els, had been cagey. 'If the PGA Tour doesn't give its blessing, then I'm not going to be able to play,' he hedged. 'Greg asked for my support and I gave it, but there's a big difference between commitment and support.'

'He was supported by a lot of his friends and then when it went public, they didn't support him,' Laura said. 'And that really hurt him.'

Olazábal was a lone voice in a wilderness of criticism. 'Please feel free to use my name as a strong supporter of the idea,' he said, in a fax to Norman.

The reaction of the golf community to 'Norman's World Tour' was outrage. While it was generally agreed that it would provide a much-needed wake-up call to the smug complacency of the other Tours, most people believed that greed lay at its heart. Any way you painted it, it perpetuated the wealth and success of an already élite minority, put money in Norman's pocket, damaged the other Tours and the image of the game, and cheapened the majors and the competition. As Jerry Tarde said in *Golf Digest*, the events would be 'little more than glorified skins games'.

Peter Thomson concurred. 'The potential to damage and even wreck the US and European Tours is real. That's not to say they don't need a good shake-up. But the Tours are professional golf's nurseries and they need to be nurtured by those who've come through the system to become famous and wealthy. That particular lucky élite would not be in clover today had those Tours not been in place for them to get started. Before they leap into the beyond, I hope they consider those they leave behind.'

Norman, meanwhile, felt that his motives had been misinterpreted. 'The perception with me with the World Tour was just ridiculous,' he says.

'It came out that he was trying to do something for Norman rather than for the good of golf,' Frank Williams said, 'and he really was trying to do something for the good of golf, or what he perceived as the good of golf – whether that's right or wrong. He took a helluva hammering from his peers and from the golf world at large ... I remember John and Scott and I sitting with Greg in his old office and we said, "You know you're going to get a lot of flak from this? They'll put their own twist on it and the twist it'll be is that, 'Wealthy guy Greg Norman's getting even wealthier.' " He said, "Oh, I don't think it'll be that bad when I explain it all." 'Course, he never got the chance to explain it. It was like everything in Greg's life, done on the run and in a hurry.'

Nick Price was of a similar mind. 'I think the mistake that he made with the World Tour was he tried to put it together too quickly. But other than that, I think his intention was to do something for the betterment of the game. I don't believe for one minute that he was doing it for financial gain because the money that he stood to make out of it was negligible. And he was absolutely right. He made the respective Tours think about golf on a global scale, especially in the US which tends to be insular. It was probably the biggest step forward that we've ever seen.'

To Norman, the most upsetting part of the entire incident was when he started getting letters from PGA club professionals who wanted to stop carrying his clothing line because he was 'ruining the game' with the World Tour. 'I was devastated by that,' says Norman. He phoned every pro individually and persuaded them to restock.

Since then, Tim Finchem and the other circuits have moved inexorably towards a mini-World Tour of their own. 'Are they ruining the game?' says Norman, who had eleven top tens to finish runner-up on the money list despite undergoing haemorrhoid surgery after the World Series. 'Of course not. Those people are doing it because they can see how much money there is on the table to be made.'

By February 1995, Norman's World Tour was dying on its feet and he had two new worries to contend with. At the Alfred Dunhill Challenge, the Southern Africa v. Australasia match held in Johannesburg, he had received more bad press after his singles match against Nick Price. At the sixteenth hole, he and Price were respectively fifteen and nine feet from the pin and all-square, when Norman suggested that they concede each other's putts. The Zimbabwean readily agreed and went on to win the last hole and the match. But afterwards both received a hostile reception from officials and other players for taking friendship too far and making a joke out of a serious event.

'Greg's got to understand he deserves better than that,' said Ken Schofield. 'He let the game down, he let the team down. Unfortunately, Nick Price conspired with him. That's not what golf is about . . . This was supposed to be a special addition to the calendar and there were players trying their guts out, but what happened between Norman and Price was absurd. Both men made an error of judgement. If the show is more important than the result, then it's not worth having.'

It was not the first time the European Tour's executive director had rounded on Norman. At the Johnnie Walker Classic in Manila that month, he had confronted the Australian on the subject of the World Tour and had been persuaded by Norman that he had been 'used' and that 'it really wasn't his gameshow'. That hadn't stopped Schofield from writing to the sponsors of the Dubai Desert Classic, the Irish Open and the European Masters to complain about another matter: the $300,000 appearance fees Norman was supposed to have received in 1994.

'A guy in my shoes has to be pro prize money and against appearance money,' explains Schofield, who has adopted a sort of Band-aid regulation in Europe whereby incentives must not be more than 25 per cent of the prize fund. 'And many sponsors would go to any apparent lengths to skewer Greg Norman.'

Norman was furious. 'To single me out in three tournaments I played in put me in a very awkward position and I don't forgive Ken for that,' he said, after a heated debate with Schofield in early 1996. 'Ken and I had known each other basically for twenty years and the twenty-year relationship ended right there, as far as I was concerned.'

' "Why me?" That's what he said,' reports Schofield. ' "Why do you pick on me? What about all the other guys?" I just said, "I'm sorry, Greg, but the issue appears to be you. It *always* seems to be you that's in the headlines – or people close to you – wishing to ram down people's throats that you can command and receive on our Tour sums that appear to break our regulations." '

On the golf course, Norman used these conflicts to drive himself forward, with spectacular success. A chance to steal Ben Crenshaw's thunder at the Masters only ended when he pulled a sand-wedge shot 70 feet left of the flag on the penultimate hole and three-putted. 'I had one hundred and six yards to the hole,' Norman explained, 'and I don't like hitting a sand-wedge that far. I like one hundred and four yards. It was a little uphill, there was a breeze coming out of the right-hand corner and I was on a hanging lie. It was one of those deals.' Norman shrugged. 'I was between yardages.' Yet in 1986, the Year of the Shark, he had told a reporter, 'When everything is going in the right direction . . . my caddie gives me half yardages . . . he'll say a hundred and thirty-one and a half yards instead of a hundred and thirty-two. He knows that if I'm really playing well I can put it to within that half-yard.'

When back spasms forced him to pull out of the Heritage Classic, he took a five-week break, relaxed, spent time with his family and didn't touch a club until the Memorial Tournament. 'You're lucky to see me this week,' joked Norman, before sweeping majestically to victory at Muirfield Village. A final-round 66 included single putts on six of the last seven greens and birdies at the seventeenth and eighteenth.

At the US Open, it was business as usual and this time Corey Pavin pipped him to the post. 'You could call it another shot heard round the Greg Norman household,' Dan Jenkins said wryly as Pavin's magnificent four-wood to the eighteenth at Shinnecock consigned the Shark, who had shared the fifty-four-hole lead, to second place in yet another major.

In August, Norman caused a huge fracas when he accused Mark McCumber of illegally repairing a spike mark on the seventh green in the first round of the World Series, effectively labelling him a cheat. In golf, there is no mud that sticks like cheating and therefore most players, even if they are 99.9 per cent certain that a partner has knowingly violated the rules, would tend to confront them in private. Norman was having none of it. He refused to sign McCumber's card after the round and, when McCumber insisted he had merely removed an insect, threatened to withdraw from the tournament. 'An ugly scene ensued in the scoring trailer,' reported *Golf World*.

'I didn't sign the scorecard for a reason,' Norman fumed, after the Tour's senior director of rules signed McCumber's card on his behalf. 'What I saw is what I saw. I'd do it again if I saw a violation that blatant. I was furious because I was disappointed in what I saw. I could've bench-pressed five hundred pounds, that's how mad I was.'

While McCumber went home with his reputation in tatters, Laura, Navarro and Finchem persuaded Norman to stay. 'They told me, "Don't compromise yourself," ' Norman said. 'They were right . . . Why compromise Greg Norman's chance to win?' Three days later, he holed a 66-foot chip to beat Nick Price and Billy Mayfair on the first play-off hole. 'The golfing gods were good to me today,' Norman said.

There was a theory in some quarters that Norman had deliberately humiliated McCumber to even the score for McCumber's outspoken opposition to the World Tour. 'Who does Norman think he is? God?' McCumber had been quoted as saying. But Price thought the World

Series was Norman's moral reward. 'Greg is a man of high principles,' he said. 'He is extremely adamant about what he saw.'

In October, Norman arrived at the Dunhill Cup, his first event in six weeks, fresh from a holiday in Belize with Nick Price. He had gone there to recover from a bout of chemical poisoning, possibly from lettuce or fruit, which caused him to lose thirteen pounds in six days and spend ten days in bed. 'Reports came in from Australia that I had cancer and in the US something else,' Norman said. 'I am fine now.'

At the end of the season, Norman won the money list with a record $1.6 million, but he was robbed of the Vardon Trophy, awarded for the lowest stroke average (69.06), on a technicality. Under the rules, any player who withdraws in mid-round becomes ineligible for the award and, by failing to complete the second round of the Heritage Classic with a back injury, Norman had disqualified himself. But there were compensations. His Australian Open victory was his first in his own country for five years. His peers voted him Player of the Year, he appeared in sepia-tone on the cover of *Men's Journal*, describing his life as a business tycoon, *Golf World* voted him Man of the Year and *Golf Australia* devoted an entire issue to him.

In the early days, when Norman had been taking his first, tentative steps towards fame and independence, Laura was involved in every last business decision. She answered all the fan mail, fielded all the phone calls. 'I remember the day that Greg said he needed a secretary,' she says. 'I said, "Oh, no, I don't want us to get that big." And I fought it every step of the way, expanding, I guess. I liked the way things were.'

Now, with Frank Williams's help, Norman was expanding Great White Shark Enterprises Inc. into a multifaceted corporation with a worldwide staff of forty-three, but Laura was still consulted on every crucial move. 'He trusts her like nobody else,' Hughes Norton says. 'And I think any of the crunch-type decisions, he would always get her input on.'

In an article entitled 'Team Norman', Australia's *Sun-Herald* discussed Norman's growing entourage, people like Tony Navarro, Pete Draovitch, Gary Stuve, Flash and John Cott, an IMG chauffeur.

'He's just weeded out people he's not comfortable with,' Laura said.

Norman had approached Williams about running Great White Shark Enterprises shortly before he left IMG. They had been good friends since 1977 and Williams had the added advantage of having absorbed IMG's knowledge while managing to avoid being cast in their mould. Born in England, he had pulled himself up by his bootstraps, starting out as a post-office clerk and subsequently selling fish on the King's Road in London. Later, he migrated to Australia and worked for Electrolux, before buying a 50 per cent share in the Australian Masters in 1980, developing the concept, selling it to IMG and ultimately heading their Melbourne office.

'Frank has wonderful skills with people . . .' Norman told Bernie McGuire in *Australian Golf Digest*. 'He's very loyal.' But he acknowledged that, 'Because of our friendship, I've probably been a little bit harder on Frank than anyone else in life.'

Williams gives a wry smile. 'If he ever sees the error of his ways, he's always been the first to apologize,' he says, 'which is something I find very difficult . . . But he has got a temper. It'll take a long time to build but when it comes to a crescendo – God! I could always make him angry if I didn't keep him informed on something or I made the mistake of thinking it's not important enough for him to know. He *hates* that, hates it with a passion. So our differences of opinion – and there have been a few – are usually a lack of communication, sometimes caused by him being so damn busy and giving me ten minutes when he should give me an hour. He's always on the go. He lives life at a hundred miles an hour. Never stops . . . I wouldn't be him for the world. But he doesn't complain about it. He just gets on with it.'

Asked if he considered Norman a principled person, he said cautiously, 'On some things.'

To Norman, no attribute is more valuable than loyalty, and friends and employees found lacking in it are ruthlessly expelled from his circle. 'I'm so much better now because I control my entire office,' he says. 'People that work for you, *you* sign their pay-cheques and you have the loyalty, you have the trust. I'm extremely loyal to people. I'll throw a blanket over people and give them anything they want if they just show me the loyalty back.'

In the eighties, Norman used to fall asleep in business meetings, bored rigid by the plotting and planning he paid others to do. When one or two expensive mistakes were made with his money, he began to sit up and pay attention. He found, to his surprise, that he loved high-risk wheeling and dealing, loved to spend days thrashing out deals over boardroom tables, loved dreaming of taking his company to the 'next level'. Gradually, he learned to trust his instincts. The Cobra gamble paid off handsomely and the Greg Norman Collection – the clothing company that grew out of his deal with Reebok but is now separate – is riding lucratively on the coat-tails of the Tommy Hilfiger, Ralph Lauren, sportswear-as-fashion boom, to the tune of some $200 million in annual sales by 1996. Even his cars were big business.

'I have one Ferrari I drive, the others are for investment,' Norman told the *Sunday Express* in 1989. 'People say I should invest in art. Bull. I understand art, not paintings. Instead of *Mona Lisa*s on the wall I have Ferraris in the garage.'

'His father is very clever and Greg's become that way,' says Toini. 'Even Greg himself says that he's more like his father these days.'

'To me, he was always what we call street smart,' Hughes Norton says. 'In the case of his Ferrari collection, he had a knack for knowing when it was the right time to buy, and it's a very fickle sort of market. He wasn't a classic businessman, traditionally trained, or what you would call a great business mind, but he had wonderful savvy.'

Norman agreed. 'I'm not saying that I'm some Harvard business graduate,' he told Bernie McGuire, 'I'm not anything. But all the people I've got to know on Wall Street, well, I would say that the majority of them are street smart. They're not Harvard graduates. They've learned the hard way.'

He told McGuire that Kerry Packer had given him 'a wonderful piece of advice in 1985 or 1986 [when] I was asked to get involved with a business. I knew he was in the media. I walked into his office and said, "KP? I need to see you. I've had this proposition. Someone has asked me to be the figurehead of something and I'm really not too sure about it." KP said, "Son, you keep out of my business and I'll keep out of your business . . ." I said, "KP, that's all I needed to hear." '

'There is no doubt in my mind that Greg will end up as a billionaire . . . because he's very innovative,' Williams says. 'A classic example is when we bought the sod farm. We were just walking around and he said, "Isn't it silly? We build golf courses but we buy the sod from another company. Why don't we buy our own sod farm?" So I went up to Avon Park, Florida, got the world rights to [Australian turf farmer] Hugh Whiting's grass and renamed it GN-1. Then we used it at the Medalist [Norman's first US course, co-designed with Pete Dye in Hobe Sound, Florida], as a marketing ploy. Currently we can't buy enough of it.'

Successes like these have helped to quadruple Norman's fortune in the four years since he left IMG. In 1995, he made a reported $11 million in endorsements alone. Along with Shark Shootout in California (which has raised over $10 million for charity), he has the Greg Norman Holden International (formerly Classic) in Sydney and his own boat-building company, Norman's Yachts Inc. He has more than twenty-five course-design projects either open or under development, each of which pays him $1 million. Two days after the 1997 BellSouth Classic was held at the TPC at Sugarloaf, his 7,259-yard Atlanta design, his office received eighteen requests for course designs.

'The homage is unmistakable,' *Golf World* said of Sugarloaf. 'It's Augusta National-meets-Royal Melbourne.' Ron Whitten concluded, 'It could be the best thing to emerge from the hills of Atlanta since Bobby Jones.'

'Greg is just a product now of twenty-five years of hard work,' Wayne Grady says.

'He's an excellent businessman,' Tom Crow says. 'He has the same focus in business as he has in golf. He has the same energy.'

But James Marshall was not alone in believing that, over the years, Norman's blossoming empire and extracurricular pursuits had detracted from his focus on the golf course. 'He knows that, rightly or wrongly, to be judged at the top level of golf, you have got to be successful in the majors, and I think that to achieve that you've got to be single-minded. For somebody like Greg, who has always been incredibly materialistic, who has always wanted to be in the lime-light, it is difficult to bring all of your energies to bear and shut out all that other stuff and concentrate on winning.'

'I guess at some stage you make a choice about whether you want to fly all over the world, building golf courses and running huge businesses, or whether you just play golf,' Mike Clayton says. 'Faldo just wants to play golf, it seems to me. I'm sure he does some of the other stuff, but golf is a major priority, whereas with Greg, I'm not sure golf is a priority. But how do you criticize the guy for not being so one-dimensional he's got no room in his life for anything else?'

As his empire has grown, the size of Norman's toy collection has increased proportionately. By the end of 1996, his Internet site was declaring that he had no idea how many Ferraris he owned (it was believed to be six). He also possessed a custom-built $8 million Gulfstream IV jet, a $4 million Bell 230 twin-engine helicopter, his 87-foot fishing yacht *Aussi Rules*, a couple of smaller boats, three Harleys, two jet-skis, a Rolls-Royce, a Bentley, a Mercedes and six Chevrolet suburbans, not to mention the mansion with housekeeper, house manager, grounds-keeper, etc., in Jupiter Island, Florida. The scale of his wealth and his perceived flaunting of it had a lot to do with the envy and hostility he aroused on the Australian and US circuits.

'I've never wanted to be the guy with the most on the block,' Norman insists, 'contrary to all this bullshit you read about Greg Norman.'

When it is pointed out to him that he certainly seems to have the most on the block, he snaps, ''Course I've got a lot, but that's not what I *wanted*. I've got a lot because I worked damn hard on the golf course and I was pretty smart with some of my business decisions. Yeah, I've got a lot, I'm not denying that, but it was not my sole objective in life to go out and get money.'

'No-one has the right to judge you on how you spend your money,' Laura says flatly. 'Greg has probably been a little more extravagant than most golfers . . . He loves spending money on wonderful things and he loves having beautiful things around him. He's always had a suite when he went some place, where other people would stay in a cheap hotel. It's just the way he is, and he can afford it and he's put down for it. When he first got a helicopter, he'd fly to tournaments and people would say, "Well, it's OK for Arnold but it's ridiculous for Greg." Well, Greg could afford it, so it wasn't ridiculous. Yet people would make a judgement on what was right or wrong with how he should spend his money. I think it comes down to jealousy.'

Norman agrees wholeheartedly. To him, he is still the same blue-eyed country boy he was at seventeen. 'People are very jealous of what I've got . . . You read about I own all these Ferraris and two helicopters and planes and a house over here and a house over there. I don't have two helicopters, I have one. I don't have six Ferraris, I have four. I have Harleys. But I enjoy them. Is there anything wrong with that?'

---

# CHAPTER FOURTEEN

# DEATH IN THE AFTERNOON

'People who talk about choking under pressure have no idea how many things can go wrong on a golf course besides nerves and fear.'

ARNOLD PALMER

THE FAIRWAYS OF AUGUSTA National dropped away from the club-house in an unblemished emerald wave, curving treacherously around the tall, spare pines and the fuchsia splash of azaleas in the dark pools. It was early but already the crowds were taking up their positions. Craned forward at Amen Corner or lolling under the pines, they were dotted decoratively around the course in that half-languorous, half-tense attitude peculiar to Augusta galleries, in any position that might afford a view of what promised to be one of the greatest final rounds in history.

Even the hardest-boiled newspapermen agreed: justice had never seemed so poetic. Greg Norman, whose ardent, unrequited infatuation with Augusta had survived some of the most wicked injustices in memory, was leading by six strokes going into the final round of the 1996 Masters. In the dim distance was his old adversary Nick Faldo. Phil Mickelson, now saddled with that unfortunate tag 'the best player in the world not to have won a major', was lying third, and everyone else was too far back to figure.

'If I have one dream left in golf it's to win at Augusta,' Norman had said two years earlier. 'If I told you different, I'd be lying, not only to you but to myself. I love everything about the tournament: the golf course, the way they run it, everything. It feels different from any other tournament in the world and I've been so close to winning it that I'd be very disappointed if I didn't some day win it. But I honestly believe I've got a lot more chances to do it.'

Out on the range, Norman felt nervous but, as he later told Laura, 'It was the right kind of nervous.' He didn't feel the curious deadness that had come over him at St Andrews in 1990, and he didn't feel as jittery and nauseous as he had at Turnberry in 1986. He felt hopeful and relaxed. Watching him, Butch Harmon thought his ball-striking was almost perfect. A constant stream of people came up to wish Norman the best. 'Enjoy yourself,' Frank Williams told him. Among the pile of good-luck notes in his locker was one from Nick Price: 'Go out and win by twelve,' his friend had written. Frank Nobilo smilingly said the same thing. Norman looked away. 'I'd rather have a two-stroke lead than a six-stroke lead,' he told the New Zealander.

In a way, there were too many well-wishers, too many people piling their expectations on his shoulders. Everywhere he turned, there were constant reminders that his family, friends and a million spectators were depending on him to do himself justice. He tried reading *Popular Mechanics* but couldn't take in a word. There was no escape, not even in the bathroom. There, he had run into Peter Dobereiner, the ailing golf writer, who had always been one of his biggest supporters. 'Not even you can fuck this up now, Greg,' Dobereiner said teasingly.

Greg Norman was contemplating catastrophe and it didn't faze him in the least. In about ten minutes all the trophies, fame and Ferraris in the world would not be able to save him as his million-dollar swing exploded into pieces, but somehow Norman was not in the slightest bit perturbed. He fixed his gaze on the horizon and listened calmly to the voice that had entered his consciousness.

'Uh, Greg, we've got a little problem,' said Lieutenant Maris 'Weasel' Luters.

After a day of training, during which he had emerged with flying colours from the ejector-seat test, the water parachute drag and the full-gear water tread, Norman was a hundred miles out of San Diego and 7,000 feet above the US Navy carrier *Carl Vinson* in an F-14. Weasel, his top gun pilot, was alerting him to the fact that the flaps wouldn't go down. It was looking ominous for them. Without the flaps, it would be impossible to slow the jet sufficiently for it to hit the deck of the carrier safely and they would have to make an emergency landing at a nearby runway. At the last possible second, the flaps released and they made it to the ship. Afterwards, Norman was asked if he had been afraid. 'Oh, no,' he said. 'It just meant we got to look at the sunset longer.'

At forty-one, when the average man is beginning to realize that it isn't necessary to be the first one off at the lights, Norman's relish for gut-wrenching, adrenaline-spewing activities was increasing daily. He stroked bull sharks sleeping in underwater caves; drove at 190 m.p.h. in Lamborghini Diablos on desert highways; hugged the wall at 180 m.p.h. in Roger Penske Indy cars; ran out of oxygen 88 feet below the sea and rose to the surface no faster than his own bubbles, suffering from only a mild case of the bends. 'Greg likes to stand right on the edge of the cliff,' Steve Elkington said.

Another favourite Norman pastime was to fly his Bell Jet Ranger helicopter – pitch black with the word 'Shark' in gold lettering on the side – at insane speeds at low altitudes or weave it through the Everglades. 'He has a qualified pilot with him but he scares the heck out of some of the people who fly with him,' Gary Stuve reports.

None the less, Norman hotly denies that he has ever undertaken any activity that might result in death or serious injury. 'I would never put myself in a position where I would be jeopardizing my life,' he says categorically. 'Never, ever. Never have, never will. There's not one thing that I do that's dangerous. Now, when I went diving with sharks I had a cage. I wasn't out there being Mr Macho Man saying I can swim with Great Whites. I was in a controlled environment. When I go up in a fighter jet, I'm in a controlled environment because I know that that pilot's not going to kill himself. Go check my driving record. I enjoy driving fast but that doesn't mean to say that every time I get in a vehicle I drive at 100 m.p.h. No. Roger Penske invited me to drive an Indy car at the racetrack. I got in there and I put that pedal flat. But you couldn't hurt yourself even if you spun out because it's got protection. And I'm not the type of driver who goes beyond my capabilities. There's never been a situation, I can honestly say, where I've jeopardized my life or anybody else's.'

In contrast, Norman was finally learning to throttle back on the golf course, to use his vast resources more intelligently and manage his game more professionally. When the core of his driver caved in shortly before the final round at Doral, he called Laura and had her rush a pile of clubs to him in his helicopter. He selected a titanium-headed Cobra and played his way coolly and methodically to a two-stroke victory. 'Greg is where he is now because of maturity and learning from mistakes,' said Butch Harmon, who had checked Norman's swing for the first time since August. 'He is more aware of his capabilities and not so gung-ho about always hitting the perfect shot. He has learned how to come down the stretch and win.'

Standing in the sunshine with Norman minutes before the start of the final round at Augusta, Harmon had no idea that those words would come back to haunt him. He watched the balls climb sweetly into the blue and savoured the fruits of their hard work. There had been a few small hitches. They had fallen out briefly over, among other things, Harmon's general unavailability, and Norman had missed back-to-back cuts at Bay Hill and the Players Championship. But they had made up and Norman bounced back the way only Norman could, with more heart and fight than ever. Harmon watched Norman's square brown hands clip another ball off the manicured turf of the practice range. He was, Harmon thought, as ready as he ever would be.

Every April, Norman walked out onto the clubhouse lawn, where Green Jackets and ordinary folk basked in the spring air and tucked into clam chowder and toasted tuna sandwiches, and fell in love with Augusta all over again. He even loved the colour of it. 'It's the only pure golf tournament we play in,' he told reporters on Tuesday. 'It's just pure golf. Over the years, you get to know the people and where they sit . . . You see the same face at the corner of sixteen, off the seventeenth green, on eighteen. Those are the type of traditions that you really love to play with and understand.'

Everybody knew Norman's feelings on Augusta, how much the green jacket would mean to him. In *Augusta: Home of the Masters Tournament*, a club member tells the author Steve Eubanks, 'I remember one time I was sitting on a golf cart with my green jacket on and Greg Norman popped out of the club and said, "Sir, may I say something? I want you to know this is the greatest golf tournament in the world." '

Asked about his game since the two missed cuts – the first time in his career he had missed successive cuts in the United States – he said his only problem was mental. 'I think there's times when you just get tired,' he explained, managing, despite this, to radiate an uncharacteristic aura of tranquillity and goodwill. 'You go at it hard and sometimes you wake up on the thirty-first of December and think, my God, I've got to go through it all again. But that's part of life.' He smiled.

'Someone wrote that everyone in life tries to overcome fear,' said a reporter. 'We are driven by fear. What is your fear?'

'Well,' replied Norman pleasantly, 'one of my great motivations in life is the fear of failure. I like the idea of pushing myself to success, you know. And the way you push yourself to success is that you don't want to fail.'

On Wednesday, Norman woke up with his work-stressed back hurting so badly that he was hardly able to swing the club. 'He was just so frustrated,' Laura said. 'It hadn't happened to him in for ever. He kept saying, "Why now, of all times?" ' But Fred Couples sent over his back therapist Tom Boers and, by the following day, Norman felt like a million dollars. On a glorious spring morning, he pushed himself to the most perfect first round of his Masters career, making nine birdies in a 63 that tied Nick Price's ten-year-old course record. It was his first opening score in the sixties since 1981 and it was, as the *New York Times* put it, 'the stuff of dreams'.

For the first six holes, Norman had made nothing but pars and a familiar tightness crept into his jaw. Then the ball started to roll for him. He was wearing an elegant cream shirt, striped sweater and black pants and, when the crowd showed their appreciation as his 220-yard four-iron shot flew out of the woods on the fourteenth and landed three feet from the hole, he laughed delightedly, bowed and doffed his hat.

Afterwards, he described it as one of the best rounds of his life. 'It was one of those things where I just let it flow,' said a beaming Norman, who was leading by two strokes from Mickelson and four from Hoch and Tway. 'You just try to keep the momentum going that's within you. You don't let it get away from you and get too excited about it. I am happy and excited but there's a long way to go.'

The most striking aspect of Norman's performance was his composure. He was as tranquil as a Zen student trimming a bonsai tree. When gusting winds sent putts scurrying off Augusta's concrete greens on the second day, he simply 'factored in' the new conditions and responded with a 69 on a day when the stroke average of the field rose to 74.43. He led by four from Faldo and six from Mickelson and Frost. 'I'm very relaxed, very comfortable within myself,' he said. 'I'm feeling good and looking forward to the weekend.'

On Saturday, Faldo entered the equation but not even he could upset Norman's equilibrium. 'Greg's going really well and I'm just trying to catch him,' the Englishman had said, after a second-round 67, but in the third round nothing went his way. His face clouded, his Harrison Ford fringe flopped over his eyes and he slumped to a 73. He wasn't the unbeatable giant he had been when he went head-to-head with Norman at St Andrews. An affair with twenty-one-year-old Arizona golfer Brenna Cepelak, a multi-million-dollar divorce, and the worst dustbin-digging excesses of the tabloids had left Faldo battered and bruised, and he hadn't contended in a major for two years.

Norman maintained his serenity even when his approach to the short twelfth was snatched by the wind and deposited on the bank between the front bunker and Rae's Creek. 'I never got mad because I hit the shot solid,' Norman explained. 'It'd be a different story if I hit a bad shot. Then it would be, "Why did you make a stupid mistake like that?" ' Instead, he walked calmly back to 81 yards – a distance from which, for reasons known only to himself, he claimed

215

he had hit 50,000 practice shots – and hit a sand-wedge to 10 yards for a lucky bogey. His eventual 71 left him on 203, 13 under par, six strokes ahead of Faldo and seven ahead of Mickelson. Scott McCarron, David Frost and Duffy Waldorf were a remote fourth on 212.

Afterwards, Faldo gave the predictable 'anything's possible with the heat on at Augusta' press conference, and Norman gave the predictable 'I'm just going to go out tomorrow and play as if we're all on the same number' speech. He seemed very contented and at ease. He was, as Butch Harmon said, 'finally at peace with Augusta'.

When Greg Norman was named Player of the Year in 1995, he told *Golf World* that he had an actual written list of things he still wanted to achieve: trek the Himalayas, dive under the polar ice-cap of Antarctica, fly in the Space Shuttle, cruise down the Amazon, land a jet on an aircraft carrier. Norman loves lists. On his Internet site were his seven favourite dives, ranked according to beauty, water quality or degree of difficulty, and the three he was planning to get to: Truk Lagoon, Micronesia, the Red Sea and Antarctica. In *Digest*'s 'One Man's Total' column, Norman claimed that he had flown 275,600 miles in 1995, used four drivers in his career, dived to 180 feet, beaten 7,000 practice balls most weeks and hit a tee shot 483 yards on the eighteenth hole of the King's Course at Gleneagles during an exhibition.

'Life, to him, is a check list,' said Rick Reilly. 'Fly F-14 jet – check; pat shark at the bottom of ocean – check. You wonder if he ever stops and says, "That was wonderful. I enjoyed that." '

At the top of Norman's check list was victory at the Masters. And there was no reason why he couldn't achieve it. Only Nicklaus had a higher top-ten finish percentage on the PGA Tour (53 per cent to Norman's 49 per cent). When the inevitable 'karma' question was asked in the Shark's pre-tournament interview, he said he believed things happen the way they are meant to. 'Sometimes you don't feel like you've got a chance to win or somebody else is running away with it and, boom, something happens and turns the whole game around just by the bounce of a ball. Why does the ball bounce that way? Those type of things you think about and reflect on. They all even out in the long run.'

On Sunday morning, Norman and Faldo stood on the first tee at Augusta, each lost in his own thoughts. It was hard not to feel that karma was at work, that it was finally evening things out for its most ill-used golfer. Up on the clubhouse lawn, Ben Crenshaw was talking to the television cameras. 'He's battling a lot of demons right now,' he speculated, about Norman's frame of mind. 'All third-round leaders battle those demons. He's said many, many times that he wants to win this one. He's prepared, his mind looks very strong. We'll see.'

On the first hole, Norman proceeded to pull his first drive and make bogey from a greenside bunker. It was an unfortunate start but he didn't seem rattled. He hit a beautiful chip to a couple of inches to match Faldo's birdie on the second, and they were off. Norman saved par at the third, bogeyed from the bunker at the fourth and parred when Faldo birdied the sixth. At the par five eighth, Norman pulled his three-wood second 30 yards left into the pines. The gallery muttered uneasily. Grimly, Norman gritted it out for par, his mouth a hard white line. Faldo birdied.

Settling down to watch the telecast in a hotel hundreds of miles away, Wayne Grady felt a sense of shock as the camera panned in on Norman, standing on the ninth tee with a three-shot lead. 'You could see in his face then that he was in trouble.'

Rodger Davis, who was in Bali doing a corporate day, experienced exactly the same feeling of dismay. 'There's not many things I'd feel sorry for Norman about, because he's made so much money and all this, but when it came on TV and I saw his face I thought, I don't believe this. He was on the eighth and he was still four in front but you could see it in his face . . . And his expression didn't change all day.'

Trevino once observed that hard hitters like Norman needed to learn to gear down in the closing rounds at Augusta. 'Once they start tucking those flags in back, you have got to sneak up on them . . . The problem with a hard hitter is he's got to fly the ball past the hole all the time. When they put them in back, you're a dead man.'

Norman was conscious only of his dwindling lead and Faldo's relentless march. On the ninth fairway, he fired a 98-yard wedge shot at a pin perched on a knoll as slippery as ice. Faldo was safely on the green, some 35 feet away. Norman's ball paused for a split second, then spun back 20 yards down the hill. There was a little gasp from the gallery and he seemed visibly to shrink. Faldo two-putted for par and Norman bogeyed. Two strokes separated them at the turn.

'The reason Nick Faldo is such a wonderful player is because he doesn't really care about being in there three feet,' Bruce Edwards says. 'He's going to put it in there where he's not going to make bogey. He won the British Open with eighteen pars which, God bless him, is how you play the game. The ninth hole at the Masters was a typical example. He didn't care that he was thirty-five feet by. He'll take his four. "Go ahead and make your mistake. Oh, you just did." '

'There's certain things you've just got to do at Augusta,' Davis says. 'Greg is a good enough player to do them, but I think at times all he sees is the flag.'

At the tenth, Frank Williams was rushing numbly down the hill in the sultry heat, panicking about Laura. 'She's a wreck,' he said. He wasn't doing too well himself. He covered his eyes as Norman missed his seventh green of the day, hit a weak chip to 10 feet and missed the putt. Faldo made a comfortable par. At the eleventh, Norman's 14-footer for birdie rimmed the hole. His hand shielded his white, frozen face. He missed the three-foot return and made another bogey. They were now level.

A sportswriter sidled up to Williams, who had separated himself from the clammy, nervous crowd and was standing beside a pine tree with his head in his hands. 'How do you feel around now?' he asked cheerfully.

Williams tried to disguise a murderous glare. 'Great,' he said. 'I have every confidence.' Crestfallen, the reporter scurried away. 'Christ,' Williams said. 'How does he think I feel?'

He walked over to Laura and Morgan-Leigh, who were clinging to each other on the rise above the short twelfth like the hypnotized witnesses of a car crash. Below them, Norman pushed his tee shot into the water. He took a double-bogey to Faldo's par. Wordlessly, Williams wrapped his arm around Laura. Norman's face had become a mask of pain. He drove woodenly into the pines on the thirteenth. A funereal silence cloaked the gallery, now in no doubt that they were helpless bystanders at the total disintegration of a champion's psyche. 'I feel sick to my stomach,' one spectator said. Another compared it to watching Old Yeller die.

In the locker room, Nick Price turned away from the television, picked up his car keys and drove to the airport. 'I couldn't watch,' he says. 'I knew how much the Masters meant to Greg. I knew what was happening and I didn't want to see it.'

'It was devastating,' Butch Harmon recalls. 'I walked around with Laura and Morgan-Leigh and it was one of those things where, as you watched it happen, you couldn't believe it. The man had played so well for three rounds. He just had such total control, not only of his swing but of his emotions. He had done everything right, and to see it all start to come apart was very difficult for a teacher to watch. More difficult for the hurt that not only he was going through, but his family was.'

Watching from the sidelines as Tony Navarro persuaded Norman to lay up, David Leadbetter was eerily perky. 'His routine has changed by six or seven seconds,' he commented. 'He's gripping the club and regripping it. He can't get comfortable.' Faldo, his own pupil, was a textbook study on how to stay calm and play smart in the pressure-cooker environment of Augusta's back nine. He hit the best shot he had hit all week, a 215-yard two-iron, to the heart of the green and matched Norman's birdie.

'We talked about this last night,' Leadbetter said breezily. 'I told him, nobody's shot a low number to win the Masters since you came from five behind to beat Raymond Floyd in 1990.'

Minute by minute, the life seemed to be ebbing from Norman's body. At the fifteenth, his 200-yard six-iron tilted towards the water but stayed up. Jaw clenched, Norman chipped for eagle. He put everything into it. His whole being seemed to centre on the hole, to will the ball towards it. Twenty thousand people held their breath as it rolled across the shiny green and slid tantalizingly close to the hole. Then it stopped cold, inches short. Norman, his putter raised in silent prayer, his face contorted with agony, fell to his knees, arched backwards and collapsed on the green.

'I hit the most perfect shot,' he says now. 'I put all my energies into it. I visualized it. Everything I know that I'm good at – feel, not executing till you're ready to go. And then when it didn't go in, I thought, Oh, shit. Then Faldo hit a great shot too, so I didn't even make up a shot. So that's when I knew. And the next shot was indicative of the emotions going out of my system.'

From that point on, Norman was, in Riley's words, 'a dead man walking'. On the sixteenth tee, his hands fidgeted, fussed and clenched the club like an executioner on his first day at the job. In a misguided attempt to pull off a miracle, he hooked his six-iron tee shot into the water. The resulting double-bogey left him four strokes behind, tottering blindly up the closing holes, gaunt with suffering.

Faldo looked shell-shocked himself. What should have been his finest hour had become tainted, and as he walked up the last, acknowledging, with the smallest of waves, the muted applause of the crowd, it is hard to imagine another player reacting with more humility, compassion or grace. Always portrayed as a cold fish – socially inept and mechanical – Faldo showed a degree of humanity in victory that brought tears to the eyes of the gallery. After holing a birdie putt on the last for a 67 to Norman's 78, he put his arms around his weary opponent and held him for a minute. 'I don't know what to say,' he told Norman, 'I just want to give you a hug.'

Afterwards, Faldo stumbled towards the cameras, choking on his words. 'From ten, eleven on, it was so nerve-racking it was unbelievable, so emotional . . .'

Norman was already headed towards his fifty-second second-place press conference, an affair of such dignity that Bobby Jones would have been hard pressed to beat it. Throughout it all, Norman was philosophical, candidly admitting that he 'played like shit . . . Call it what you want to call it, but I put all the blame on myself . . . My thought pattern was good but my rhythm was out,' and then using gentle humour to explain the worst collapse in major championship history.

'Greg, is it humanly possible not to dwell on a day like this, at least for a while?' someone asked.

Norman smiled thinly. 'Watch,' he said.

He glanced up at the television screen, on which Ben Crenshaw was helping Faldo into his third emerald blazer. '*God*, I'd love to be putting the green jacket on,' he said, 'but life's going to continue. I'm sad about it. I'm going to regret it. I've let this one slip away and I've let others slip away. But it's not the end of my life. I'll continue to win golf tournaments. I'm not going to fall off the face of the earth because of what happened here.'

Asked if he felt like screaming, he said softly, 'I don't know how I could ever convince you guys that I know I screwed up today, but it's not the end of the world for me. It's really not. I've got forty million bucks . . . If I had won today and all those other championships, my life might be totally different. But I didn't win. I am upset inside, but I'm not going to run around and be like a Dennis Rodman and head-butt an official. I'm not that way. I respect the game of golf we play. I love the game of golf. It's given me a lot and it's going to give me a lot more.'

'I honestly, genuinely feel sorry for him,' said Faldo, who hoped that this victory would be remembered for his performance rather than Norman's loss. 'What he has been through is horrible. If it had happened to me like that . . .' His voice trailed off. 'Greg's a great player, a great competitor, he really is. He's a great guy too. He's a credit to the game and the game needs him out there all the time. I think he's fantastic. The man's got the drive and the commitment and he'll be back.'

In the locker room, Harmon waited anxiously for Norman. He had walked off the course when the Shark hit his tee shot in the water at the sixteenth, unable to take any more. 'When he came in, I just went up to him and put my arms around him and said, "Greg, I can't tell you how bad I feel and how sorry I am for you," ' Harmon says. 'And he said, "Butchy, I just didn't have it today. My good shots weren't good enough and my bad shots were pitiful." And that was pretty much it.'

When it was all over, Norman drove out to the airport to board his jet. He was deeply touched that a small group of supporters had come to offer words of comfort and to praise him for his sportsmanship in defeat. He stood with them for a few minutes, signing photographs and chatting quietly. Then he climbed slowly up the steps to the aircraft, where his devastated family and friends were waiting. He looked at their pale, sad faces. 'I'm sorry I let you all down,' Norman said.

When they took off, Norman had a beer and talked to Laura. Somewhere over Florida, the mists closed in on him. 'Sorry for drifting off for a minute,' he said to Laura.

'Greg, you drifted off for over half an hour,' she told him gently.

When the plane touched down at West Palm Beach, they stayed on board and got deliriously drunk. 'Greg felt disappointed for us, and we felt disappointed for him, and nobody really knew what was going on or how anybody felt,' Laura recalls. 'We sat there for hours on the tarmac in the plane, just talking. Greg needed the support of the people around him. The loss was disappointing, of course. I know how badly Greg wanted to win the Masters. But he accepted it so much better than everybody else. I was very angry with a couple of the reporters, the way they described it like it was a funeral in our family. You know, we have such a good perspective on what's really important, and although a golf tournament is important, it isn't as important as the things that are going on in the world, people dying, people getting sick. As bad as everybody felt, we didn't think it was the end of the world.'

After the agony came the dissection. In Britain, the *Independent* documented the seven times the Shark had led a major going into the last day, winning only the 1986 Open, under the heading 'Norman's Chokes'. The *Augusta Chronicle*, the paper that helped create Norman's heroic nickname, used it against him on Monday: 'Shark Skinned,' screamed a banner headline. Jim Murray, the columnist who eulogized about him when he finished fourth in his first Masters, told his readers that, 'There's only one golfer on the planet that can regularly beat Greg Norman in a major tournament. That's Greg Norman.' The *Philadelphia Inquirer* said that the life had leaked right out of Norman. 'And if you took any pleasure at all in witnessing that then your heart is as hard as a tombstone.' *Golf Digest* compared it to other catastrophic collapses – Sam Snead's eight on the seventy-second hole of the 1939 US Open, and Arnold Palmer's 'bizarre unhinging' in the 1966 US Open when he squandered a seven-stroke lead in nine holes. In *The Times*, Mel Webb said, 'Norman seems to be a man specially selected by Kismet to be its stool-pigeon.'

Most players felt for him from the bottom of their hearts, but Chi Chi Rodriguez believed that Norman's collapse was 'God's way of punishing him for what he did to Mark McCumber. I don't think you ought to destroy a man's character that way.'

Callahan thought the epilogue to the Masters was more curious than the tournament. 'In the press-room post-mortem, the fifth word out of Norman's mouth was scatalogical. But the news that went out was how "classy" he was. "He's a real man," said the man from *Sports Illustrated*. "He is more a man for it," wrote the man from the *New York Times*. So manliness got a good going-over into the bargain. Be a man. Take it like a man . . . A minority in the audience thought Norman took it too much like a man, too blithely anyway. His eerie smile bothered them.'

On Sunday night, hours after the tournament, Norman and Laura went walking along the beach in Hobe Sound. They tried to discuss what had happened but little came of it. 'Never in my career have I experienced what happened between the tenth and fifteenth holes of Augusta last year,' Norman told *Golf* the next season. 'I was totally out of control. And I couldn't understand it.'

'That was his worst disaster, that one,' Peter Thomson says. 'There was no excuse for that, and there was no excuse of ill luck for that one. He did that himself. He just held on too tight. He has a faith in strength, whereas the real golfer is the opposite. The reason Hogan took about forty-five waggles before he ever hit a shot was to get the lightest possible grip of the club and still have it under control. He was about a hundred and eighty degrees from where Greg was at Augusta. [Greg] was trying to hang on tighter and tighter in the mistaken belief that that would get him where he wanted to go. And that was his downfall. When I watched him, he was trying to crush the club. It's a wonder the shaft didn't buckle. That was the worst thing that ever happened.'

When 'choking' – the ugliest word in the language and the cruellest, a word denoting cowardice and chronic fear of victory –

was held up as the cause of Norman's demise, Thomson refused to accept that Norman might have been eaten alive by nerves: 'He's never lost because he's been afraid, which is what choking's about. That's absolutely untrue. There was never that. But he had a faith in, I think, the wrong things, like hanging on tight and using strength.'

'You can't win seventy-one tournaments and be a choker,' Nick Price said flatly. 'You can't win ten tournaments and be a choker. I can tell you the guys on the Tour who are the chokers. They are the guys who are good players but they've won two tournaments in their whole careers. Something stops them playing well under pressure, and whether that's guts or that they're afraid of success . . . Those guys are the chokers.'

To Price, Norman simply lost confidence and never recovered it. 'But again, when he started playing poorly, he could have started playing more conservatively.'

'Greg does all right until the head comes off and the turnip goes on,' Jack Newton told *Golf Digest*. 'I don't think it's bad luck. He's had some bad breaks but you make your own luck, I think. Technically, there isn't much wrong either. The biggest flaw in his game is his course management. The bottom line is, it sucks.'

'Well, of course, Norman has got an awful lot of talent,' Cary Middlecoff told *Australian Golf Digest*. 'But he hasn't got a whole lot of sense, I don't think, about golf . . . What he did at Augusta this year was unbelievably bad. There are about eight or ten places on that golf course, no matter what the weather conditions, you avoid. He just made every mistake that he could make.'

But the sports psychologist Bob Rotella felt that, to victory-motivated players like Norman and Palmer, losing by one stroke or twenty made no difference. 'A lot of the world has trouble understanding that because most people are embarrassed to death about shooting a high number. A guy like [Norman], he wants to win or he doesn't care. They're the kind of guys who couldn't live with themselves if they didn't go for the flag.'

Everyone was an expert with an opinion. The teacher Peter Kostis thought that Norman would benefit from a ball with a lower spin rate. Johnny Miller said there were twenty-five ways Norman could have won but he chose the one way he could lose. Others felt that Faldo was a crucial factor. Faldo agreed. 'The key was for me to play with him on Sunday. If you're right there, then he can really keep a close eye on things.'

Butch Harmon thought the eleventh, where Norman hit two perfect shots and a near-perfect putt and made bogey, was the turning point. 'That, to me, was when all the air just went out of him.' Tom Callahan believed the twelfth, when Norman 'went for the pin . . . which small children know not to do,' was a classic miscalculation. 'That's when "good old match play" kicked in. That's when Janet Leigh went back into the shower.'

'The question is, was Greg Norman playing "Greg Norman" at Augusta or was he playing smart?' Mike Clayton wonders. 'You can have the image of Superman, flying round the world, but you have to be careful that you don't start playing the part of yourself in your own movie. You've got to say, "Well, I'm not going to be a Hollywood hero this time, I'm just going to be a regular guy . . ." Maybe he plays "Greg Norman" too much. Maybe he should start pretending he's Jack Nicklaus or Peter Thomson, instead of doing what people expect Greg Norman to do. You never saw Nicklaus make one of those mistakes, never mind five in a row.'

'It's one of those situations where everyone tried to put their finger on what happened,' Harmon says frustratedly. 'David Leadbetter said that his swing wasn't sound, which was ridiculous because it was very sound when he shot sixty-three and sixty-nine in the first and third rounds . . . I think it was more mental than physical.'

'I have to say, he might never recover from the Masters,' Newton says. 'The Larry Mize thing was big at the time but I think, being as resilient as he is, he got over it. This one he's got a real hang-up about because everyone, including me, has always thought that if he was going to win an American major it would be at Augusta because it's made for him . . . He may never recover from that. He wouldn't admit that.'

Eighteen months on, Norman believes he has recovered, that nothing could ever hurt him like the Mize defeat. 'It's just one of those things that just got away. That's the simplest way of putting it. I mean, it *hurt*. Tony [Navarro] hurt just as much as I hurt. Because it got away. There wasn't anything we could do about it. I should have been able to do something about it, personally and internally, but I couldn't. It was just one of those things that happen in life, and it happened for a reason . . . I'm a fatalist. I wish I had won it, but when I look back on it, I ended up a better person because I lost it. To me, that might be the shining light that comes out of it.'

# CHAPTER FIFTEEN

# GHOSTS OF AUGUSTA

'Destiny, the alchemy of fate and luck.'

JANE MENDELSOHN, *I WAS AMELIA EARHART*

ABOVE THE LUSH FLORIDA forests, the out-of-season hotels and the empty beach tapering into the distance, the sky was a gun-metal grey, shot through with sheet lightning. Terrifying white forks split the ocean. At Great White Shark Enterprises, Frank Williams was in his office with the blinds drawn. He was recovering from the migraine, which had caused him to spend most of the morning lying prone in the darkness. A big man, with wavy grey hair, fair skin and a booming voice as cosmopolitan as Norman's, he is as tenacious in business and as much in thrall to wealth and the good things in life as the Shark is. But like Norman he is softened by kindness.

Williams has known Norman for nearly twenty years, but when he took on Norman's management early in 1994, few people thought it would last longer than six months. 'He's not a great one for giving you continual pats on the back,' Williams admits. 'I mean, in four years he's told me perhaps three times what a great job I did for him. He's always ribbing me – "God, I think you could have done better"

– spurring me on, type thing. At times it's been a very stormy passage.' In the summer of 1997 they went for three months without talking until finally Williams couldn't stand it any more and marched into Norman's office. 'Is it over now?' he demanded.

Norman looked up from his papers. 'Is what over?' he asked innocently, knowing full well what Williams meant. Then they cleared the air and were friends again.

'When I first joined Greg as his manager, Steve Williams said to me, "From now on there will always be conflict, every day," ' Williams remarks. ' "If there's a hard way and an easy way, Greg will find the hard way." Now that's not one hundred per cent true, but there's a lot of truth in it. But that's what makes champions champions. They are different, they do go against the tide.'

If a man's character could be judged by the contents of his office, it would be virtually impossible not to like Norman. Laura's décor is almost poetically beautiful. From the Persian rugs to the dappled elevator casing, the fragrant bathrooms to the shark sculpture on the boardroom table, there is nothing in the building that doesn't look as if it cost a million dollars, and yet, with the exception of the giant blue mural of Norman beside the autograph-signing room, the overall picture is one of elegance. Even the pervading smell, of clean, expensive wood, is unforgettable.

Norman's office is large but not disproportionately so. Behind his chair stands a vibrant painting of the rich red earth of the Australian outback, and an organizer testifies to his frantic schedule. The walls are hung with framed photographs of the Shark with Nicklaus – 'To a great pro and friend, best regards, Jack' – with Clint Eastwood, Nigel Mansell, Ben Hogan and Nelson Mandela, and there are letters from Bill Clinton – 'I really appreciate you making time to play with me . . . I've been one of your biggest fans for a long time' – and Al Gore, among others. His shower is an appropriately macho blend of black marble and fluffy cream towels, and his bookshelves are dotted with little models of his various planes and boats, photos of his family and dog Foster, and books on game-fishing records, wine and fish.

Williams reaches up to his own bookshelf and takes down the most gratuitously cruel item of media coverage published since Norman's collapse at Augusta in 1996. A German magazine has used photo-manipulation to show Faldo putting a green jacket on Norman's shoulders. Williams has never forgotten the morning after the Masters nightmare. When he arrived at the office, he and Nina, Norman's secretary, took one look at each other and burst into tears. 'Greg came in and was a pillar of strength. You'd never have thought anything had happened. I don't know to this day how badly it affected him, I really don't. He does not dwell on the past. *Ever*.'

It was a changed Greg Norman who went to Hilton Head Island after the Masters. This being the most damning of all his defeats, he steeled himself for the worst, for the most vicious criticism and savage personal attacks. He wasn't prepared for compassion or kindness or for the ten thousand faxes and letters that poured into Great White Shark Enterprises, and onto his boat, *Aussi Rules* – moored near the MCI Classic – at a rate of one every three minutes. He wasn't expecting a national outpouring of emotion and empathy. 'I'm sick of getting tears in my eyes reading them,' Williams said. 'So many of them are about kids. So many of them are about how Greg was such a perfect role model for how to handle adversity.'

'My son said I'm still his hero, so that's all I ask,' Norman said.

When phone calls, telegrams and notes on his locker were added to the volume of support, Norman was visibly humbled and overwhelmed. 'Laura said to me, "You know, maybe this is better than winning the green jacket. Maybe now you understand the importance of it all." It's extraordinary how I reached out and touched people by losing . . . It's almost as though, like Laura said, you've won some aspect of it all but you didn't get the green jacket. It's like nothing that's happened and there are a lot of things I'll be able to cherish . . . The thing that makes me gladdest about all of this is that I've seen life in a different light. That's what I'm happy about.'

Everywhere Norman turned people were cheering for him, and his fellow professionals – the ones he thought were incapable of feeling anything but jealousy and scorn for him – shook his hand warmly and told him he was the best player in the world and that his graciousness in defeat was a credit to the game. Nicklaus, Floyd and Couples all telephoned. 'You know, I don't think Greg really realized how much people like him,' Davis Love said. 'I think one of the things that's come out of this is that he knows now how much the Tour players did not want to see it happen to him and that they wanted him to know that they didn't want to see it happen to him.'

Playing with Norman in a practice round, Price told him, 'You've earned more respect and more friends by handling yourself the way you did in the adversity that you faced than if you'd won three Masters in a row.'

Whether by accident or design, Norman was paired in opening rounds with Paul Azinger who, in the three years since he beat the Shark in the US PGA Championship play-off, had endured a horrific battle with cancer. 'I think I might have been the perfect pairing for Greg, as far as putting things into perspective,' Azinger said. 'We grind it out, but the reality is, he lost a tournament, I could have lost my life. In that regard, I might have been the guy he needed to look at for two days.'

Human nature being what it is, there was always going to be someone who took pleasure in Norman's misery and at Hilton Head it was an inebriated man the local police identified as Thomas J. Yarrington. 'Do you have a problem?' demanded Norman, when Yarrington heckled him on the eighteenth tee on Saturday.

'Why'd you choke last week? You cost me a lot of money,' the man yelled belligerently. Tony Navarro pounced on him and wrestled him to the ground. 'That's assault and battery and I'm going to sue Greg Norman,' yelled Yarrington, before being removed from the course and charged with disorderly conduct.

But every minute more letters came from good people, genuine people, people who cared, so many of them that Norman, who tries to reply to all his mail personally, paid $45,000 for full-page thank-you ads in *Golf World*, *Golfweek* and the *Sydney Telegraph*. Notes came from George Bush, Byron Nelson, Bob Hawke, Christopher Dodd from the US Senate, Augusta chairman Jackson T. Stephens, Butch Harmon, Tom Watson, Danny Sullivan and Scott Hoch, but often it was the ordinary people who said the most. Like ten-year-old David Tiffenberg from Forida:

> I have been playing golf since I was four years old. I hate, hate, hate to lose, but if I won every tournament I would quit golf

230

tomorrow. We can't always have our heart's desire, but failing can make us stronger. You are the best golfer in the whole world. Be happy and know that there are a million kids like me who love and respect you.

In response to Dave Anderson's lacerating critique of Norman in the *New York Times*, Robert M. Schmon wrote:

What makes Norman extraordinary and so utterly compelling to watch is not his indifference, but his obsession to win. This, mixed with his propensity for shot decisions that push the envelope, that are bold and often foolhardy, pull him apart from the ordinary, the safe and the bland, and into the wonderful world of our golfing fantasy and imagination.

By the time he finished thirteen strokes behind Loren Roberts and one ahead of Nick Faldo on Sunday, Norman knew that there had been an intrinsic change in his personality. 'The best thing is that I'm less cynical now, which is going to make my approach to the game much easier as years go by. It's easier to deal with situations when you know that people really care about you, it picks you up when you're feeling down. It's been an amazing few weeks. Missing two cuts, practising at home, playing great, playing at the Masters and then coming here. It's been a lifetime of experiences.'

In retrospect it was strange how quickly Norman reverted from the state of grace he found in the immediate aftermath of the Masters to his former cynicism. It was not immediately obvious. He returned from a three-week holiday full of vim and vigour and in no time at all was on his Gulfstream jet, rushing from a whirlwind site inspection of the TPC at Sugarloaf to the Memorial Tournament, and telling the *New York Times*, 'I want to be the hunted again. I want to have that six-shot lead again going into a Sunday of the US Open or the Masters . . . There'll be a situation where I'll be the hunter, sure, where I'll be a Faldo sitting four or five back. But I want that lead again, to be hunted, more for myself than for anything else.'

He conceded that there had been strategic errors at Augusta. 'I like my strategy ninety-eight per cent of the time,' he said. 'But when I think back at things I should have done at the Masters under those extreme firm conditions, maybe there are times, maybe half a dozen to ten shots out of seventy-two that you play differently. Think of the guys who have won the most majors – Jack Nicklaus and Ben Hogan – two of the most conservative guys who have ever played the game of golf. There's a reason why.'

Racing through America at 45,000 feet, Norman was full of fun and laughter, the picture of health after a week of diving and catching sailfish off the coast of Mexico with Laura, and Nick and Sue Price, and two weeks alone on the waves in the Bahamas. He had even found time to play recreational golf at Cat Cay with his brother-in-law and two crew members. 'In eighteen holes, I had eighteen beers,' Norman said, with a grin. 'When we ran out of beer, we went home.'

But when he reached Lytham for the Open in July, all memory of these happy moments had vanished without trace from his mind. 'I was a little bit down,' Norman said. 'I was not in the place I wanted to be. I did not have a good three-week break after Hilton Head. I didn't do anything that I planned on doing.'

To make up for it, he had just taken another two-week trip to the South of France and the Mediterranean. He appeared to be enjoying life but there were signs that he was suffering a delayed reaction to the Masters. There had, for instance, been the Greater Hartford Open débâcle. The defending champion, Norman had been forced to dis-qualify himself on Friday night after finding he'd played a non-conforming ball during the tournament. He was lying fourth at the time. A series of frantic phone calls to Maxfli and PGA officials confirmed that the balls Maxfli had given him to experiment with, an XS-7, XS-8 and XS-9, but had forgotten to tell him not to use in com-petition, were not on the USGA's list of conforming balls.

'It's been a Jekyll and Hyde season for me,' Norman said at Lytham. 'I had a good start, but the last six or eight weeks have not been very stellar at all. I think it is a patch that I'm going through and hopefully I will dig myself out of that patch this week with a victory . . . Like any job, you get into a rut, that's all. You have to figure it out, do something different, take a vacation to stimulate what you're going back to.'

At the Open, Norman was stimulated enough to tie for seventeenth place but back in the United States his life began to unravel. In the first instance, he dispensed with the services of Butch Harmon. 'If you look at Greg's record in 'ninety-three, 'ninety-four, 'ninety-five, he was by far and away the best player in the world,' Harmon says. 'I don't know how anybody could play better than he played. But in 'ninety-six, he started to stray away from some of the things that I liked him to do and he wanted to go back to some of the stuff he did back in 'eighty-six – get his swing a little steeper, get his swing longer. He felt it took the pressure off his back. And for some reason we just started to grow apart, teaching-wise . . . I worked with him up to the US PGA and then we decided to go our separate ways.'

According to Harmon, their parting was personal, not swing-related. 'Greg and I had a misunderstanding . . . He was upset about something I had talked to one of his companies about and it just irritated him so much that he said, "In the best interests of our friendship, I think it's better that we should go our separate ways." Which actually, honestly, worked out best for me because I was not going to be able to work with both Greg and Tiger Woods.'

Norman's initial reaction to the 'misunderstanding' was to go berserk. As long as he had worked with the Shark, Harmon had worn Greg Norman Collection clothing, emblazoned with Cobra logos, but when Cobra was sold and Tiger Woods was on the verge of signing with Nike, Harmon's agent suggested they get a Nike deal.

Harmon claims he told his agent to try to do a deal with the president of Norman's company first, because he would be 'very uncomfortable walking out on a tee with Greg Norman wearing Nike clothes'. At the time, Woods was still an amateur and Harmon says he felt loyal to Norman. Frank Williams's version is a little different.

'Butch's agent rang and said, "I'd like to get in touch with the guy at Reebok,' Williams recalls, 'so I put him in touch with Richie, who runs Greg Norman apparel, and he was apparently making demands of Richie for X amount of dollars and Richie got a little pissed off about it and told Greg and Greg blew up. To Butch, it was a very petty thing. To Greg, it was a major thing because Greg is, "You're either for me or you're against me. You're either one hundred per cent – not *ninety-nine per cent* – one hundred per cent with me, or you're not with me," and that's the way he is. Butch tended to blame me. He said some pretty nasty things about me, too, and I never did anything but good for Butch. I made him a lot of money. And that was the whole reason he left.'

'It really wasn't that they were going to *pay* me,' insists Harmon. 'I was going to do a number of clinics or exhibitions for him at my fee and that's how I would get repaid for wearing the clothes, which Richie had no problem with. But unfortunately when the story got back to Greg, he was told something totally different and he just flew off the handle . . . He got extremely upset with me and that's really what the whole deal was about. Since then he has apologized to me and said he was totally wrong, he was given the wrong information and the thing that he said that made me feel so good was, "I don't know why I was so mad because you have the right to get any deal you can get." As I told him later, "Greg, I was trying to do the right thing by you." '

While the Harmon situation simmered away in the autumn of 1996, Norman busied himself with another feud, this one with David Graham. At Lytham, Norman had attended a meeting on the Presidents Cup, a Ryder Cup-type duel between the United States and the Rest of the World, during which Graham was unceremoniously ousted as captain.

'The Presidents Cup was about the worst insult I ever had in golf,' Graham, the former US Open Champion, told the golf writer Lorne Rubenstein. However, he was less concerned about the circumstances that led to him being forced to resign than about the role Norman played in the situation. This was not entirely unreasonable. Norman had been very vocal about Graham's organizational abilities, or lack thereof. 'We're all very concerned,' he said in late June. 'It's like walking into a room full of fog – you don't know what the heck's going on. You've got to get the team camaraderie going early. It's like we're not even playing a golf tournament.'

Two years earlier, Norman had been forced to withdraw from the event when he had haemorrhoid surgery. When he turned up on the last day to support his team, CBS asked him if he would wear a microphone for the telecast. Graham put his foot down. 'The Presidents Cup is not Greg Norman's tournament,' Graham said

234

nastily. 'It's a twelve-man team, it's not Greg's team.' Norman was spitting mad.

During the second Presidents Cup, Graham received two phone calls from the Shark, one of which was an attempt to convince him that he had not instigated Graham's departure. 'The second was to tell me what he thought of me in no uncertain terms, that our friendship was over and that he never wanted to talk to me again,' Graham recalled. 'I said, "Hey, your choice." I don't know why he said those things.'

Probed by Rubenstein, Norman admitted it was true. 'David was way out of line for telling you that,' he said. 'It was a private conversation. But I did tell him those things. Did he also tell you that at the end of our conversation he apologized for accusing me of wrongdoing?'

In actuality, Graham did not own up to saying sorry at all. 'I've even told Greg on the phone that if he could prove to me that he was not responsible, then I certainly owe him an apology,' he explained. 'But on the other hand, I can't stop thinking that I've known Greg Norman for over twenty years, and he was the number-one ranked player in the world, and part of the responsibility of being the number-one player in the world is to ask, "Now, what's right and what's wrong in this situation?" . . . The thing that hurts me the most is that he didn't try to stop it.'

At the end of the day, it didn't matter who was the ring-leader at the meeting, only that victory was so important to the members of the International team that all twelve of them sanctioned the casting aside of Graham. Gary Player described the way those dozen players handled the situation as 'a total disgrace, a humiliating embarrassment' for Graham, which had damaged the image of the game. The PGA Tour bowed to pressure from the foreign players and Peter Thomson was installed as captain.

'A lot of guys were gunning for him,' Mike Clayton says of David Graham, who has been left scarred by the experience. 'He'd pissed off Ernie Els because he had criticized Ernie the time before for not playing when Ernie had committed to play in the Dunhill Cup, and it's pretty hard to piss off Ernie. A lot of guys, when they came back from the first Presidents Cup, said he hadn't done that great a job.'

Frank Williams says that Norman, whose team lost by a point to the United States, was taken totally by surprise when he was made the scapegoat for Graham's departure: 'At the British Open meeting, apparently one started complaining, "Well, David never tells us anything and he's so arrogant and he made my wife leave in the middle of the banquet," and then another guy chipped in and then they all chipped in and they all had their own little grievances about Graham.'

Steve Elkington and Nick Price backed him up. 'It had nothing to do with Greg,' the Australian said.

A year on, Graham remains bitter about Norman's perceived role in the mutiny. 'It'll take more than that son-of-a-bitch to put me out of business,' he said.

All in all, it amounted to a blood-pressure-raising September for Norman. He also found time to have a blazing row with Tim Finchem, cornering him in the lobby at the Westfields Conference Center in Virginia during the Presidents Cup. Shortly before the start of the singles matches on Sunday, the US Tour commissioner had announced the formation of a 'federation' that would sanction three World Tour-type events in 1999. 'I've had it up to here with Tim Finchem,' Norman raged the next day. 'It's the end of the rope for me. He hung me out to dry.' He was particularly angry that Finchem appeared not only to have stolen his World Tour idea but to have taken advantage of Fox's interest in golf. 'Hopefully, Greg and I can work through this,' Finchem said feebly.

Norman's response to this series of controversies was to endeavour to prove that when he had 'forty million bucks' in winnings to keep him happy, he really meant it. 'With my performance thus far in 1996, which includes a win at Doral, my career earnings are now over ten million dollars,' he wrote on his Internet site. Two weeks after the Hartford incident he had signed an $18 million deal with Maxfli, and he skipped the World Match Play to clinch a deal in Chicago. He failed to appear at the pro-am for the prestigious, season-ending Tour Championship, first citing mechanical problems with his jet and then saying, 'I just had to reshuffle some things,' and then left before the final round.

He was still seething over the World Tour business. 'It's like somebody cutting off your arm. You can try to mend it but you never really get it back.'

On Norman's parking plaque at the Tour championship, somebody had written: 'GONE FISHIN'.'

Greg Norman, shiny under the glare of the television lights, sat on a sofa beside Laura wearing an expression that could have been bemused rapture but might just as easily have meant 'Too fucking little, too fucking late.' It was September and an Australian presenter was waving that famous red book. 'Greg Norman, this is your life,' he cried, as he wheeled out Arnold Palmer, Bob Hope and the usual procession of childhood acquaintances Norman had probably hoped he would never see again.

Then they brought out Toini and Merv. Norman embraced his mother warmly and gave a quick, cool hug to his father, taking care not to allow his immaculate Nehru suit to touch Merv's body. 'So,' enthused the presenter, 'did you think Greg would end up as [the world's best] golfer?'

'He could have spread out into a few other things, but this one will do,' Merv said.

For much of his adult life, Norman had tried to penetrate Merv's reserve, to cut down the emotional wall that would allow his father to put his arms around him and say, 'I love you, I'm proud of you.' But to no avail. A product of his generation, Merv found it difficult to display physical affection and even harder to accept Norman's lavish lifestyle. 'Sometimes I used to think, Wouldn't it be great to give my dad a big hug? God, wouldn't that be great? I haven't seen him in so long,' Norman told *Sports Illustrated* shortly before the Masters. Instead he went for months without calling him. 'What's the point?' he said. 'I can't get anything out of him anyway.'

There is little doubt that Norman's personality – his obsessive drive and his constant need to reinvent himself in different superhero modes (saviour, top-gun, petter of sharks) – is inextricably bound to his relationship with his father. 'My father made me the individual I am because of his strength of character and my mother gave me the emotions,' Norman says, and Laura is not alone in thinking that the events of Augusta and Norman's lifelong conflict with Merv might be linked.

'We tried to discuss what happened at the Masters,' says Laura.

'You know, I do not believe Greg choked. He works his butt off to win, he loves that feeling. Greg has been there too many times to choke. Some people say, well, the whole thing with his dad came up, he wanted to please his dad too much. Who could ever know what happened? It could be very complex, it could be very simple. Maybe he did want it too much and he put too much effort into it. The fact is, it didn't happen.'

'In America, the cliché – maybe because there are so many fatherless kids in the ghettos – is that when you home in on a lineman at the Superbowl, he always goes, "Hi, Mom!" ', says Tom Callahan. 'I think that if they homed in on golfers, they'd all go, "Hi, Dad!" because I think it's a father's game. Deacon Palmer is the clue to Arnold . . . Harry Player was that goldminer . . . Payne Stewart, his father died and if you mention it today, he'll start weeping . . . All the guys who have the most vinegar in them, the way to sweeten them up is to say, "Tell me about your dad." '

Callahan's theory has Tiger Woods and Jack Nicklaus as the ultimate dad guys. 'When Charlie Nicklaus died, Jack lost weight, took charge of his life, got off the phone with Charlie and became a man. Barbara will tell you that. The year his father died, Tom Weiskopf, who everyone regarded as a wasted talent, became the best player in the world. The kind of Rosetta stone to all these guys, to me, is their dads. They're all dad guys with two exceptions: Faldo and Greg Norman. They're mom guys. Faldo's mother probably couldn't break an egg but she'd be in the kitchen and he'd be on the porch, he's practising his swing and she's saying, "Give me one more knuckle." And Norman's mother was a player. But mom guys in golf are pretty rare.'

Frank Williams compares Merv to the father of Ken Venturi, who scoffed at his son's dreams and then, when he became successful, told him to prove it wasn't a fluke. Only on the day that Venturi came to him and said, 'Dad, I don't know if I'm going to be able to play golf again, I think I'm going to lose three fingers,' did he reveal the depth of his feelings. 'Don't worry,' he told his son. 'I've seen the best, and it was you.'

'The doctors could have cut my arm off, it wouldn't have mattered,' Venturi said.

'I think it's that kind of relationship,' Williams says of Merv and Norman. 'I think his father wants him to achieve again and again, and I think he's doing what Venturi's father did to him . . . We all like to get recognition from our parents – it's the ultimate recognition . . . I don't know if Greg has ever got the feedback that he would like . . . I'd say his father's not used to hugging people. But I've always found Merv OK. I think he's a strict, down-the-line, black-and-white guy.'

'His father was a rather severe, tough individual, whereas his mother was a very gentle, very supportive individual,' James Marshall recalls. 'I would say Greg had a lot of conflicts with his father. His mother was a wonderful woman . . . I think his father probably found it hard to turn to Greg and say, "Well, done, that was bloody good." Whereas, his mother was very supportive.'

Tom Ramsey is one of the few who have seen a different side to Merv. 'I think his father's a tremendous fellow, really a good and genuine man. I really like his father. I relate to his father very well. I find his father very much a warm, people person, and I think Greg is not a people person, even though that's his image.'

'There were a lot of things said about his dad not being support-ive,' Laura says. 'His father is very proud of him. He doesn't know sometimes exactly how to show it but he has his own way of doing it. People around his father know he's very proud of Greg. It's just that he's from the old school. He doesn't understand Greg's lifestyle, the way Greg is. Greg is so different from his dad. Greg is very flam-boyant in a lot of ways, his dad is extremely conservative. So there's conflict there but it isn't that his dad didn't support him. He did but his mother was the golfer. She was the one who, while his father was working, would drive him to the golf course and pick him up.'

At the same time, she admits that Norman's desperation to please his father is a likely key to both his character and his success. 'I think that sometimes that can happen . . . It could be that because he was looking for approval and wanted to show his father how good he was, that's what spurred him on. I don't know. One psychologist could say, "That's the reason." Another could say, "How come those guys who have really supportive fathers that were golf coaches are so good?" I think it's unfair to make an assumption of that. It's very possible that

Greg could have become so successful for that reason, but I just think Greg is a very driven person. He wants to be good at everything. That's just his personality. So whether that originated from trying to please his dad or not, I don't know ... I think that Greg could also get to the point where he could start thinking, Is it my dad? I don't think he really knows. And I don't think that anybody will ever know.'

Partly because of his background and partly because of the animosity his wealth and attitude arouses on the PGA Tour, Norman has, he feels, always struggled to form close bonds with other men. 'I feel sorry for Greg,' Laura told Rick Reilly. 'What's happened is really sad. I know Greg would love to have a close male friend, someone to get drunk with and just tell anything. But there's nobody.'

What made this statement slightly disturbing is that for years Norman had talked about his friendships with everyone from Jack Nicklaus to Nick Price, and yet when it came down to it, he seemed to feel he had left his real friends behind in Australia. 'My best friends, outside my wife, are the people I pay a salary to,' Norman says.

Bruce Edwards didn't find this surprising in the least. 'Curtis Strange used to be his best friend, won't talk to him any more. Curtis Strange used to joke with me and refer to Greg as "our buddy. Hear what our buddy did the other day?" But that's what he does. He likes to surround himself with the top people and then when they're no longer the top people or they put him off, they're out. There was a football player who was a great running-back with the New York Giants, Tucker Fredrickson. He was one of Greg's big mates in Palm Beach. I asked someone the other day: "Have you seen Tucker Fredrickson?" He said, "Oh, he and Greg aren't talking." And I thought, That doesn't surprise me at all. It just follows the course with Greg. And it's too bad. That's why he's lonely. That's why he doesn't have any friends.'

Even Norman's friendship with Nicklaus has cooled. 'I don't see Jack that much,' Norman explains. 'His life and career have gone in a different direction. I hardly ever see the man. Yeah, we're still friends, but not like Nicky Price or Ray Floyd.'

'Greg's an extremely loyal person,' Steve Elkington told Hodenfield. 'If you're on the right side of him, fine. If you're on the wrong side, he won't give you the time of day. That's the way a lot of people are in Australia. We don't buddy up with everybody. And in his position, everybody wants to be his friend.'

'I get hurt when I read in the paper that he hasn't got any friends,' Frank Williams says. 'I mean, he has twenty or thirty friends that work for him. I don't think Greg realizes how good some of his friends are.' He sighs heavily. 'There's a part of Greg that's very private. I consider myself a friend of his but there will always be a part of Greg that I will never get to know. I think he just holds that last bit back. But I know that if I was ever in trouble or I needed him, he'd be there. Good friend to have. Terrible enemy. I get very emotional about Greg, I really do. I don't like to be emotional – he's the only male that I am emotional about apart from my kids – but he brings it out in me for some reason. I feel passionately about him, and a lot of the people around him do.'

But either Norman doesn't see that or he chooses to overlook it. When Laura first came out on the Tour, she recalls the wife of a top player telling her not to expect to have many friends if Norman became the best golfer in the world. Now she feels it's true. 'Part of it is Greg's personality. Greg makes a wonderful friend because he's a very giving, caring, considerate person, but I think people are intimidated by him. They're just not sure how to approach him and over the years he's become a little defensive so maybe he's more unapproachable now. And I think as you get older you don't need as many friends. You don't have as much time for them. In our life, anyway.'

The strange thing is that people who care deeply about Norman and feel they share a bond with him are everywhere. 'He's a great guy,' says Elkington, who enjoys fishing, hunting and sharing a beer with Norman. 'He's fun to be around.' Price talks glowingly about their relationship. 'People don't see the side of him that I see and a lot of his close friends see. He's a very generous and warm person. In our time as friends, we've had a really good time together and I've enjoyed every minute of it. What people don't realize is that he's very generous to kids, to other Australian guys and other professionals.'

Bill Longmuir has remained a loyal friend to Norman and Norman to him throughout the years. 'He's terribly misunderstood,' Longmuir says. At the 1995 Open at St Andrews, he bumped into the Australian in the locker room, not realizing that Norman was suffering excruciating back pain and had played poorly as a result. 'There wasn't any talk of his bad finish, it was just, "You'll make the cut," ' Longmuir remembers. 'We got chatting. I'd had a bit of a bad time with my personal life and he mentioned it, said he had heard. Just then a couple of R & A officials came down into the changing room. And this is what you have to understand about Greg to understand the man. We were having a personal conversation and these two officials walked up and said, "Greg, could you give us your autograph?" I thought he was going to punch their lights out. He said, "Just wait over there, please," and then we continued talking with these guys listening. I felt so awkward. I don't get much time with him and it was a precious moment. And to have these guys break in on it . . .'

Away from the Tour, with its broken dreams and fleeting bonds, Norman's home life is, in spite of persistent rumours to the contrary, secure, happy and relatively normal. He works extremely hard at being a good father, offsetting his long absences by spending quality time with his children when he is at home, helping them with their homework or taking them fishing. At tournaments and at home, Morgan-Leigh and Gregory come across as well-mannered and well-balanced kids. 'I don't think people realize what a wonderful father Greg is,' Laura says.

'One of the most fascinating things in my life now is being a parent,' Norman says.

Williams envies Norman's ability to communicate with his children. 'He's loving, affectionate, firm, converses with them at length . . . I think he's a much more involved father with his children than perhaps his own father was. I think that's an education process from Laura, because Americans . . . show their feelings. They're not afraid to embrace or kiss, whereas the English and the Australians and people of that extraction are . . . So I think, in that respect, Laura has been exceptionally good for Greg. You know, he portrays this macho image. I'm not sure he's as macho as he makes out. I think he's much more caring and feeling than he lets on. I think he has an enormous amount of softness in him that he doesn't want to show.'

'I think there's a sensitive guy in there,' Elkington agrees. 'Not super-sensitive, but I think he cares about things.'

'As you get more successful, you become more reclusive in a lot of ways, so you become very close to the people around you,' Laura says. 'Greg and I have become so family-oriented and towards each other that we really are best friends. The way we're different is that he's like the Energizer Bunny. Gregory and I are homebodies, and Morgan and Greg are more "Let's see how much we can do in one day." That's great because we keep each other in balance . . . If I was like him, we would go until he ran out of juice.'

When he is at home, Norman rises at 5 a.m., answers his e-mail, takes his children to school, exercises, eats breakfast and is off and running. His Hobe Sound house, built in 1902, sits on eight acres of land between the ocean and the intercoastal waterway. It has a gym, a beach-house, two guest flats, a putting green, a basketball court and Labradors VB, Foster and Miller – named after beers.

'His house is beautiful,' says Bruce Edwards. 'I mean, it's everything money can buy. He's got all the toys . . . But I think he's very lonely, if you want the truth.'

'His home life is very ordinary,' Williams says firmly. 'It's a big home, beautifully decorated, but it's a house which, although opulent, is very comfortable. When you sit down, you don't feel as if you're in a show house . . . [Greg] cooks the barbecue, helps with the washing-up, helps around the house.'

'Our home is a home,' Norman says. 'It's not overstated.'

Laura describes their life as simple. 'People expect our house, for some reason, to be glitzy. Our house is really a home. We've got two kids that have friends over all the time. Our house is just big over-stuffed furniture. It's really comfortable, nothing pretentious at all.' But in the midst of all this ordinariness, there is the extraordinariness that famous people have a tendency to see as normal. The *Hello!* version of down-to-earth existence. 'When we added on a new wing to the house,' Laura continues, 'from the main house to the children's wing, I put in this gallery, and that's where the trophies are now. I don't have golf pictures up in the house or the office. The trophies are with us, as they should be, but they're not all over the house . . . At the end of the day, Greg and I are just normal everyday people. Our lives are very high profile because of Greg's job, but we are no different than we were before Greg became successful. Even though we have a butler, I send him home and we do the cooking and Greg helps with the dishes and we go out and walk the dog. We do all the things that other people do.'

To her, Norman's best quality is 'his sensitivity towards his family, the way he is with the children, the way he is towards me. His biggest strength is his mind. He's the one person I've seen that I believe could do anything he set his mind to. His weakness is probably his vulnerability. He does get upset about the things that are said about him. When he's out on the golf course, he hears things and he gets angry. Now I wish he wouldn't let that stuff bother him, but he does, and he gets back to his old days of being an Australian kid who wants to come out fighting. That part of him is a weakness. He lets too much outside stuff affect him.'

# CHAPTER SIXTEEN

## THE POLITICS OF ENVY

'Greg, as I say, thrives on the press. If the press stopped writing about Greg, or he didn't get the attention he gets, it would be like taking the sun away from a flower.'

JAMES MARSHALL, MARCH 1997

FOR WEEKS CLEAN-CUT secret servicemen had been there, with their hammers and fibre-optic phonelines, poring over the beach cottage with a magnifying glass. They were preparing for President Clinton's visit. Following the success of their friendly game of golf at New South Wales Golf Club in Sydney in November, Norman and Clinton now spoke on a 'weekly basis' on the phone, and Norman had invited the 13-handicap, golf-mad President to spend a night at his home in Hobe Sound before they teamed up for a two-day member-guest tournament at the Medalist in March 1997.

Because the events of the 1996 Masters had entered international vernacular, Clinton had spent much of the previous year cautioning anyone who expressed optimism at his lead in the polls with the words 'Remember Greg Norman.' It didn't bother Norman. He himself was a staunch Republican but he maintained they got along well. 'There's really a nice chemistry between us,' he said. 'I think we share some personality traits. We have a similar attitude toward life. I think he's a real man's man.'

He was looking forward to showing the President around the Medalist. 'It's a great honour but it will be very low key,' Norman said. 'The President wants to play golf, work out in my gym, putt on the green in my backyard, have a few cold beers and a couple of quiet dinners. He values occasions when he can be a regular guy.'

Clinton was continuing a long tradition of White House golfers, but Norman's depiction of a close friendship between them was met with a degree of scepticism. 'There's an awful lot that, I'm afraid, is total utter bullshit,' James Marshall says sorrowfully. 'Who said he talks twice a week to Clinton? I would personally doubt it. And if Greg said it, I certainly wouldn't believe it. See, he's given to gross exaggeration sometimes . . . it's hard to draw the line between what's fantasy and what's real . . . That [story] that it was the Air Force or golf. It's a load of bullshit. Greg no more would have qualified academically to get into the Australian Air Force than fly to the moon. Greg was no Einstein when he left school and that story that has been perpetuated over the years that he was either going to be a fighter pilot or a golfer is sheer garbage.'

Tom Ramsey was of a similar mind. 'I think he's opinionated about too many things other than golf, when he doesn't have the background, or the education, to be.'

'Greg was fortunate that he was blessed with a gift for playing golf,' Marshall continues. 'That has been his passport to success in life . . . Greg is not the sort of person, in my view, about whom you could say had he not been a golfer he would have been a rocket scientist or a doctor . . . I think, if you take away all the façade and all the bullshit, Greg is just a very ordinary guy. He's not a Peter Thomson, who would have been highly successful in any field. He's not a Graham Marsh, who is a very bright guy.'

That said, preparations continued apace for the President's visit on 13 March. 'The Secret Service looked at everything,' Laura says. 'There was this patch of grass and they said, "If he's going to walk from here to here, we need to have you put in some paving stones, if you wouldn't mind." They were very nice about it. And we said, "No problem."'

When Clinton finally arrived, he was late. It was after midnight and Laura was in bed but she got up to watch from the window as the motorcade rolled up the drive. Clinton stood on the front steps talking to Norman. Food had been prepared for him over at the beach cottage, but he wanted to come into the main house. Contrary to popular belief, he refused a beer and drank a Diet Coke. He was plainly exhausted and kept yawning. Laura drifted in and out of sleep, catching snatches of conversation.

'I've always been impressed about the man being a man,' Norman said enigmatically, 'but as I said to him . . . "You're just a damn good person."' They discussed 'life', China and the Constitution, on which Norman had a few thoughts.

A little before 2 a.m., Laura woke with a start as a dark figure loomed at the end of the bed. 'They've just taken the President away in an ambulance,' Norman said plaintively.

Laura sat up in bed with a shriek. 'I said, "Come on, that's not funny,"' she recalls. 'Because he knew my biggest fear was that [Clinton] would get food poisoning or get shot while he was at the property. You know, something awful. He said, "Word of honour, they've just taken him away in an ambulance." And I can't even describe what that feels like. The President of the United States has fallen down your steps. Greg caught him, thank goodness, because he would have gone back and hit his head, but it was a traumatic time.'

At 1.20 a.m., Norman had been escorting the President to his quarters when Clinton tripped on a step that had been coloured to blend in with the concrete landing and tore the quadriceps tendon in his right knee. By one forty-five, he was on his way to a hospital in Bethesda, Maryland, for an operation. He would spend up to eight weeks in a leg brace and his summit with Boris Yeltsin would have to be postponed.

Chaos reigned as America woke up to pictures of an ashen President emerging from hospital in a wheelchair. Helicopters circled Norman's house, photographers camped out in the bushes, boats ferried tourists past the infamous steps where the President took a tumble, and Norman was inundated with interview requests from every talk show in the country – all of which he turned down – all wanting to know exactly how Clinton came to suffer a freak accident

247

at the home of golf's most star-crossed player. 'Every time I turned on the television, there was this picture of him, and I kept thinking, My God, this happened at our house,' Laura says. 'It was an awful feeling.'

On the other side of the planet, far from Norman's glamorous, power-broking existence, Charlie Earp sat on the peaceful, lager-scented balcony of Royal Queensland. He was contemplating his ex-pupil's future. 'If he could win one of the majors, it would make a big difference to Gregory Norman,' he said. 'Dear God, let him win one.'

He was a little put out that Norman had traded his more traditional methods for new-fangled teachers like Harmon and, more recently, Leadbetter. 'I just teach natural stuff. I don't go in for any of this bio-mechanical business,' he says. 'The golf swing's been going for three or four hundred years, and the things they're trying to do! Robot stuff. I'm what Greg would probably refer to as an eye coach . . . I can *see* the problems. A lot of the old coaches can. I just don't go for the gurus. They're just trying to teach everybody to play the same way. Everybody's different to me.'

In October 1996, Norman had gone to see Leadbetter at Lake Nona at the suggestion of Nick Price. They had spoken on the phone once before when Norman wanted advice on improving his short-irons, and Leadbetter had told him to point his thumb at his ear at the top of the backswing. 'He doesn't like to get into detailed mechanics. He's such a great natural athlete, he just likes to stand up to the ball and hit it.'

When Norman came to see him about a full-time coaching arrangement, Leadbetter was struck by how different he was from his image. 'He's actually quite an introvert. You know, he's really a nice guy and he's got a lot of high values . . . He's a workaholic, too. He's certainly a fun-loving guy, but he's very private too. He really has very few close friends. He's very family-oriented.'

Inevitably, they discussed the Masters. 'To be honest, the problems he had last year at Augusta were more physical than mental,' Leadbetter says. 'They became mental after a period, but initially they were physical. He didn't have any trust in his swing.' Watching him hit shots, he thought Norman's swing was too flat, too tight and too restricted, and that the clubface was shut. 'Coming into the ball, he really had to manipulate his body out of the way to try to hit it. So he was losing a lot of distance and really didn't have a lot of control with his irons, which was very noticeable at Augusta last year. I suggested that we narrow his stance, get him turning behind the ball, and get him freed up to the point where his swing is somewhere between where Butch Harmon got it and where he used to be many years ago. The turning action is really what's helped his spine and his back in general. And he's very confident. He says, "Hey, my swing feels great, David . . . I'm feeling good about it." '

Likening himself to Nicklaus, Norman told *Golf World* that he had switched to a flatter swing for exactly the same reasons the Bear did after the 1986 Masters – because he was unhappy with his swing. 'At first it worked,' reported Norman, 'but soon he was struggling . . . In my case, I was fed up with golf after a slump in 1991. That was when Butch Harmon convinced me to take an extra-wide stance and make a flat swing. Like Jack, I played great for a while. However, let me go on record for the first time and say that this swing always felt unnatural, led to over-rotation of my forearms, hips and shoulders and was hard on my back. This flatter action failed me at last year's Masters, where I mishit shots under pressure.'

In an intriguing twist, Bruce Edwards says that Harmon told Tom Watson and himself that, before he turned to Leadbetter, Norman asked Nicklaus if *he* would consider coaching him. 'Jack said, "Greg, I'm not a coach, I'm a golfer. I'm not one of those Leadbetters." '

In December, two weeks after he started working with Leadbetter, Norman won the Australian Open by eight shots. In the first weekend of January, he collected $1 million for beating Scott Hoch in the Andersen Consulting World Championship of Golf – one of those surreal multi-million-dollar events nobody cares about with a format that demands a Mensa membership. At that point, he had been the world number one for 291 of the 560 weeks the rankings had been in existence. Curiously, he had won the world money list just once in its thirty-year history, in 1986. Nicklaus had topped it seven times.

Two months later, he lost a three-man play-off for the Dubai Desert Classic, handing the title to an Australian rookie called Richard Green. It was his first full tournament since October and he was relaxed and charming after a three-month break to rest his ailing back. During that time, he had taken a two-week golf-design trip through Asia, dropped into Morocco for twelve hours for a dinner engagement, changed from a wound to a two-piece ball, put a little work into the World Pitch and Putt Company, prepared to open a chain of restaurants called Greg Norman's Down Under Grille in Myrtle Beach, South Carolina, Orlando, Palm Beach, etc., and endorsed a golf aid called The Secret.

'Greg doesn't need Lead, he's got The Secret,' Faldo said facetiously.

At the back of Norman's mind Augusta loomed large, the crucible of humiliation to which he had to return. He had already begun receiving huge quantities of supportive mail. After the 1996 Masters, he had taken more time off than ever before, had dropped to 149th place in greens in regulation, seen his scoring average rise by three-quarters of a shot per round and missed four cuts for the first time in his career. Asked at Doral how he was going to deal with this year's Masters, he said simply, 'I never run away from anything, guys. I've always stood facing the music.' He grimaced. He had a baseball cap on and his blond hair dripped with sweat. 'I accept the fact that I made a mistake. It was all my fault. If you people want to keep talking about it, writing about it, so be it. It's not going to affect me. I look forward to going back to the Masters with just as much passion as I had before things happened last year.'

He had decided that his Tuesday press conference at Augusta was positively the last time he was going to speak about it. Until then, he resigned himself to discussing it at the Players Championship. He was less happy to talk about Clinton. 'I think from my wife's point of view and mine, we were looking forward to having a friend over for a couple of days,' Norman said, making the President's visit sound like a pyjama party, 'and as it turned out, that friend hurt himself . . . But looking behind every dark cloud, there is a silver lining. Maybe slowing him down a little bit might have been good for him.'

At one stage, Tim Finchem arrived to help Norman dispel the notion that a cross word had ever passed between the two of them. They sat like a couple of born politicians making the kind of candy-floss talk that politicians specialize in. 'There never has been a feud between the two of us and there probably never will,' Norman assured his audience.

'Probably,' beamed Commissioner Finchem.

'Probably,' said Norman, with less certainty.

The World Tour furore had driven Norman closer than he had ever been to retiring. 'I could see him saying, "To hell with this. I don't need this,"' Frank Williams says.

'Retirement,' Norman said immediately when he was asked at the TPC what the long-term prognosis was for his back. 'I think that would be the best bet. I can tell you that when I didn't play golf for three months I never had a hip problem, never had a back problem ... Believe me, I enjoyed waking up every morning without having an ache and a pain and having to stretch out to get myself going for that day. So that's the answer.'

And then the Masters was upon him.

Of all the golfers on earth, there are only two men capable of controlling, and even manipulating, the emotions of the press, through a subtle blend of charm and brazen self-confidence: Seve Ballesteros and Greg Norman. At Augusta, Norman was at his best, thanking reporters profusely for their support since the previous Masters, and then later dropping it in that he hadn't read a golf article in a year.

'Whenever a guy says, "I don't read it," you get a picture of him poring over it with a jeweller's loop,' Tom Callahan remarked.

Dan Jenkins made fun of Norman's post-Augusta 1996 comments that he only made two mistakes all day, and that he had so much confidence in his own abilities that, 'If I wanted to be a brain surgeon and take the time to study that, I could,' suggesting that he would lose the 1997 Masters 'when he: a) Blows a ten-shot lead . . . while hitting only three bad shots, and b) Dies after thirty-six holes while performing brain surgery on himself.'

It turned out that Norman had spent the previous day with Tony Robbins, a motivational speaker, who had worked with Olympic swimmers, André Agassi and the military. Robbins told him that most athletes have one or two keys they use to motivate themselves. Norman, it transpired, had forty-eight. Describing one, he explained, 'If you keep thinking about the worst round you've ever had in your life, you're going to keep playing that same shitty round. I don't want to keep thinking about it. Flush it on out.'

He looked so thin and hollow-eyed that several people asked if he had lost weight. 'I don't think so,' Norman said. He had just spent two hours in a traffic jam and astounded Laura by managing to refrain from attacking the dashboard or screaming curses out of the window. He returned to his day with Robbins. 'One thing he did say . . . was that I had two worlds going on. I had the outer world and the inner world. And I've been worrying about the outer world. I've got to get back into worrying about my inner world.'

Three days later, Norman missed the cut. When his ball rolled off the apron of the fifteenth green into the water on the second day, he abandoned hope. 'He didn't want to play after that, it appeared,' said Nicklaus, his partner. 'It took all the wind out of his sails.'

When the blood began to gush from the bull's neck, Norman leaned forward, a broad smile on his rugged face. The dying animal bellowed in agony but in Madrid the cheering crowd drowned it out. They cheered again when the matador bowed and presented the Shark with his hat, a great honour. A Spanish newspaper showed Norman craning forward in a state of high excitement, face alight.

In the year since the Masters disaster, there had been a revolution on the PGA Tour – namely the arrival of Tiger Woods. In April, Woods had electrified the golf world by winning the Masters by a staggering twelve strokes. In the space of eight months, he had acquired some $60 million in endorsements and become a global phenomenon, and he was as far ahead of most players, in terms of power, charisma and technique, as Nicklaus was in his heyday and Norman was at his best. At 330 yards, he was almost 50 yards longer than the Australian off the tee, and Norman said that every course was a 68 for him. 'I remember the days when courses were par sixty-eight for me, too,' he said wistfully.

Despite Norman's insistence that he cherished the arrival of the new world number one, it was no coincidence that he altered his schedule to take in events he hadn't entered for years, like the St Jude Classic in Memphis and the Spanish Open in Madrid.

'Greg's playing in the Spanish Open as a favour to Seve, and then

Seve's going to play in Greg's tournament in Australia,' Frank Williams said. 'They've been friends for years.'

Ballesteros appeared to have slept through the entire relationship. He claimed that his manager, Roddy Carr, had asked him if it was OK if Norman played in the tournament. 'I said, "Fine," ' Ballesteros said. 'Greg has been the number-one player for many years and it is good for the tournament. Apparently, they make a deal that I go and play in Australia. I never said that. Maybe Roddy Carr will play in Australia.'

In November, Ballesteros, after making strings of prima-donna demands for air-tickets, hotels, $100,000 appearance fees and assorted luxuries for his wife, children and nanny, would pull out of the deal to play three events in Australia. 'Greg is furious,' Williams said, knowing the Spaniard would get away with murder, while Norman's softness would render him unable to sue.

Back home in the States, a row was beginning to sizzle over Norman's comments following Jumbo Ozaki's victory in the Chunichi Crowns tournament in Japan at the end of April. At the second hole in the final round, Norman accused Ozaki – who is more powerful than the Prime Minister in Japan – of improving his lie in the rough. It was a brave but ultimately foolhardy call. 'All I did was issue a warning to Jumbo as a friend,' Norman said. 'I told him, "You can't put your driver behind the ball and then pull out an iron." I didn't accuse him of doing anything.'

All of these things added to Norman's grim countenance and defensive attitude. Throughout the season, as he emerged victorious from two events and signed more multi-million-dollar deals, he hardly cracked a smile. 'There's an evolution through time, an evolution through two decades of pressure,' Norman told *Golf.* 'In [the] Australian Open, people compared me to Tiger Woods, who was smiling all the time. Hell, when I was twenty-one years old and didn't have a care in the world, I smiled a lot, too.'

The change in him was the subject of frequent debate. He was noticeably more abrupt and on edge. 'People think that you just go out there and play golf and have a good time,' Norman says, 'but there's so much more to it, so many sacrifices. So obviously I'm very cynical because of that, which I hate. It's a shame because my nature

253

has changed and my attitude has changed, which saddens me most out of my life ... I know I'm not the same guy now as I was seven years ago. I'm not the same guy now as I was twenty years ago. I'm not the same guy I was a year ago.'

'There are two Greg Normans,' Butch Harmon explains. 'Away from the golf course, he's great. He's fun to be around, he's tremendously adventurous – shark-fishing and landing on carriers, he loves to push everything to the limit. I thoroughly enjoy being around Greg away from the course. At the golf course, he seems to be irritated all the time. He doesn't seem to be having a good time. He always seems to be upset, whether it's with himself or with somebody else, and I don't like that side of him. I wish he'd go back to the way he used to be. There's nothing wrong with being intense. If you look at Tiger Woods, he's intense when he's playing but you see him smiling and laughing. You never see Greg like that in a tournament and I think that's hurt his golf game. I think his intensity has caught up a little bit with his nervous system over the years.'

'I've seen him get very angry,' Williams admits. 'There a lot of anger in him, a *lot* of anger. I don't know why he does get so angry sometimes.'

Stewart Ginn, Norman's friend from the early days in Australia, felt he knew the exact cause of the Shark's unhappiness. 'Of course he's changed,' he says. 'I think the pressures have got to him. I feel sorry for him. I've seen him in situations where he's got a mobile in one hand, he's got a beer in the other, three people are waiting in the hotel lobby, two people are in the room with him, he's leading the tournament by five or six shots and we're trying to go out to dinner. He's got no peace. None. He's turned harder in a lot of ways because he's had to. I think a lot of people are jealous of what he has. I feel sorry for him. But the thing I like is that we can still have a laugh together.'

It was hard to tell whether what happened at the Kemper Open was the result of these pressures or one of the indirect causes of them. Standing on the tee with Tom Lehman on the morning of the third round, Norman listened idly as the starter introduced him and said he was one of the game's great players. 'But if he ever invites you to his house to view his trophy collection, I would advise you to respectfully decline,' Bill McGuire continued, in a tongue-in-cheek reference to the Clinton incident.

Andy Martinez, Lehman's caddie, was amused. 'I thought it was kind of funny. I thought it was overblown, but you're in Washington DC. The place is full of clowns and criminals. I laughed, but then I looked at Greg. Greg was not laughing. He kind of turned and looked at the guy and he glared at him for about two or three seconds. Then he turned and hit his tee ball and the guy introduced Tom and Tom hit his ball. I looked at Greg and he's making a beeline for the tent where they keep the drinks [to confront McGuire] and there was some serious talking that went on. He was not happy. Then he got off to a bad start because it seemed like he was so agitated.'

Norman was not agitated, he was furious. Back home in Florida, Clinton's little accident had spawned a thriving – not to mention embarrassing – industry in T-shirts and coffee mugs, and it had worn on his last nerve. He chewed McGuire up one side and down the other and then went after his fourball and started horribly.

'What really got to Greg was that he was in contention . . . and he was very psyched up,' Laura explains. 'He hears this and it just sends him off the edge. And I don't blame him. A lot of people said, well, he overreacted. They don't understand that when these guys are trying to win a tournament, their mind is very much into what they're doing . . . Greg was just standing there perfectly innocent and this man said something very stupid at a time when Greg was focused on his golf. Then they say there was nothing wrong with what the guy said. That was so totally wrong and it was unfair to Greg, it really was.'

Not altogether surprisingly, the *Washington Post* gave Norman a roasting. 'This kind of humiliation was totally unnecessary,' Tony Kornheiser wrote. 'McGuire tried to make a joke, and Norman ran over him with a tank . . . It's not like he intimated that Norman pushed Clinton down the steps . . . Golfers and tennis players amaze me with their sense of entitlement . . . What should the guy have said? "Ladies and gentlemen, here's God"?'

The next day, when a spectator heckled Norman with some nonsensical American remark which sounded like, 'Chum it in the water, Greg,' he flipped the guy the bird.

From Kemper, where he shot 67 to finish third, Norman went to

Congressional for the US Open. On the eve of the tournament, when the mud-slinging was at its height, the Normans took Gregory and Morgan-Leigh to the White House to meet the President. It was a beautiful blue day, and afterwards Norman suggested they should show their children, who have been brought up as Catholics, the church where they were married. 'It was lovely,' Laura says. 'The priest blessed our rings. It was very special because it's been sixteen years. The priest said it was so nice to see someone come back because they almost never do.'

That night, Norman held a press conference to announce, to general amazement, that he was trading in his Gulfstream IV jet for a $40 million Boeing 747. He had also signed a seven-year agreement to be an ambassador for Boeing. According to Norman, who covered 442,600 kilometres in 1996, the bigger plane would allow him to take more staff and make fewer refuelling stops, as well as providing space for a boardroom, a private suite with toilet and shower, a gym and an advanced satellite-communications facility.

'Has it occurred to anybody that this deal might be a better deal than the one he's got at the moment?' Frank Williams demanded as the *Australian* reflected the general reaction with a montage of Norman's house, his custom-built boat, his jet, his Harley and the Boeing 747, illuminated like a prop in a David Copperfield show. 'He can have all the comforts of home,' Williams said, of the Boeing, for which Norman paid cash.

Williams was on his way back to Australia to take up the reins of Norman's company there as executive vice-president, while Bart Collins, the smooth, IMG-moulded American, who headed Norman's company in Australia, was returning to the United States as president of Great White Shark Enterprises. Despite reports to the contrary, it was a fairly amicable arrangement. 'Everybody', Norman explained, beaming, 'is extremely happy at my company.'

On Thursday, Norman's father was admitted to hospital with heart trouble. On Friday, Norman missed the cut. On Sunday, the *Post* ran a column in which readers were invited to offer their opinion on the Kemper controversy. 'There's no excuse for Greg Norman's boorish behaviour . . .' railed Mark Nelson from Vienna. 'Palmer and

Nicklaus are always class acts. Norman's me-against-the-world bit is wearing thin.'

'Gee, I wonder if Jay Leno and David Letterman know that "it is just wrong . . . to make jokes" about the President's activities,' said Steve Durante from Potomac.

Most of the letters were critical, variously describing Norman as juvenile, petty, sour, mercurial, arrogant, egotistical and self-absorbed. Curtis Werner, aged seven, was one of only four supporters. 'If it makes you feel any better, I would love to come over and see your trophies,' he told Norman. 'However, my dad wants me home by nine.'

In Australia, the media seized on Norman's latest blunder with glee, quoting the *Post* in full and making spiteful insinuations about choking. 'Where once he held a special place in people's hearts for his thrilling, take-no-prisoners approach to tournament play, and the stoic way in which he accepted the slings and arrows of outrageous fortune when he came unstuck,' the columnist Charles Happell wrote, 'he is now threatening to try their patience.'

The *Herald-Sun* began a column, 'Message to Greg Norman: Go away. Take your private jet back to Florida. Come back when you have rid yourself of your hubris.'

Over the winter, the Normans had held a family vote to decide whether they should move to Australia permanently. It had to be unanimous and since Gregory, now eleven, didn't want to go, the idea was put on hold. But Norman had given up trying to appease the Australian press or anyone else. 'They kill me,' he says. 'Two years ago, I was so close to never going back down there.'

Ten days after being condemned for missing the US Open cut, Norman made three closing birdies to win the St Jude Classic in Memphis.

The more one analyses it, the more Norman's life resembles a hall of mirrors, a shifting corridor of reflections and split images. There is the granite-jawed, Lone Ranger figure the public see, surrounded by jets, Ferraris, butlers and heads of state, forever poised on the knife-edge between agony and ecstasy. There is the unstintingly kind, private and down-to-earth man his friends know – the friends he doesn't always believe he has. There is the Norman his family knows, and then there is the Norman only Norman knows.

Norman cherishes this secret corner of himself. So certain is he that he is the only one acquainted with his true nature that he doesn't believe even Laura is privy to it, far less the media. 'The media don't have a clue about Greg Norman,' the Shark says categorically. 'I pick up newspaper articles and read about Greg Norman and what he's like and what he's done and they're one hundred per cent not true . . . And that's what, believe me, out of everything, irritates you to death. If I retired now, my only regret in life would be the media and the slant they put on things. Because I know the majority of it isn't right '

'I think it's really sad that his ability to sit down with the press and open himself up has really backfired on him,' Laura says. 'They think they know him but they don't know him at all.'

To Norman, there are three major misconceptions about him:

(a) *He is egotistical.* 'I don't have an ego,' Norman said at Doral, when he was asked if he was bothered by the prevailing Tiger mania. This gave rise to the joke: 'Greg Norman doesn't have an ego. He has two.'

(b) *He is arrogant.* 'I know I'm not an arrogant guy,' Norman says. 'I'm actually the other way. I'm not one who enjoys the hype. I *never* have. I've never enjoyed the limelight. I hate the limelight. All that stuff I don't enjoy. I don't like cameras in my face. But people think I do.' Laura supports this. 'There is a bit of arrogance about Greg, but anybody who's very good in their profession has a bit of arrogance. His confidence in himself might come across as being egotistical but that's a misconception . . . When we go to functions at school with the children that he's not used to, Greg sort of stays in the background. He's very shy in a lot of ways still.'

(c) *He is materialistic.* 'I'm not a materialistic individual,' Norman says. 'I mean, I can buy and sell things in a heartbeat. I don't get attached to materialistic things.'

Herein lies the essence of Norman's problem: he sets himself up to be targeted. There is every reason to believe that he is, as Williams says, the same big-hearted kid that he was at seventeen, but over and over again he provides fodder for those who would prefer to be amused by his perception of himself as a country boy at heart. 'I've never been afraid to ask a question,' Norman says. 'I've never been afraid to go up to a president or a Jack Nicklaus, because most of the time people love to give advice when they're of the stature of the President of the United States or a Jack Nicklaus or the Prime Minister of Australia. They enjoy being recognized as someone special.' He sees no contradiction between this and his desire to be accepted as the boy-next-door. When Jana Wendt of Australia's Channel Seven suggested that one of the 'bug-bears' Australians had with him was 'that you have such a well-developed sense of your own worth', Norman interpreted that as a compliment. 'A wave of joy and gratitude swept over his face,' reported *Inside Sport*. 'Thank you,' he said. 'I'm glad someone has *finally* realized that. Because yes, I do. Like I said, I'm very in tune with myself and my business, and what I can do and produce for people.'

Remarks like these convey all the characteristics Norman claims to despise and reveal none of the traits the people closest to him love: his generosity, compassion and consideration. 'He's a very kind man,' Charlie Earp says. 'He'd do anything for you. If he thinks he owes someone a favour, he does it. He can't stand nonsense, can't tolerate it. But he can make an excuse for someone, forgive them. I've got a video of his fortieth birthday. Very private, very caring, tears. His mother read a poem and he loved it. He has to be the other way because he's a salesman for golf.'

'I've been a good friend of his for ten or twelve years,' John Cott says, 'and from what I've seen, he deserves everything he's got. You can talk about all the toys, but he's out there working all the time. It annoys me. I hear "Greg Norman this" and "Greg Norman that", but if they worked as hard as he does, they'd probably be up there too. He's just such a down-to-earth, great guy. He's so generous, he's so funny. Laura and the kids are his whole life. It's an honour to be around them because they're unique people.'

Collins once said that the only common thread in Norman's life is Laura. Through every storm she has always been there for him, supporting him unconditionally. 'I don't know anyone who doesn't love Laura,' says Williams.

'The only person who really knows me is my wife, and I bet you she doesn't know me completely,' Norman says. 'She hasn't seen sides of me I know I have, that I don't think she needs to see. I don't mean that in a bad way. Like I tell her, "You've never seen me mad yet." Nobody's ever seen me mad yet, except a couple of people.'

'His family come first,' says Cott. 'Second is his golf.'

Greg Norman was higher than nature ever meant man to be, and he was still climbing. Muscles straining, breath uneven, he heaved himself up until finally he stood on top of the Sydney Harbour Bridge, where Paul Hogan once worked as a rigger. Far below him, the Opera House jutted like a toy fan into the twinkling waters of the harbour, and yachts flecked the bay like stars. 'Action!' cried the director. Above Norman's head, a cameraman leaned from the hovering Channel Seven helicopter and prepared to shoot.

Norman had arrived in Australia at six-thirty the previous morning, flying into Sydney in his Gulfstream IV jet. 'Why don't I live here?' he asked a couple of hours later, relaxed and laughing as he enjoyed a meal in Rose Bay. 'He's very emotional about Australia when he first comes back,' says Williams. 'Until the media start on him.'

Later, when Williams jokingly suggested Norman spend the afternoon watching the Australian PGA, he jumped at the chance. 'Do you know,' said the Shark, sprawled out in the sunshine in a T-shirt, shorts and sneakers, 'I've never done that.' Williams was flabbergasted. At the New South Wales Golf Club, Norman wandered happily through the crowds, signing autographs and watching other players compete.

Driving back through Circular Quay a few hours later, they stopped at traffic lights. Beside them, a wedding party had gathered on the steps of a cathedral, the bride in white, the groom immaculate in a suit. All of a sudden, the groom's expression changed. He shot out an arm. 'That's Greg Norman!' he cried. 'That's Greg bloody Norman!'

Norman grinned out of the window. 'He seems pretty excited,' he said.

The lights went green. John Cott, who was driving, moved off. 'Hold on a minute,' Norman said. He jumped out of the car and walked over to the wedding party, with its flowers and suits and radiant faces. There, on the steps of the cathedral, he kissed the bride, put his arm around the groom and posed for a few photographs. 'That's when Greg's at his best,' Williams said. 'That's when he's happiest.'

On Sydney Harbour Bridge, an icy wind blasted Norman's strong brown face and pushed back his blond hair. In six days' time, the man who had been golf's world number one for the best part of a decade – and its most magnetic, exciting, loved and inexplicably flawed exponent – would tie the Australian Open with scores of 68, 67, 66, 73, then lose to Lee Westwood after three-putting the fourth play-off hole. Now he faced the cameras with a smile. 'I look forward to seeing you all at the Greg Norman Holden International on the fifth to the eighth of February 1998,' he said. 'In one of my favourite cities in the world, Sydney, the Olympic city.'

It was November 1997, and Norman was reaching the end of another triumphant season, during which he had overtaken Woods as the world number one. When he won the World Series in August, sweeping four shots clear of Phil Mickelson, with a stylish and aggressive performance, Price called him the greatest player of the last twenty years.

'Greg Norman is one of only two people who transcend the game,' says Clayton. 'Tiger Woods is the other. Even Nicklaus didn't do that.'

Norman used to feel that he would play his best golf in his forties. In 1993, when he devised his secret seven-year plan, his focus was the year 2000, by which time he would be forty-five, his children would be almost ready to leave the nest, and retirement, from golf at least, might be a possibility. But lately, he had begun to wonder if he shouldn't bring it forward – if the misconceptions, the needling and the constant reminders of his failures and belittling of his achievements were really worth the fleeting moments of ecstasy.

'There's never been anybody who tried harder than Greg and he gets precious little credit for that,' Peter Thomson says. 'He's got great courtesy and manners. People win things and there's a temptation to rest on your laurels and take up the soft life. That's an easy way to go and to his great credit Greg has never done that for an instant.'

Perhaps this is the key to Norman's continued survival in the face of blows that have felled greater men like oaks: hard work, plain and simple. Or perhaps, as John Cott says, he has been saved by his priorities: family first, golf second, business and fishing somewhere in between.

Never once has he shied from the harsh benchmark of history, the one that says that despite winning almost eighty titles around the world in snow and wind, on links and parkland, despite meeting triumph and tragedy with dignity and equanimity, he must be lumped in with those who were *almost* great.

'I look at our careers,' Price says, 'and I've won three majors and he's won two. And that's weird. To me, he's an eight-major person. I look at Faldo [with his six majors] and I think, Greg should have won more than he has. Faldo's got a very clinical game, but he's a plodder. He doesn't have the ability to hit the ball three hundred yards if he wants to, or stop a five-iron on a dime. He doesn't have the flair that Greg has.'

'Greg has always had tremendous potential, hasn't he?' Gary Player says. 'Unbelievable potential. He has had a career that could have been unbelievably sensational. He's had an opportunity to set a record that would have been just phenomenal, and things have happened so that he hasn't. But he's not too old still to accumulate a great record.'

'When you look at his career, when you look at everything about the man, he's one of the greatest players we've ever seen,' says Butch Harmon. 'And yet everyone is judged by the majors. I don't agree with that. I think his statistics speak for themselves – his scoring averages, his Vardon Trophies . . . Those are the things that count.'

'It wouldn't surprise me if he won a major at forty-five or fifty,' Mike Clayton says. 'He's so much fitter than I imagine Nicklaus ever was. Phenomenally fit, still got a great game. But if he stopped now, how would history measure his career? I think there is a parallel with Weiskopf. Their careers will probably be judged the same way. So, in the end, do you lump them in with Larry Nelson, or do you just say, they were great players who could have won more majors? Then again, put Nicklaus where Norman was and he'd have won eight majors. So can he be called a great champion? I don't know. He's definitely a great golfer. He can hit shots not many guys can hit or ever will. Best driver of the golf ball there ever was. Great bunker player. Terrific iron player. Good putter. Gutsy. The crowd love him. Charisma. Everything the game cries out for.'

'Lord knows, he's a good player,' Cary Middlecoff says, summing it up. 'But he does a lot of funny things.'

To Norman, majors mean a lot, but they are not everything, not life and certainly not death. 'My sweetest victory was my first one, the West Lakes Classic,' he says, 'because I would never have won the British Open if I hadn't won that one first. Then comes Royal St George's and then maybe Turnberry.'

Through it all, Norman has soldiered on, golden, proud, adventurous, thrilling, damaged and compulsively watchable. 'There've been times when I haven't wanted to go on,' Norman admits. 'But when you really think about it, why deprive yourself because of other people's opinions? I *love* doing what I do. I don't care what anybody else thinks about me. I do what I think is right for me, my wife, my family and my friends. And if I keep that priority, everything else will fall into place.'

After four rounds of the Australian Open, Norman's name was in its customary place: at the top of the leaderboard. Soon it would be Christmas, and he would take a much-needed break with his family, enjoying a little tranquillity before it all began again in the new year. 'Quite honestly, if I retired tomorrow, they're going to forget about me in a very short period of time,' Norman says. 'But all I've done and all I've structured for myself and my family, I've got for the rest of my life, and that's the most important thing. That's when you go and really savour what you've done because you've got time to sit back and reflect. And I'll enjoy that, I really will. There'll be no better feeling.'

# APPENDIX:
# GREG NORMAN'S VICTORIES

---

1976
West Lakes Classic (AUS)

1977
Martini International (EUR)
Kuzuha International (JAP)

1978
Festival of Sydney Open (AUS)
Traralgon Loy Yang Classic (AUS)
South Seas Classic (FIJI)
New South Wales Open (AUS)

1979
Traralgon Loy Yang Classic (AUS)
Hong Kong Open (HONG KONG)
Martini International (EUR)

1980
French Open (EUR)
Scandinavian Open (EUR)
World Match Play (EUR)
Australian Open (AUS)

1981
Australian Masters (AUS)
Martini International (EUR)
Dunlop Masters (EUR)

1982
Dunlop Masters (EUR)
State Express Classic (EUR)
Benson & Hedges International (EUR)

1983
Hong Kong Open (HONG KONG)
Australian Masters (AUS)
Open de Cannes-Mougins (EUR)
World Match Play (EUR)
Kapalua International (HAWAII)
Queensland Open (AUS)
New South Wales Open (AUS)

1984
Kemper Open (USA)
Canadian Open (CAN)
Victoria Open (AUS)
Australian Masters (AUS)
Australian PGA (AUS)

1985
Australian PGA (AUS)
Australian Open (AUS)
Dunhill Cup (Australian team) (EUR)

1986
Panasonic-Las Vegas International (USA)
Kemper Open (USA)

**British Open Championship (EUR)**
European Open (EUR)
Dunhill Cup (Australian team) (EUR)
World Match Play (EUR)
Queensland Open (AUS)
New South Wales Open (AUS)
South Australian Open (AUS)
Western Australian Open (AUS)

1987
Australian Masters (AUS)
Australian Open (AUS)

1988
MCI Heritage Classic (USA)
Lancia Italian Open (EUR)
Daikyo Palm Meadows Cup (AUS)
ESP Open (AUS)
Australian TPC (AUS)
New South Wales Open (AUS)

1989
The International Greater Milwaukee Open (USA)
Australian Masters (AUS)
Australian TPC (AUS)
Chunichi Crowns (JAP)

1990
Australian Masters (AUS)
Doral Ryder Open (USA)
Memorial Tournament (EUR)

1992
Canadian Open (CAN)

1993
Doral Ryder Open (USA)
**British Open Championship (EUR)**
Taiheiyo Masters (JAP)
PGA Grand  Slam of Golf (USA)

1994
Johnnie Walker Asian Classic (THAILAND)
Players Championship (USA)
PGA Grand Slam of Golf (USA)

1995
Memorial Tournament (EUR)
Canon Greater Hartford Open (EUR)
Fred Meyer Challenge (with Brad Faxon) (USA)
NEC World Series of Golf (USA)
Australian Open (AUS)

1996
Ford South Australian Open (AUS)
Doral Ryder Open (USA)
Fred Meyer Challenge (with Brad Faxon) (USA)
Australian Open (USA)
Andersen Consulting World Championship of Golf (match play;
    tournament finished 5 January 1997) (USA)

1997
FedEx St Jude Classic (USA)
Fred Meyer Challenge (with Brad Faxon) (USA)
NEC World Series of Golf (USA)

# INDEX

271